A Pathway to
Social Work Competence

cognella®

SAN DIEGO

A Pathway to
Social Work Competence

A Step-by-Step Process to Integrate the Nine Competencies
into the Social Work Practicum

Maria Ortiz Bustos

Bassim Hamadeh, CEO and Publisher
Amy Smith, Senior Project Editor
Rachel Kahn, Production Editor
Emely Villavicencio, Senior Graphic Designer
Kylie Bartolome, Licensing Coordinator
Natalie Piccotti, Director of Marketing
Kassie Graves, Senior Vice President, Editorial
Jamie Giganti, Director of Academic Publishing

Cover image copyright © 2016 iStockphoto LP/saemilee.
Cover image copyright © 2021 iStockphoto LP/EKATERINA BONDARUK.

Competencies 1–9 are excerpted from Educational Policy and Accreditation Standards, pp. 8–13. Copyright © 2022 by Council on Social Work Education. Reprinted with permission.

Printed in the United States of America.

cognella® | ACADEMIC PUBLISHING
3970 Sorrento Valley Blvd., Ste. 500, San Diego, CA 92121

To all who contribute to the well-being of others, especially those who have supported the dreamers.

Brief Contents

Detailed Contents

CHAPTER 4

Competency 4: Engage in Practice-Informed Research and Research-Informed Practice   61

CHAPTER 5

Competency 5: The Requirement to Engage in Policy Practice   86

CHAPTER 6

Competency 6: Engage with Individuals, Families, Groups, Organizations, and Communities   104

Acknowledgments

I want to thank my husband Daniel Bustos for his support and encouragement and for giving me the opportunity to expand my view of this world. As a first-time writer, I am very grateful for the support of everyone at Cognella. I am especially thankful for the support and guidance provided by Kassie Graves and the constructive feedback provided by Elisa Adams. I want to thank Tony Bobadilla for reading the first few chapters of the draft of the book and providing useful feedback, especially on Chapter 4. Finally, I want to thank my family and friends for being part of my life and teaching me about faith, love, compassion, integrity, and resilience.

Introduction

The social work practicum is an exciting learning experience. Your achievement—and challenge—is switching from learning in the classroom to learning by doing as you develop and practice your social work skills in the real world. This chapter outlines the steps in the learning-by-doing process that will get you there and will provide you useful tips and strategies you can use along the way.

The Learning-by-Doing Process in the Social Work Practicum

This book is different from most textbooks you have encountered. While all textbooks provide the fundamental facts, this guide will provide you with a method for engaging in the learning-by-doing process required in the field practicum setting. The social work practicum gives you the opportunity to take on the role of a social worker, with the guidance and support of an experienced social worker serving as mentor.

Your personal commitment to learn the requirements of each competency and implement it during your social work practicum experience is a crucial step in your competence development journey. It will take effort to explore the meaning of competency concepts and to implement those concepts during practicum.

The nine competencies set out by the Council on Social Work Education (CSWE, 2022) are our starting point (Figure I.1). As you explore the essential concepts imbedded in each phrase of the competency description, you will start developing a better understanding of their use in social work practice. The exercises in this guide are designed to give you an opportunity to learn the competency requirements and practice their implementation.

The development of professional competence is an individual process, and the level of professional development you achieve during your practicum will depend on the knowledge, skills, and abilities you bring to it, and your willingness to engage in learning by doing. If your goal is to become a competent social work professional, you should understand that the learning process includes making errors, and that learning from our errors in practice is a necessary step. Therefore, consider your professional relationship with your social work instructors and mentors as your first opportunity to practice behaving as an ethical and professional apprentice.

You likely have taken or will soon take courses that provide you with fundamental knowledge related to each of the nine competencies. For example, most social work programs will have at least one research course, at least one policy course, and several social work practice courses that focus on the engagement, assessment, and intervention process as well as the evaluation of social work practice. You may have taken a course dealing with diversity and difference in society,

Competency 1:

Demonstrate Ethical and Professional Behavior

Competency 9:

Evaluate Practice with Individuals, Families, Groups, Organizations, and Communities

Competency 2:

Advance Human Rights and Social, Racial, Economic, and Environmental Justice

Competency 8:

Intervene with Individuals, Families, Groups, Organizations, and Communities

Social Work Competencies from the Counsel on Social Work Education (CSWE) 2022

Competency 3:

Engage Anti-racism, Diversity, Equity, and Inclusion (ADEI) in Practice

Competency 7:

Assess Individuals, Families, Groups, Organizations, and Communities

Competency 4:

Engage in Practice-informed Research and Research-informed Practice

Competency 6:

Engage with Individuals, Families, Groups, Organizations, and Communities

Competency 5:

Engage in Policy Practice

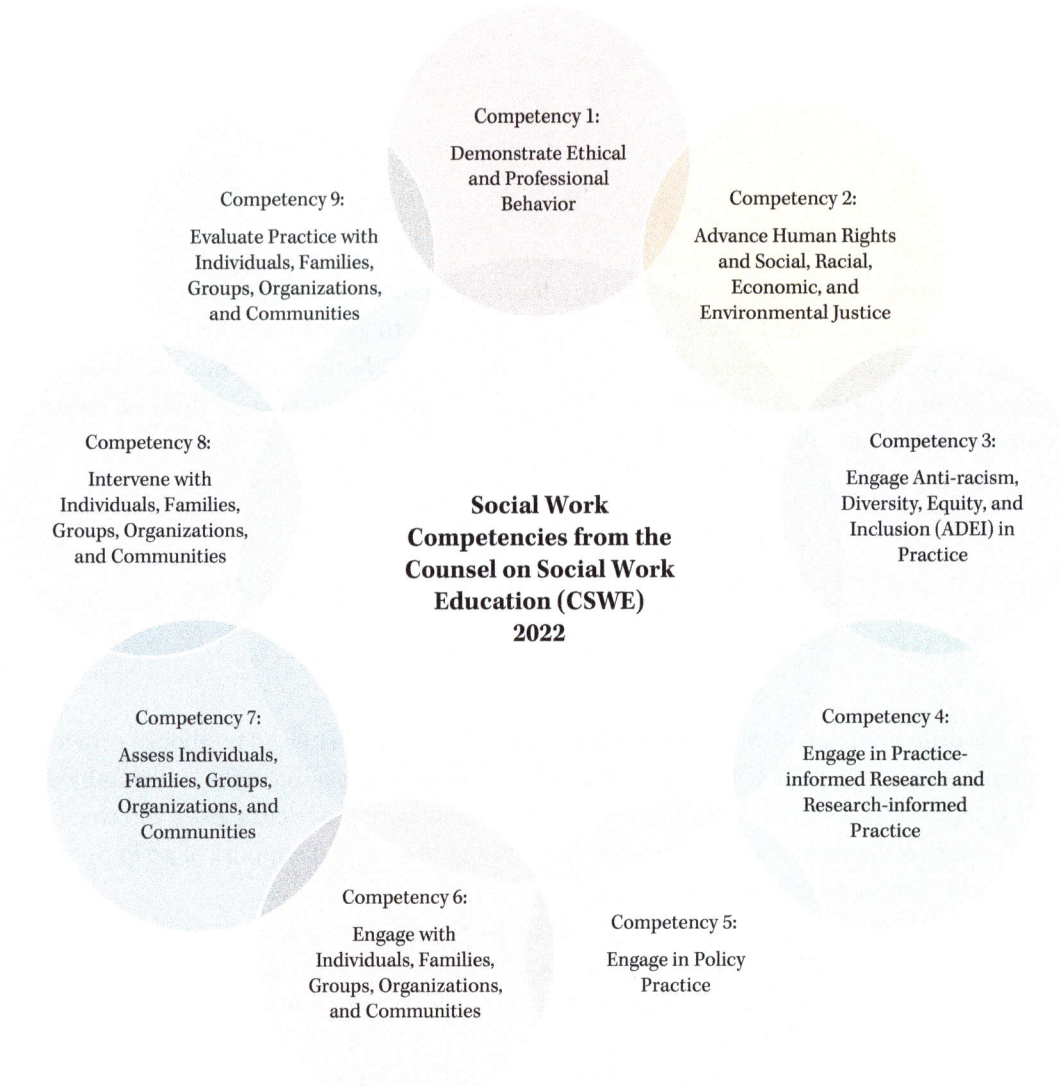

FIGURE I.1   The nine social work competencies provided by CSWE.

and several courses that offer an opportunity to become familiar with the National Association of Social Workers (NASW, 2021) Code of Ethics.

The nine CSWE competencies contribute to the complete concept of professional competence in social work practice. Social work professionals demonstrate ethical and professional behavior as they interact with clients, colleagues, and the community, and they need to demonstrate the knowledge, values, and skills related to every one of the nine competencies as they perform social work tasks on a daily basis. Developing research skills or acquiring information about social policy is not enough. An ethical social work practitioner needs to be able to read and evaluate research studies to learn about the issues that affect their clients' well-being and the social policies that affect client services.

Figure I.2 illustrates why learning about the nine competencies in the classroom setting is only the beginning of your professional development process. As you start your practicum experience, you transition from gaining conceptual knowledge to using that knowledge in the

The classroom

Acquire the knowledge, values and skills relevant to the social work profession

Learn about the nine competencies

The social work practicum

Practice implementing the knowledge, values and skills relevant to the social work profession

Use the nine competencies to inform your decisions during your social work practicum

The goal

Become a Competent and Ethical Professional Social Worker

Consistently demonstrate professional competence by integrating the nine competencies to perform social work tasks and make the commitment to continuous professional development

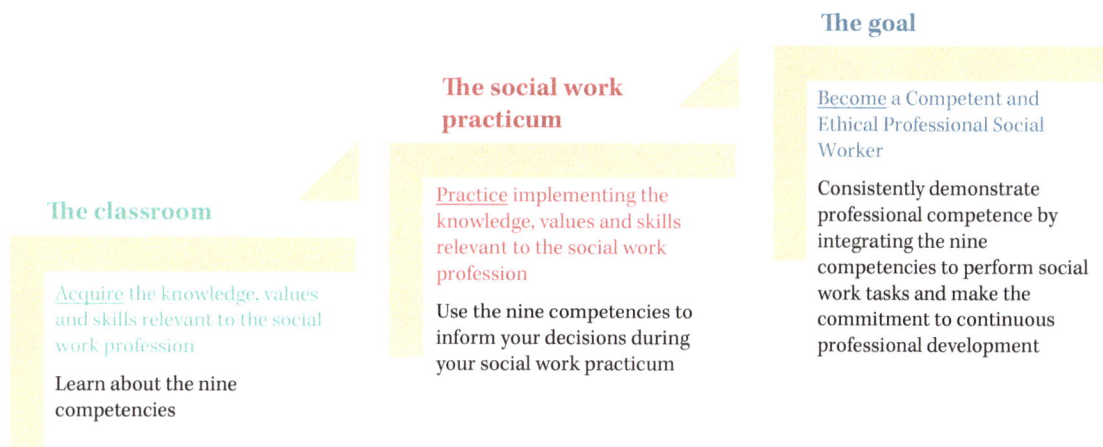

FIGURE I.2   Adding practical experience to classroom learning leads to the goal of becoming a competent and ethical social worker.

real world. It takes time, effort, and commitment to gain competence in any profession. Social work is a particularly complex profession because you must work effectively with people who are dealing with complex problems that do not have easy solutions, and who might even resent the notion that they need help.

Many students benefit from taking a personal inventory to assess who they are and their reason for wanting to become a social worker. Some have experienced personal difficulties and strongly desire to make a positive change in the world. However, personal issues that have not been resolved can hinder their ability to set clear boundaries between their personal life and the professional relationships they need to develop during their practicum. CSWE includes "affective reactions" as a key component of professional judgment in practice situations because your emotions will influence how effectively you work with people. If you have experienced trauma in your life, addressing it will make you a more effective social work student and eventually an ethical social work professional. Unresolved issues, however, expose you to the risk of being triggered by your client's traumatic experiences. Most colleges and universities have a counseling center, or you can use community resources to address your own emotional issues before they come up during practicum or after you have become a social worker.

Since competence is a quality that can be demonstrated only when you handle real-life situations with precision and accuracy, you need to prepare yourself mentally for the discomfort of exposing yourself to new situations. Experimenting with new behaviors includes the possibility of making errors. Identifying those errors and learning how to correct them in real situations is an important part of the learning-by-doing process, and the ability to communicate honestly with your social work instructors and mentors then becomes indispensable.

Figure I.3 depicts the step-by-step process used in this textbook to guide you through the professional development process. As you can see, the first step is to identify and acquire the fundamental knowledge associated with each competency to develop an understanding of the requirements related to it. The use of critical thinking skills (discussed later) is essential in the next step since you will need to distinguish between the relevant and the irrelevant in a vast amount of information. In the third step, you need to be familiar with the profession's code of ethics and implement it in your social work practice.

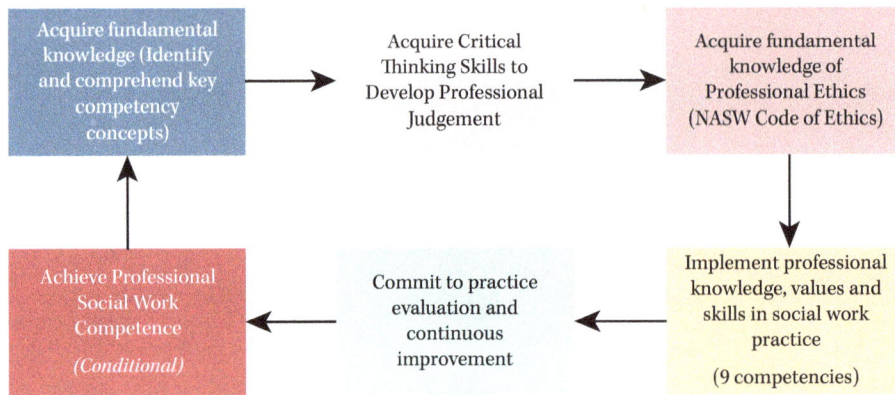

FIGURE I.3   The professional social work competence development process used in this book.

The goal of the social work practicum is evident in the fourth step, when you develop and utilize the professional knowledge, values, and skills necessary to effectively function as a social worker. In the fifth step, you discover that a commitment to continuous learning is an essential component of ethical social work practice, because we live in a continuously changing world. Although professional social work competence is the goal and the sixth step, it is conditional because we remain competent only if we are willing to keep up with changes in policy, practice, and social issues that affect social work practice.

Step 1: Identify Key Concepts

As you can see from Figure I.4, before you can integrate competency behaviors into your social work practice you need to make sure you understand key competency concepts and develop an understanding of their utility. As you consider the different kinds of information needed to provide social work services to clients, you will notice that the main tool you need to fine-tune is your own brain. Becoming a social work professional will require you to engage in cognitive processes that allow you to make professional judgements. And because we are human and our emotional responses to ideas and people influence our professional behavior, we must become aware of our emotional reactions and learn to manage them to maintain professionalism during emotionally charged situations.

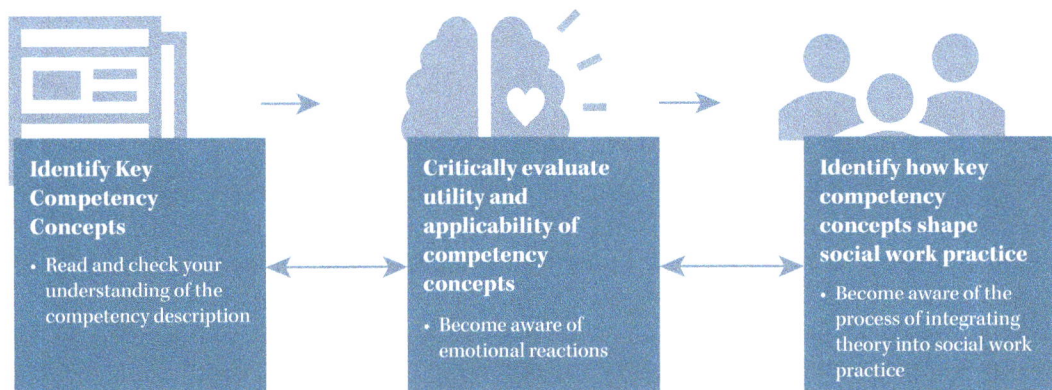

FIGURE I.4   The first step of the learning-by-doing process is to identify key concepts.

This guide will provide you with a process to examine each sentence in the competency description, and you need to check your understanding of competency concepts to evaluate their utility and applicability to your social work practicum. As you begin to identify key concepts, search for definitions of competency concepts, and critically examine the requirements of the competency to explore their relevance to social work practice, it will be useful to also use your practice experience to inform your search for the information you need to implement the competency so that you can become aware of the process of integrating theory to practice. However, make sure you use academic and scientific sources of information, such as your textbooks and scientific articles you can access through your university library, because the internet contains a great deal of misinformation. Be selective about the information you integrate into your social work practicum experience. Additionally, when you read a sentence in the competency description you should be able to clearly explain how the competency requirements imbedded in that sentence contribute to effective social work practice and how you can effectively demonstrate those competency requirements during practicum. You can skip the process of identifying key concepts, searching for competency relevant information, and critically examining the requirements of the competency and just write your reflective writing practice and then complete the application, follow-up exercise, and self-evaluation. Some students will benefit from investigating each sentence in the competency description to fully comprehend competency requirements, while others can demonstrate competency integration more quickly if they already have a good understanding of the competency requirements and their utility in social work practice.

Step 2: Use Critical Thinking Skills

In the second step of learning by doing (Figure I.5), you critically examine the requirements of each competency to develop a clear understanding of them. Your use of critical thinking skills in this process is essential because you will encounter conflicting theories about how the world works. You will need to make informed and unbiased decisions about their utility and relevance as you select information to integrate into your social work practice and to apply to each specific situation. This is how you develop your ability to formulate professional judgments.

The development of critical thinking skills requires effort and focus. Among the many tools you can use, the *Miniature Guide to Critical Thinking Concepts and Tools* by Richard Paul and Linda

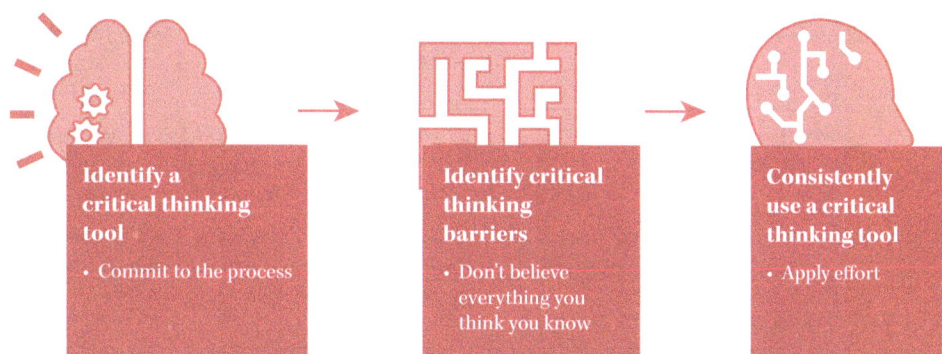

Identify a critical thinking tool
- Commit to the process

Identify critical thinking barriers
- Don't believe everything you think you know

Consistently use a critical thinking tool
- Apply effort

FIGURE I.5   The second step in the learning-by-doing process is to use critical thinking skills to develop your professional judgment.

Elder (2019) can be a good start. It offers a useful step-by-step process to critically examining scientific research articles.

Another big step in developing critical thinking skills is questioning your own beliefs and making a conscientious effort to avoid letting personal biases interfere with your decision-making. If your goal is to successfully work with diverse client populations, the ability to consider diverse points of view will be essential. By consistently using critical thinking, you can develop the habit of questioning the validity, reliability, and utility of all kinds of information, including your own ideas, and since your brain is the main tool you need to sharpen as a future professional social work professional, the more you practice considering divergent points of view, the better. The next time you speak with someone who has a different culture or political or religious view, make an effort to listen without judgment. Consider the possibility that their point of view is the correct view. Ask yourself how your life would be different if you lived in accordance with those views. If you can engage in this kind of mental exercise at least once a week, you will learn a lot about your own biases.

A third way to develop critical thinking skills is to ask who, what, where, when, why, and how when you explore any issue. These are the questions journalists ask when they investigate an event or issue, they are writing about, but you can easily adapt them to explore social work topics as well. If you use them to guide your learning, you can increase your capacity to think critically. In Table I.1, those questions are used to explore the NASW Code of Ethics. You might come up with different questions and different answers. For example, you might want to know more about the history and evolution of the Code of Ethics, who participated in writing the first version, and

TABLE I.1   Critical Thinking Questions and the NASW Code of Ethics

Questions	NASW Code of Ethics	Possible Answers
Who	Who wrote the NASW Code of Ethics? Who benefits from it?	Social workers in the United States. Social workers benefit from having professional standards of practice and clients who are harmed can seek redress.
What	What is the purpose of the NASW Code of Ethics?	To describe social work as a profession and to provide professional social work practice standards.
Where	Where does it apply? Where is it enforced?	In the United States professional licensing boards can use it to create guidelines to grant or revoke a license, and NASW can enforce the code among its members.
When	When is it useful? When is it enforced?	When social workers face ethical challenges. When social workers engage in unethical behavior and should be reported for ethical violations.
Why	Why is a social work professional code of ethics necessary?	Professional codes of ethics provide guidelines to protect both professionals and clients
How	How is the NASW Code of ethics used?	It is an educational tool to provide novice social workers behavioral guidelines, and it sets social work practice standards.

TABLE I.2   Critical Thinking Questions to explore any topic.

Topic	
Questions You Want to Explore	**Answers You Found by Investigating the Topic**
Who	
What	
Where	
When	
Why	
How	

how changes to the document have been made throughout the years. The main idea to keep in mind is that to develop critical thinking skills, you need to be intentional and consistently use a method that will allow you to generate questions to explore any issue more precisely.

Table I.2 is a template you can use to explore any topic you want to know more about.

Step 3: Demonstrate Professional Ethics

Professional and ethical social work practice is the first of the nine competencies. Although all nine are interrelated, developing a working knowledge of the NASW professional Code of Ethics is essential. While the guidelines do not include an implementation process, by consistently using an ethical decision-making tool (Figure I.6) you can develop your own mental habit of thinking through the ethical decision-making process. CSWE focuses on educational standards, and the NASW Code of Ethics focuses on professional ethics, but both require a commitment to professional growth and development.

Ethical decision-making tools are necessary because they provide a process to identify specific factors that contribute to a problem in social work practice and its ethical resolution. If you have taken an ethics course, review your textbook to identify an ethical decision-making tool you can use during your social work practicum experience. If you have not taken an ethics

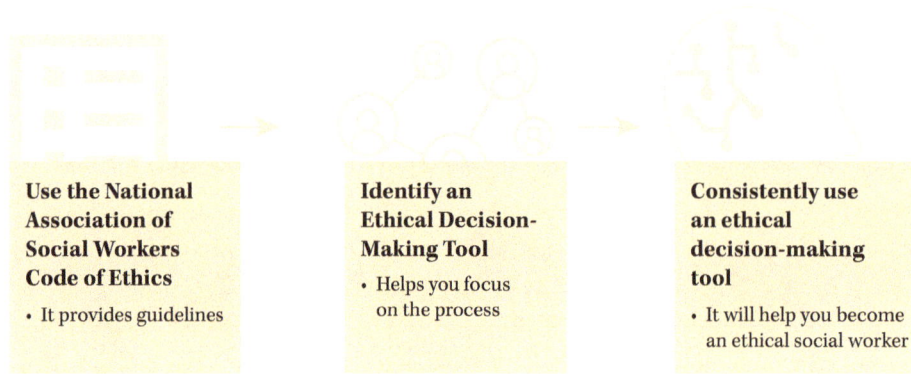

Use the National Association of Social Workers Code of Ethics	Identify an Ethical Decision-Making Tool	Consistently use an ethical decision-making tool
• It provides guidelines	• Helps you focus on the process	• It will help you become an ethical social worker

FIGURE I.6   The third step in the learning-by-doing process is to integrate professional ethics.

course, a good book to read is *Ethical Decisions for Social Work Practice* by Dolgoff et al. (2012). It provides several tools you can use, and it would be wise to select a tool you can use during your practicum before you need it, in part because reviewing the tools will make you more aware of possible situations when ethical concerns should be addressed.

Step 4: Practice the Nine Competencies

As you can see in Figure I.7, in the fourth step of the learning process you develop and practice all nine competencies during your practicum experience. Competency 1 means completing practicum assignments on time, treating clients and peers with dignity and respect, and accurately performing assigned tasks from the 1st day of your practicum.

Social work as a profession promotes human rights and social justice, and as you work with clients you might become aware of barriers to equity that social work clients face in daily life. Honing competencies 2 and 3 means demonstrating the ability to be antiracist when working with clients from different cultural and ethnic backgrounds than your own.

You are required to become familiar with and follow the policies that guide social work services, and you need to use research to learn about the issues that affect clients and client services. Those tasks are described in competencies 4 and 5.

As you become familiar with social work services in your practicum, you might be able to engage with clients, assess their needs, identify and implement interventions, and evaluate the results of those interventions. Those tasks are included in competencies 6, 7, 8, and 9.

Mastering all these skills is obviously a big task, but the best way to develop competence is to implement the competency requirements in the real world. And this book is designed to give you specific steps you can take to increase your knowledge and skills. Here are two examples.

The Reflective Writing Practice in each chapter asks you to identify how and when you can utilize the competency requirements as you work with clients. By writing a few sentences describing what you are learning and how you plan to integrate your conceptual knowledge into your practicum, you can identify key competency concepts and their relevance to social work practice.

In the Application Follow-up in each chapter, you will identify a specific date when you have been able to integrate the competency requirements into real-life situations. CSWE provides specific behaviors that should be demonstrated for each competency, and you will get an opportunity to practice demonstrating those behaviors first with a fictitious case, and then ideally with your own practicum case.

Competency 1:

Demonstrate Ethical and Professional Behavior

Competency 9:

Evaluate Practice with Individuals, Families, Groups, Organizations, and Communities

Competency 2:

Advance Human Rights and Social, Racial, Economic, and Environmental Justice

Competency 8:

Intervene with Individuals, Families, Groups, Organizations, and Communities

The Social Work Practicum is your opportunity to develop and demonstrate the nine competencies as you engage with clients under the guidance of an experienced social worker

Competency 3:

Engage Anti-racism, Diversity, Equity, and Inclusion (ADEI) in Practice

Competency 7:

Assess Individuals, Families, Groups, Organizations, and Communities

Competency 4:

Engage in Practice-informed Research and Research-informed Practice

Competency 6:

Engage with Individuals, Families, Groups, Organizations, and Communities

Competency 5:

Engage in Policy Practice

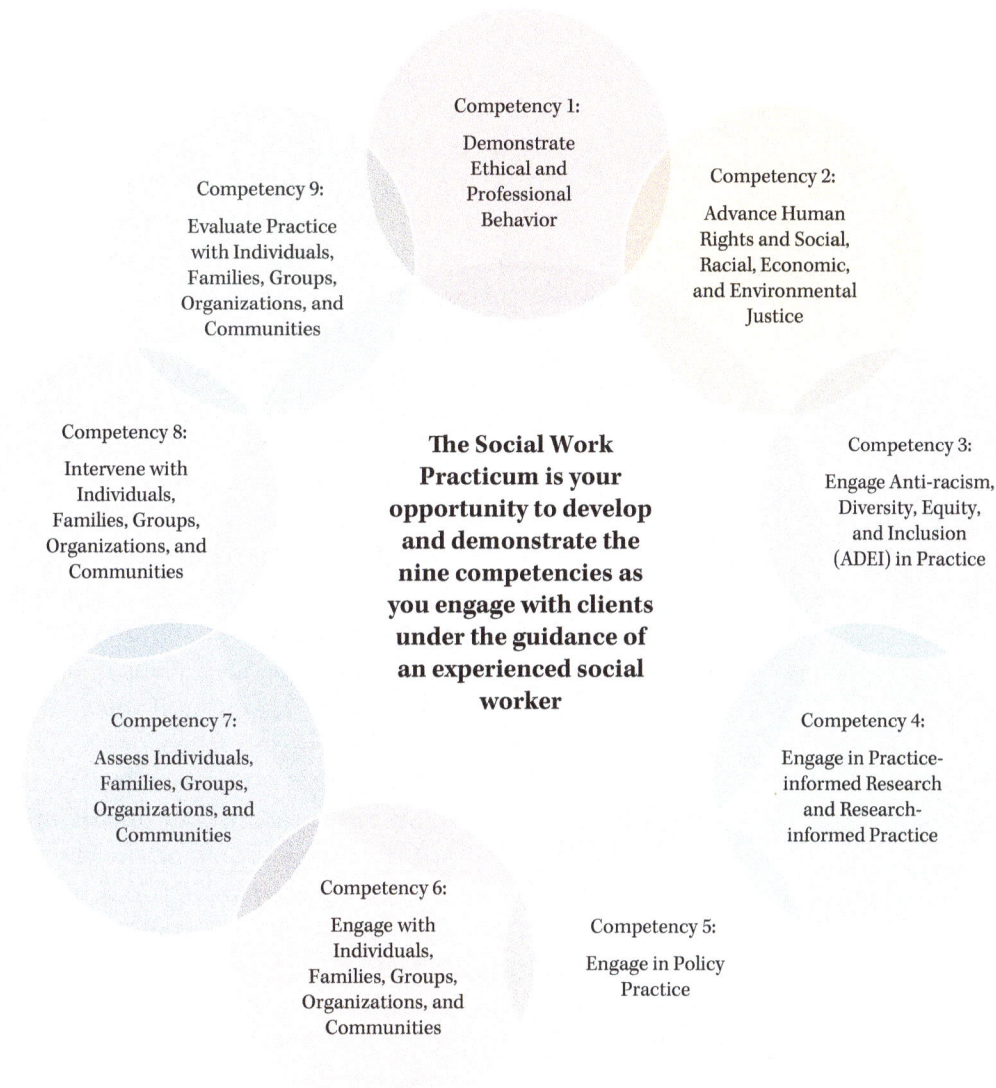

FIGURE I.7   The fourth step in the learning process is to implement your professional knowledge, values, and skills—the nine competencies—into your social work practicum.

Be both assertive and patient during this process. If there is a clear plan to allow you to practice the nine competencies, be patient if your instructor puts limits on the kinds of interactions you have with clients. If you are not interacting with clients, identify opportunities to practice your social work skills and approach your social work field instructor with ideas about becoming more involved in client services. The faculty in your social work field office can also assist you if you are not seeing the connection between competency requirements and the tasks you are being assigned at your practicum placement.

Step 5: Commit to Continuous Improvement

Making a commitment to continuous learning is the fifth step in the process of acquiring professional social work competence. Figure I.8 illustrates an evaluation process you can apply to your overall social work practice or to each competency or part of a competency. The first step

Identify the goal
and the process to
evaluate results

Identify what
went right to
replicate

Identify
improvement
needs

Address
improvement
needs and
implement
changes as
needed

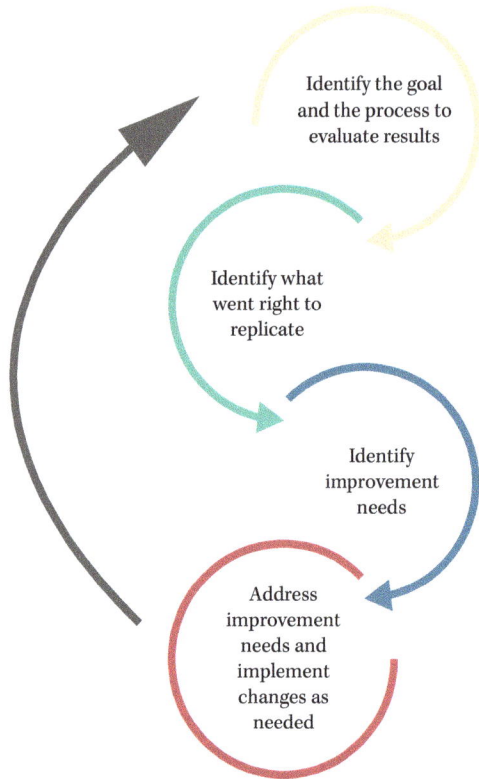

FIGURE I.8 The fifth step of the step-by step learning process is to commit to continuous evaluation and improvement of your skills.

is to identify your goal and a process for evaluating results. Identifying what went right in the competency implementation process is useful because you need to continue practicing even your effective skills. Identifying improvement needs is also essential if your goal is to increase your knowledge and skills. The last step, addressing improvement needs and identifying a process to implement changes, is the step that allows you to grow and improve.

The self-evaluation rubric in Table I.3 will help you develop a habit of routinely evaluating your integration of each competency into your practicum. Keep in mind that it would be unusual for someone to successfully use conceptual knowledge in practice situations on the first attempt, especially without any prior work or volunteer experience. Unsuccessful attempts are an important part of the learning-through-practice process, and you can save yourself a lot of frustration if you give yourself permission to make errors as long as you are committed to learning from them. In fact, if you are not making any errors in your practicum, you might be stifling your learning process by trying to achieve perfection prematurely. Talk with your field instructor about ways to minimize the kinds of errors that could harm clients.

If by the end of your practicum you have achieved more successful attempts to demonstrate competency requirements, and you can clearly identify your knowledge and skill gaps in the developing section of this tool, you will be on track to becoming an ethical and professional social worker. Being able to identify competency gaps makes you more aware of the continuous learning process required to achieve expertise in your field. On the other hand, if you are unsuccessful at demonstrating competency requirements for most of the competencies by midterm, you need to speak with your program faculty member and your field instructor to make sure you are getting an opportunity to develop and practice social work skills during your practicum.

TABLE I.3 Self-Evaluation Rubric

✓	**Successful**	I can effectively demonstrate these competency requirements during practicum, and I can explain how these competency requirements contribute to effective social work practice.
✓	**Developing**	I can identify the information I need and am able to apply it in some practicum situations, but I am also aware of some knowledge and skill gaps that I need to address.
X	**Unsuccessful**	Currently, I am not able to successfully demonstrate these competency requirements in practicum.

Step 6: Achieve Competence

Achieving proficiency requires experience as well as a commitment to professional growth and development (Figure I.9). As a student, you are not expected to become a proficient social worker by the end of practicum, but it should be your personal goal to become a competent social worker once you enter the profession and acquire experience. You are in the learning phase of your career, and you will return to this phase each time you change jobs, encounter policy changes and new or altered social work procedures, or learn of intervention innovations that require new skills. Since both social systems and people change over time, social work professionals need to be willing and able to adjust to both systemic changes and clients' growth and development needs.

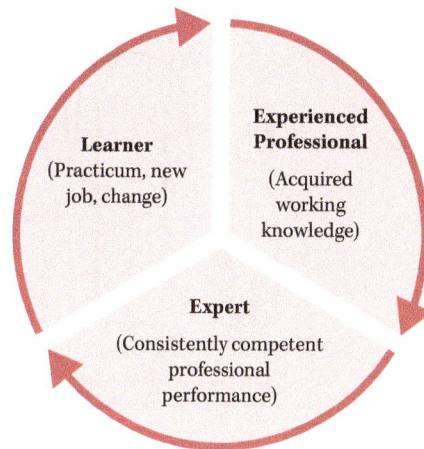

FIGURE I.9   The sixth step of the step-by step learning process is to begin to achieve professional competence.

Applying the Competencies: The Smith and Johnson Family

Throughout this book a fictitious case will be used to explore the competencies and how competency concepts contribute to effective social work practice with clients. You will be asked to imagine that the Smith and Johnson family are your clients. However, it will be important for you to consult your social work field instructor to select a real-life practicum specific case that you can use to explore the implementation of the nine competencies and corresponding behaviors as you complete your practicum experience and move through the competencies in this textbook. That process will allow you to develop your professional skills as you connect theoretical concepts with your practicum experience.

Carefully read the Smith and Johnson case, which begins in the following box. Please note that when you start working with clients, you will not have access to a complete history of your clients or the issues that affect clients. The case provides some general information, and as we explore the competencies, reflective questions will be provided for you to consider additional factors that might relate to this family. You will not need to answer the reflective questions; they are only meant to help you recognize the fact that when you consider competency requirements and their relevance to your work with clients you will have to explore additional factors that will influence how you approach your work with clients. Additionally, the titles Mr. and Mrs. are used in the case example, because social work requires us to work with diverse client populations, and in some cultures, it is inappropriate to use the first name to address an elderly person you do not know, so it is best to use respectful titles to address clients until they ask you to use their first name.

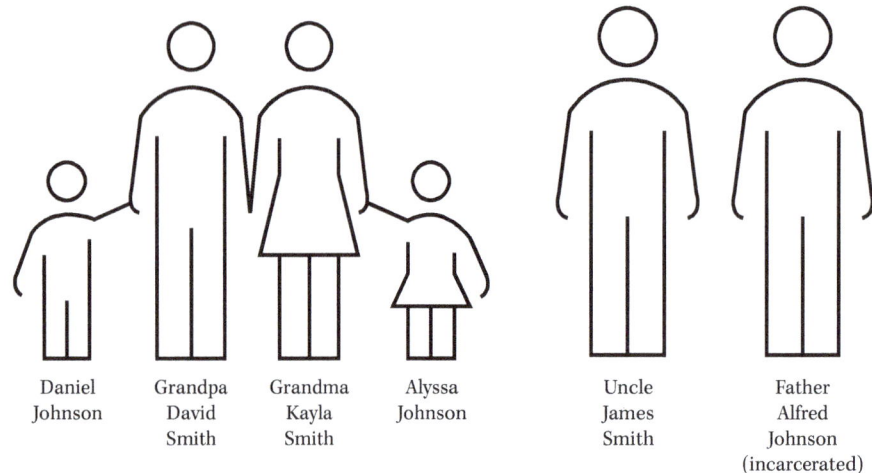

FIGURE I.10   The Smith and Johnson family.

The Smith and Johnson Family

Mr. David Smith is 72 years old, and his wife Kayla is 62. Mr. and Mrs. Smith have been raising their two grandchildren for the past 5 years. Alyssa Johnson is 10 years old, and Daniel Johnson is 12. Seven years ago, Mr. Alfred Johnson, the children's father, was arrested on drug charges. Mrs. Emma Johnson moved back into her parents' home a year later, when she was unable to keep up with the mortgage payments, and her parents offered to help her with housing and childcare while she went back to school. Mrs. Johnson was killed in an automobile accident 5 years ago.

Mr. Johnson is serving a 20-year sentence. He would like to stay in touch with his children, but it is not easy because the prison is in another city, and Mr. and Mrs. Smith are not able to take the children to visit him. Mr. Smith is retired, and Mrs. Smith used to supplement their income by cleaning apartments, but she stopped doing that 2 years ago when she was diagnosed with diabetes. Her energy level has diminished, and she often feels tired and irritable.

Daniel has been getting into trouble at school. His usual agreeable manners have changed, and he has been failing to do his homework assignments. Last week, Daniel hit a student and was suspended from school. Alyssa has not presented any problems at school, but her teachers have noticed that she now spends more time by herself.

Mr. and Mrs. Smith have a 45-year-old son. James Smith works as an airline pilot and tries to be a father figure to the children. He usually comes to visit once per month, and he takes his parents and the children to dinner or a movie or plans other fun activities that all can participate in. His last visit was the weekend prior to Daniel's school suspension. When he went back to work, he was asked to take a test for COVID-19 by his employer because one of his coworkers was ill and tested positive. James also tested positive and was asked to self-isolate.

Mrs. Smith meets with the school social worker to discuss Daniel's school suspension, and she mentions that she is very worried about her son's health. She feels sad about not being able to be there for her son because he lives so far away.

Seminar and Instructional Supervision Meetings

Most social work programs offer a seminar during the practicum, led by a licensed social worker who serves as a field liaison between the program and community social workers who serve as social work field instructors. Seminars usually meet once per week and present a great opportunity for students to share their learning experience with peers and learn about the practice settings available in the community.

The seminar course is usually structured to guide students in the process of identifying opportunities to develop and demonstrate competency-related behaviors. Therefore, at the end of each competency chapter, this book provides competency-grounded field seminar discussion ideas. Often, the explanation one student provides helps other students see the competency requirements from a different perspective. If your social work program does not offer a seminar, you might want to form a study group and use the seminar discussion topics provided to examine your competency development needs with the help of your peers. You might be able to identify an insight that is outside your own experience. At the same time, by sharing your own successes, you might help your peers understand competency requirements from a different perspective.

Similarly, most social work programs require weekly supervision meetings between social work students and their social work field instructor during practicum. Instructional supervision has two components. First, social workers need to ensure that students are provided with an orientation to appropriately function as a social work practicum student within the agency. This usually includes an initial training regarding an agency's policies and procedures as well as agency workspace and expectations of students during the practicum experience.

Second, the supervision schedule and instructional expectations need to be discussed and agreed on between the student and social work field instructor to ensure that students are offered an opportunity to develop and practice social work-related skills in the real world. If supervision meetings are unstructured, it is easy to spend supervision time discussing agency-related work needs and forget to make the connection between agency tasks and competency development requirements. The social work field instructor meeting discussion ideas at the end of each competency chapter are meant to give you a tool to ensure that you bring specific competency development concerns into your social work field instruction and supervision meetings.

As you can see in Figure I.11, prior planning will make the time you spend in seminar and during instructional supervision more productive. By completing the reading and writing exercises provided in this workbook, you will engage in the independent learning process required to achieve professional development. If you review your notes and your social work practicum performance to identify competency development needs as well as achievements, you will be better prepared to contribute to seminar and supervision discussions. If you use the self-evaluation tool provided, you will easily identify those parts of the competency that you have successfully integrated into your practice as well as the parts of the competency requirements that you have not yet successfully demonstrated. Formulating specific questions before seminar and instructional supervision meetings will help you focus on your own professional development needs.

Mentally preparing to take on the learner role during seminar and instructional supervision will make you a more effective learner. Listening can be difficult, but it is an essential skill in social work practice, and the more you practice listening attentively even when you think you already know something, the easier it will be to become an effective listener. Make sure to avoid distractions by putting your electronics away during seminar.

Competency Development Focus	Prior Planning	During Seminar and Supervision
• Seminar discussion topics specific to each competency • Supervision topics that focus on competency development and implementation opportunities during practicum	• Completing the reading and writing exercises will give you the opportunity to engage in independent learning. • Review your notes and your social work internship performance to identify your learning needs. • Prepare questions to address your competency development needs	• Listen and seek to understand • Ask clarifying questions • Make the commitment to learn independently and from others • Find satisfaction in your own professional development and growth

FIGURE I.11 Competency grounded topics for your practicum seminar and educational supervision meetings, prior planning, and your role in the learning process.

Becoming a professional requires effort and commitment, so you need to remember your reason for wanting to become a social worker. Celebrate the small steps toward acquiring social work skills and appropriately demonstrating them. When you observe your social work field instructor effectively working with clients, keep in mind that at some point your social work instructor went through the same learning-by-doing process you are experiencing now, and someday you can also become an experienced ethical and professional social worker who can mentor other students.

Commitment to Developing Professional Social Work Competence

Keep in mind that your personal learning gains will come from your willingness, commitment, and ability to accurately perform social work tasks as you engage with clients during practicum. Developing professional competence is an individual achievement. Some of the steps provided in this guide will be relatively easy for you because you already have the knowledge and skills needed for that particular part of the competency, but some competency requirements will require more effort, depending on your physical and mental health, your workload as a student and as a member of society, your self-care and time-management skills, and your academic knowledge and skills.

If you have not considered how your personal behavior might influence your professional behavior, think of the most professional person you know. Have you seen them disheveled? Are they posting pictures of themselves drinking on social media? Do they make excuses for not meeting deadlines? The personal and the professional are intertwined because we are one person. Therefore, a big part of developing your ethical and professional competence as a social worker will include assessing how you are going to manage your personal life to ensure that what you do as a private citizen is in line with your professional goals. The process also works in reverse. Your professional goals should support the kind of life you want to live, because the whole purpose of working for a living is to earn sufficient money to provide for yourself and your family.

Achieving work-life balance is an essential aspect of professional success. Helping clients increase their well-being will be much easier if your own life is in balance. Self-care prompts will be included throughout the book, so you can consider your personal growth both as an individual and as a future member of the social work profession. Take the self-care inventory in Table I.4 and consider how each action will contribute to your professional development.

TABLE I.4   Self-Care Inventory

Self-Care Tasks	Yes	No	Impact on My Personal and Professional Life Goals
I sleep at least 7 hours every night.			
I manage my time to make sure that I can fulfill my school, work, and personal care goals.			
I make sure to schedule at least 30 minutes of physical exercise three times per week.			
I know how to use my instructors' office hours and use the opportunity to discuss/ask for assistance when I am struggling to understand the course material.			
I make sure to eat whole fruits or vegetables at every meal and avoid highly processed foods to ensure that my diet keeps me healthy.			
I make sure to drink plenty of water every day.			
I do not smoke or consume drugs			
I am aware that alcohol is a drug, and I minimize its consumption.			
I have access to health care, and I use it appropriately.			
I have the capacity to be a supportive friend and have at least one friend that I can count on.			
I can contribute to the well-being of my family, and my family contributes to my well-being.			
I can set boundaries and avoid people who disrespect me.			
I know how to access mental health care, and I am willing to use it.			
I live my life in agreement with my spiritual beliefs.			
I pray, meditate, or keep a gratitude journal.			
I make sure to schedule time to rest and recover every day.			
I celebrate my progress toward my life goals.			

Who Will Benefit From This Book?

This book is structured to be used in introduction to social work practicum courses or social work practicum courses in a Bachelor of Social Work (BSW) or in the foundation year of a Master of Social Work (MSW) program. The requirements of each competency are explored to make the knowledge, values, skills, and cognitive and affective processes outlined by CSWE visible. The goal of this practicum guide is to provide students and social work field instructors a step-by-step process that can be used to develop and practice integrating the nine social work competencies provided by CSWE into the social work practicum experience. Every exercise in this guide provides a pathway to develop professional competence. The nine competencies outlined by the CSWE are elements that contribute to the complete concept of professional social work competence. Developing one of the nine competencies is not sufficient to demonstrate professional competence; it is only through skillfully incorporating all nine competencies that professional social work competence is achieved.

Summary

This practicum guide provides you with a step-by-step process to acquire the fundamental knowledge and skills of the social work profession. A six-step process is used to examine the requirements and implementation of the nine social work competencies, and you are asked to consider how the competencies shape your interactions with clients like the Smith and Johnson family as well as the real clients you will encounter in your social work practicum. The use of critical thinking skills is an indispensable part of the learning-through-practice process, and incorporating the NASW Code of Ethics into your social work practicum will increase your ability to develop accurate professional skills. If your goal is to become a competent social work professional, you will need to identify and consistently use a professional performance evaluation tool because most of us behave in ways we believe to be correct, but if we do not evaluate the impact of our actions, we might be doing harm without knowing.

As you can see in Figure I.12, this book has been designed help you explore the requirements of the nine social work competencies offered by CSWE by investigating the meaning of each sentence of the competency description and its imbedded requirements to make their relevance to social work practicum visible and doable.

There are no shortcuts. The learning-by-doing process requires time and effort. If you have a commitment to become a competent and effective social work professional, you will need to invest the time and effort required to increase your knowledge base, develop your critical thinking skills, and evaluate your ability to accurately use competency concepts in your work with clients. Although the nine competencies intersect, it is important to keep in mind that each competency contains specific requirements that contribute to the overall concept of ethical and professional social work competence. If you complete the exercises provided in this guide, you will be able to integrate the knowledge, values, skills, and cognitive and affective processes described by CSWE by the end of your social work practicum.

CSWE - 9 Social Work Competencies

Examine each sentence in the competency descriptions

(Do you understand it? Can you imagine implementing it during practicum?)

If not, search for meaning of competency concepts to gain a better understanding of competency requirements

Self-Evaluation: Did you effectively demonstrate competency requirements during practicum?

Application Follow-up: Date you have used competency concepts during practicum

Reflective Writing: How will you demonstrate competency requirements during practicum

If not, what steps can you take to gain the knowledge and skills to demonstrate competency requirements?

If yes, how can you ensure consistent competent performance?

Ethical and competent social work practice requires continuous professional development

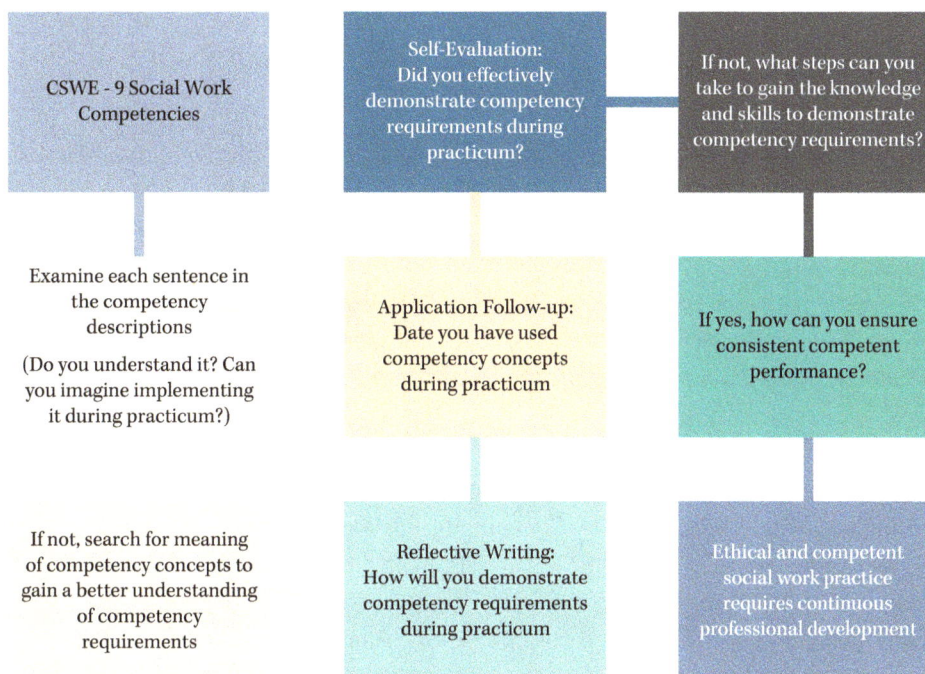

FIGURE I.12   The process used in this book to examine the requirements imbedded in the competencies and their application in the social work practicum.

Recommended Reading Materials

Books/Resources	Description
All social work coursework textbooks	The textbooks selected by your social work faculty are a key source of theoretical knowledge relevant to the social work profession and the instructional goals of your social work program. Throughout this workbook you will be asked to consult your coursework textbooks and/or search the internet to explore competency specific concepts. Remember, the practicum is an opportunity to integrate the conceptual knowledge you are learning in the classroom with the practice experience the social work practicum provides, so your class notes could also be useful.
The NASW Code of Ethics	The NASW Code of Ethics provides the ethical guidelines for the social work profession. Reading this document is not sufficient; you need to study this document because you need to fully understand the ethical responsibilities you will have as a social work professional.
National Research Council. (2000). *How People Learn: Brain, Mind, Experience, and School: Expanded Edition.* National Academies Press.	Professional competence requires a commitment to an intentional learning process. This book explains how people learn. If you want to become an expert in your field, you might want to start by learning how to learn intentionally and effectively.

References

Council on Social Work Education. (2022). *Educational policy and accreditation standards.* https://www.cswe.org/getmedia/94471c42-13b8-493b-9041-b30f48533d64/2022-EPAS.pdf

Dolgoff, R., Harrington, D., & Loewenberg, F. M. (2012). *Ethical decisions for social work practice.* Cengage Learning.

National Association of Social Workers. (2021). *Code of ethics of the National Association of Social Workers.* https://www.socialworkers.org/About/Ethics/Code-of-Ethics/Code-of-Ethics-English

Paul, R., & Elder, L. (2019). *The miniature guide to critical thinking concepts and tools.* Rowman & Littlefield.

CREDITS

CHAPTER 1

Competency 1

Demonstrate Ethical and Professional Behavior

In this chapter you will examine the first of the nine social work competencies provided by the CSWE. The competency description and its practice behaviors are dense with meaning, and translating the requirements imbedded in the description of the competency will require you to gain a good understanding of the meaning of the concepts used to describe the competency. You will need to critically examine the significance of each sentence and be able to envision its use in real-life situations to effectively apply it in practice. The exercises in this chapter constitute a process of searching for information, critically examining that information, and taking the necessary steps to apply it to your social work practicum.

You will use the same process for each one of the nine competencies, and at times the requirements will intersect. For example, in competency 1 you will identify the federal, state, and local policies that guide social work practice in your practicum setting, and competency 5 will require you to learn more about the impact of social policy on social work practice. However, the requirement in competency 1 is an introduction to the role of policy in practice, while competency 5 goes more deeply into developing the knowledge, values, and skills required to effectively use policy in practice and to advocate for policy change as needed.

Using the same process for each competency may seem repetitive, but repetition is an essential part of the learning process. When we are watching the Olympics, for example, we do not see the hundreds of hours world-class figure skaters spent practicing their routines or the many times they fell during practice, and the judges give them credit not for their efforts but for results. Social work development will require a similar commitment of the time necessary to reach a professional level of ethics and proficiency.

During practicum, you will have a mentor who will help you identify, develop, practice, and improve your social work skills. There will be times when even your best will need to be improved. Willingness to listen to constructive critique is an essential component of the learning-by-doing process, and a humble attitude will be most useful.

One last general point to keep in mind is that your mastery of each of the nine competencies affects your ethical and professional application of all the others (Figure 1.1). Consider, for instance, how clients might respond to a social worker who appears professional and speaks the language of the profession but lacks empathy or displays racist behaviors. Or perhaps the social worker demonstrates empathy but lacks the skills to effectively assess clients' needs or appropriately implement interventions. Becoming an ethical and professional social work practitioner requires the commitment to acquire the knowledge, values, and skills necessary to demonstrate every one of the nine competencies.

Competency 1 Description as Provided by CSWE: Demonstrate Ethical and Professional Behavior

As you read this description of ethical and professional social work practice, consider the knowledge and skills you need to develop during your social work practicum.

CSWE Competency 1

Demonstrate Ethical and Professional Behavior

Social workers understand the value base of the profession and its ethical standards, as well as relevant policies, laws, and regulations that may affect practice with individuals, families, groups, organizations, and communities. Social workers understand that ethics are informed by principles of human rights and apply them toward realizing social, racial, economic, and environmental justice in their practice. Social workers understand frameworks of ethical decision making and apply principles of critical thinking to those frameworks in practice, research, and policy arenas. Social workers recognize and manage personal values and the distinction between personal and professional values. Social workers understand how their evolving worldview, personal experiences, and affective reactions influence their professional judgment and behavior. Social workers take measures to care for themselves professionally and personally, understanding that self-care is paramount for competent and ethical social work practice. Social workers use rights-based, antiracist, and anti-oppressive lenses to understand and critique the profession's history, mission, roles, and responsibilities and recognize historical and current contexts of oppression in shaping institutions and social work. Social workers understand the role of other professionals when engaged in interprofessional practice. Social workers recognize the importance of lifelong learning and are committed to continually updating their skills to ensure relevant and effective practice. Social workers understand digital technology and the ethical use of technology in social work practice.

Social workers:

a. make ethical decisions by applying the standards of the National Association of Social Workers Code of Ethics, relevant laws and regulations, models for ethical decision making, ethical conduct of research, and additional codes of ethics within the profession as appropriate to the context;
b. demonstrate professional behavior; appearance; and oral, written, and electronic communication;
c. use technology ethically and appropriately to facilitate practice outcomes; and
d. use supervision and consultation to guide professional judgment and behavior

---

As you can see in Figure 1.1, professional ethics in social work practice encompass every aspect of social work practice. Ethical and professional behavior cannot be demonstrated in isolation; it is in the process of engaging, assessing, and intervening with clients that social workers either demonstrate ethical and professional behavior or do not. Demonstrating ethical and professional behavior requires being able to demonstrate every one of the nine competencies.

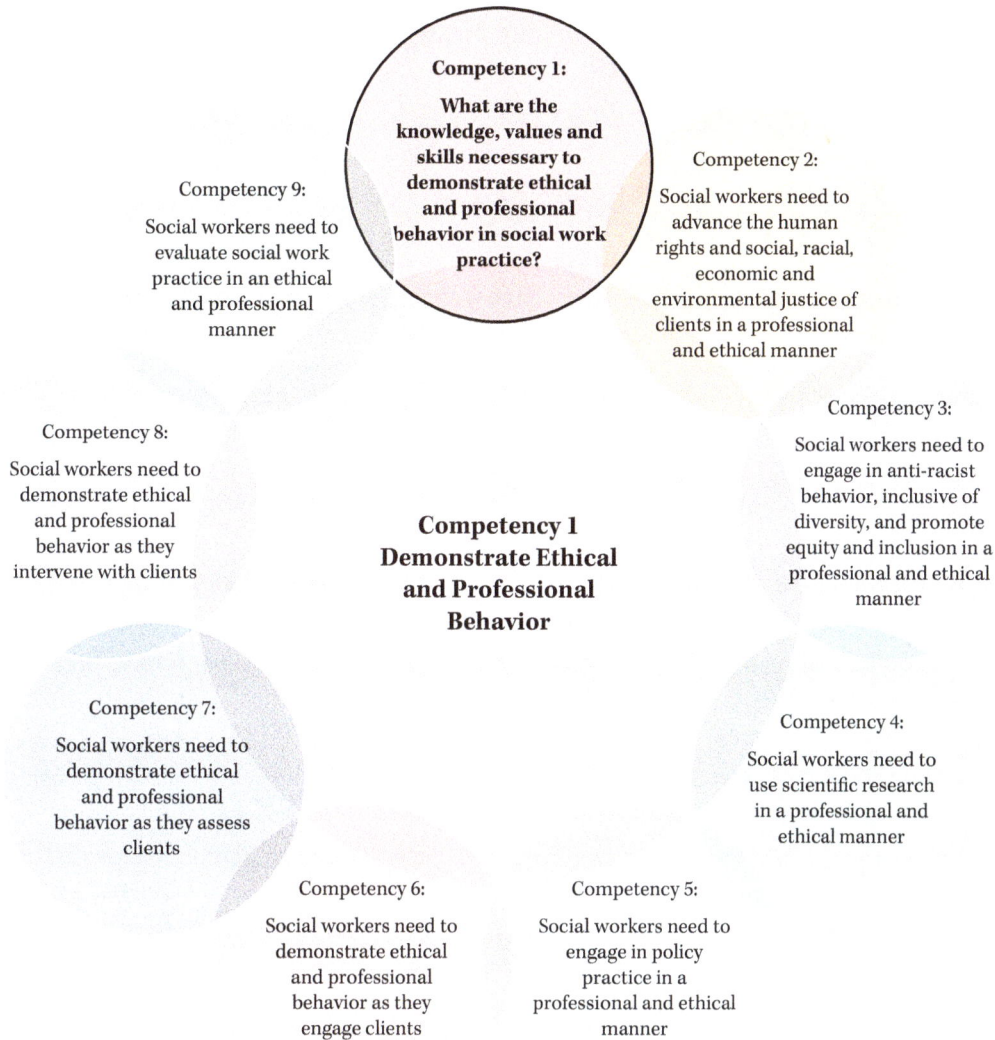

FIGURE 1.1   The relationship of competency 1 to the rest of the competencies.

Applying Competency 1

As you read each chapter in this book, consider the relevance of each competency to the fictitious case example of the Smith and Johnson family, previewed in the Introduction. Think about how the same competency requirements apply to your interactions with the clients at your practicum. If you are working in a school setting, you could be assisting children in circumstances similar to those of Alyssa and Daniel Johnson, but you may also be working with a family in similar circumstances if your practicum is a homeless shelter, a prison, a health clinic, a food bank, or any other community organization that provides social work services.

The more you can relate to the members of this fictitious family and identify the similarities to real cases in your social work practicum, the more you can learn. Even if you are not working with individuals and families like those in the case example, you can still benefit from mentally applying the competencies to a single case and using the same process to contemplate their relevance to your professional development during your social work practicum.

Reflective Questions on Competency Application

Carefully read the following questions and reflect on the professional and ethical requirements relevant to the Smith and Johnson family. You do not need to answer these questions since they are only meant to help you consider some aspects of the competency and their application in practice. However, you might want to explore the answers to those questions that directly relate to your practicum setting.

- If the Smith and Johnson family are your clients, what do you need to know and be able to do to demonstrate ethical and professional behavior?

- Can you identify at least two ethical standards from the NASW Code of Ethics that you can use to guide your work with the Smith and Johnson family?

- How would you demonstrate respect for client's self-determination if you are working with this family? If the clients are the children, are there limits to self-determination?

- Can you identify and explain the policies, laws, and regulations that will guide your work with the Smith and Johnson family?

- Think of your practicum placement; is there a possibility that you will work with a family like the Smith and Johnson Family? If so, do you have working knowledge of the agency's policies regarding clients' access to their records? Who has access? How is access granted?

- Do you have sufficient knowledge to clearly inform clients about the purpose of the services provided by the agency? Are you able to explain agency services and limitations to clients like Mrs. Smith?

- Going through the COVID-19 pandemic made it necessary to use technology for distance learning. If you are in a school setting, do you know if children like Alyssa and Daniel were able to keep up with their studies?

- Do you understand and are you able to explain the policies concerning the use of technology in the provision of social work services? If you are working with the grandparents, do you know if they are able to use technology successfully?

- If technology is used, how do you assess the clients' intellectual, emotional, and physical ability to use technology to receive social work services?

- How would you know if your client lacks the capacity to provide informed consent? Are there differences between a school setting and a clinic or other social work settings when it comes to informed consent?

- How would you demonstrate respect for the role of other professionals when engaged in interprofessional practice in a school setting, a clinic, or any other setting where you might interact with the Smith and Johnson family?

- The Smith and Johnson family could be Black, White, Native American, or Hispanic. What do you need to know and be able to do to demonstrate a rights-based, antiracist, and anti-oppressive social work practice?

- Can you identify and describe the agency's policies and procedures to address the needs of clients who do not speak English?

- Do you have sufficient knowledge and skills to demonstrate awareness and cultural humility when working with clients who come from backgrounds that are different from yours?

Can you describe and apply the concept of cultural humility when working with diverse clients? Are you committed to develop the knowledge and skills necessary to engage with the Smith and Johnson family with cultural humility?

What are the social work values that you need to demonstrate in your work with the Smith and Johnson family?

How can your personal feelings, values, and experiences influence your professional judgment and behavior as you work with the Smith and Johnson family?

What do you need to do to identify potential conflicts of interest as you work with this family? If you need to make a referral, what can you do to make sure you are not referring clients to someone who will directly or indirectly benefit you? What steps can you take to ensure that the family will benefit from a referral?

What steps can you take to protect the confidentiality of all information obtained during your interaction with the Smith and Johnson family?

Do you have the skills to operate all equipment related to retrieving and storing client information?

Do you know how to set clear boundaries to avoid engaging in physical contact with clients when there is a possibility of psychological harm to the client because of the contact?

What can you do to set clear boundaries to avoid the sexual exploitation of clients and their relatives?

How do you avoid using derogatory language in written, verbal, or electronic communications to or about clients?

Do you know the process to take reasonable steps to avoid abandoning clients who are still in need of services?

As you work with the Smith and Johnson family, you might become aware of your knowledge and skills gaps. How might those knowledge and skills gaps impair your competence? What steps can you take to address them?

As a social work practicum student, do you understand the limitations on the services you are allowed to provide with consultation and supervision?

What can you do to use consultation and supervision effectively?

Do you know the process to transition cases back to your social work field instructor once practicum is over?

As you consider these questions, think about the clients you work with in your social work practicum. Are these questions relevant to your work with clients? What other questions would be relevant to explore as you attempt to engage in ethical and professional social work practice?

Investigating Each Sentence in the Competency Description

In this section, you will explore the meaning and application of the concepts relevant to competency 1. You will use your basic research skills to explore the knowledge base of the competency, finding and studying research articles and other relevant sources such as the NASW website and the NASW Code of Ethics, along with your textbooks and course notes. While the exercises in this chapter call for you to do some independent learning, you should also explore your university library and consult with the librarian and your instructors to ensure that you are using scientific sources of knowledge.

> **Competency 1**
>
> ## Demonstrate Ethical and Professional Behavior
>
> Social workers understand the value base of the profession and its ethical standards, as well as relevant policies, laws, and regulations that may affect practice with individuals, families, groups, organizations, and communities.

Identify Key Concepts, Search for the Meaning of Those Concepts, and Critically Examine the Requirements of the Competency

1. Read and analyze the NASW Code of Ethics to identify the values of the social work profession (https://www.socialworkers.org/About/Ethics/Code-of-Ethics/Code-of-Ethics-English).

   a. What are the values of the profession? How would you demonstrate those values in your work with clients?

2. Consider those to whom you as a social worker owe ethical conduct, illustrated in Figure 1.2. Can you identify the ethical standards relevant to your practicum?

3. The first step to become familiar with relevant policies, laws, and regulations is to read your practicum agency's policies and procedures manual.

   a. What are the relevant policies, laws, and regulations that you must follow to provide client services during your social work practicum?

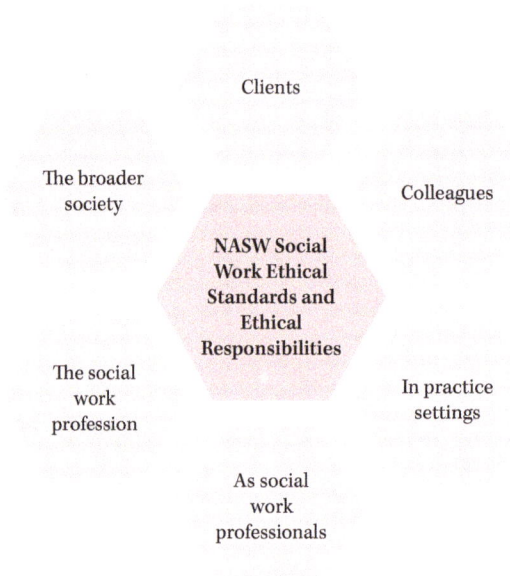

FIGURE 1.2   NASW social work ethical standards.

4. Identify and read at least one federal policy that impacts social work services at your agency.

    a. Identify the connection between agency policies and federal policies.
    b. Identify the consequences of neglecting to follow the federal mandates.

Reflective Writing Practice

In a few sentences, describe how you will use what you learned from reading the NASW Code of Ethics and your practicum agency policies and procedures to guide your work with clients during your practicum experience.

_____

_____

_____

_____

_____

Application Follow-Up

Date you used the agency policies and procedures information and the NASW Code of Ethics guidelines to assist a client at your practicum: _____

In a few sentences, describe what you learned from the process of utilizing the agency's policies and procedures and the NASW Code of Ethics in your work with clients.

_____

_____

_____

_____

_____

Self-Evaluation

Successful	I can effectively demonstrate these competency requirements during practicum, and I can explain how these competency requirements contribute to effective social work practice.
Developing	I can identify the information I need and am able to apply it in some practicum situations, but I am also aware of some knowledge and skill gaps that I need to address.
Unsuccessful	Currently, I am not able to successfully demonstrate these competency requirements in practicum.

> **Competency 1**
>
> **Demonstrate Ethical and Professional Behavior**
>
> Social workers understand that ethics are informed by principles of human rights and apply them toward realizing social, racial, economic, and environmental justice in their practice.

Identify Key Concepts, Search for the Meaning of Those Concepts, and Critically Examine the Requirements of the Competency

1. If you have a social work ethics textbook, review the index to identify a chapter on ethical principles and analyze it to identify how ethical principles are used. If you don't have an ethics textbook, you can find and use *Ethical Decisions for Social Work Practice* by Dolgoff et al. (2012).

   a. Identify the principles of human rights that are most relevant to social work practice.

2. Read the American Declaration of Independence and the U.S. Constitution and identify the human rights principles relevant to social work practice found in those documents.

3. Read the Universal Declaration of Human Rights and identify the human rights relevant to your social work practicum.

4. Conduct an internet search with the phrase "principles of human rights" and identify the social, racial, and economic justice issues related to the principles you identified.

Reflective Writing Practice

In a few sentences, describe how human rights principles relate to ethical social work practice and how you might use what you learned from reviewing these documents in your social work practice.

_____

_____

_____

_____

Application Follow-Up

Date you used the ethical principles you identified to inform your work with a client during practicum: _____

In a few sentences, describe what you learned from the process of applying principles of human rights during your social work practicum.

_____

_____

_____

_____

Self-Evaluation

Successful	I can effectively demonstrate these competency requirements during practicum, and I can explain how these competency requirements contribute to effective social work practice.
Developing	I can identify the information I need and am able to apply it in some practicum situations, but I am also aware of some knowledge and skill gaps that I need to address.
Unsuccessful	Currently, I am not able to successfully demonstrate these competency requirements in practicum.

Competency 1

Demonstrate Ethical and Professional Behavior

Social workers understand frameworks of ethical decision making and apply principles of critical thinking to those frameworks in practice, research, and policy arenas.

Identify Key Concepts, Search for the Meaning of Those Concepts, and Critically Examine the Requirements of the Competency

1. Identify a framework of ethical decision-making. You can find it in your social work ethics textbook, or you can search the internet, but if you use the internet, make sure the source is in line with social work ethics.

2. Conduct an internet search to find a definition of "principles of critical thinking."

    a. How might you use those principles to address ethical challenges during your social work practicum?

3. Identify a critical thinking tool. (This is an important step, since you should use a critical thinking tool to analyze everything you read as you are developing your professional knowledge and skills.) you can find and use *The miniature guide to critical thinking concepts and tools by Paul, R., & Elder, L. (2019).*

    a. How are you going to use the tool you identified?

4. Identify the population you serve at your practicum setting. Are you working directly with clients, or are you working with communities, doing research, or contributing to policy development and evaluation?

    a. Are there different critical thinking tools you can use depending on your client population?

Reflective Writing Practice

In a few sentences, describe how you will use the framework of ethical decision-making you identified as you complete your social work practicum. How might using a critical thinking tool to examine the ethical decision-making framework you identified impact your use of that framework?

_____

_____

_____

_____

Application Follow-Up

Date you used the ethical decision-making framework you identified to work through an issue at your practicum: _____

In a few sentences, describe what you learned from the process of using critical thinking to address an issue during your social work practicum.

_____

_____

_____

_____

Self-Evaluation

Successful	I can effectively demonstrate these competency requirements during practicum, and I can explain how these competency requirements contribute to effective social work practice.
Developing	I can identify the information I need and am able to apply it in some practicum situations, but I am also aware of some knowledge and skill gaps that I need to address.
Unsuccessful	Currently, I am not able to successfully demonstrate these competency requirements in practicum.

Competency 1

Demonstrate Ethical and Professional Behavior

Social workers recognize and manage personal values and the distinction between personal and professional values.

Identify Key Concepts, Search for the Meaning of Those Concepts, and Critically Examine the Requirements of the Competency

1. Conduct an internet search for personal values and identify at least 10 values that you believe are fundamental to who you are as a person.

    a. Explore the meaning of living your life in integrity with your personal values.

2. Identify the values of the social work profession (found in the NASW [2022] Code of Ethics).

    a. Explore the meaning of demonstrating the social work professional values as you interact with clients, peers, and supervisors during your social work practicum.

Reflective Writing Practice

In a few sentences, describe the differences between the values you identified for yourself and the values of the social work profession. Describe how you will manage your personal values as you interact with clients who might have different personal values.

_____

_____

_____

_____

Application Follow-Up

Date you recognized the difference between your personal values and professional values and used the values of the profession to guide your behavior at your practicum: _____

In a few sentences, describe what you learned from the process of applying the values of the social work profession to guide your behavior at your practicum.

_____

_____

_____

_____

Self-Evaluation

Successful	I can effectively demonstrate these competency requirements during practicum, and I can explain how these competency requirements contribute to effective social work practice.
Developing	I can identify the information I need and am able to apply it in some practicum situations, but I am also aware of some knowledge and skill gaps that I need to address.
Unsuccessful	Currently, I am not able to successfully demonstrate these competency requirements in practicum.

Competency 1

Demonstrate Ethical and Professional Behavior

Social workers understand how their evolving worldview, personal experiences, and affective reactions influence their professional judgment and behavior.

Identify Key Concepts, Search for the Meaning of Those Concepts, and Critically Examine the Requirements of the Competency

1. Conduct an internet search to find a definition of "worldview" and identify the factors that have shaped your worldview (socioeconomic status, education, culture, etc.).
2. Conduct an internet search to find a definition of "the impact of affective reactions in professional development" and think about how your feelings will influence your reactions when working with people in distress.
3. Conduct an internet search to find a definition of "professional judgment in social work practice" and identify an emotional issue that has impacted your life. Consider how emotion might impact your professional judgments. For example, if you grew up with a parent who is an alcoholic and have strong negative feelings about addictions, what steps are you willing to take to be able to work with clients who are struggling with addiction? Is there a possibility that you and your clients might be best served by your ability to select a social work practice setting where addiction is not the focus of social work intervention? What can you do to address your own emotional issues before you work with clients?

Reflective Writing Practice

In a few sentences, describe the steps you can take to increase your awareness of how your affective reactions will influence your professional judgments and the steps you can take to increase self-awareness, self-regulation, and self-care around those issues.

_____

_____

Application Follow-Up

Date you recognized how your personal experience shaped your worldview and how those experiences impact your professional judgments: _____

In a few sentences, describe what you learned from the process of increasing your awareness of how your affective reactions will influence your professional judgments.

_____

_____

_____

_____

Self-Evaluation

Successful	I can effectively demonstrate these competency requirements during practicum, and I can explain how these competency requirements contribute to effective social work practice.
Developing	I can identify the information I need and am able to apply it in some practicum situations, but I am also aware of some knowledge and skill gaps that I need to address.
Unsuccessful	Currently, I am not able to successfully demonstrate these competency requirements in practicum.

Competency 1

Demonstrate Ethical and Professional Behavior

Social workers take measures to care for themselves professionally and personally, understanding that self-care is paramount for competent and ethical social work practice.

Identify Key Concepts, Search for the Meaning of Those Concepts, and Critically Examine the Requirements of the Competency

1. Search the internet for self-care resources and ideas and identify your self-care needs:

   a. How are you taking care of your mental health?

   b. What are your emotional health care needs? How are you addressing those needs?

   c. How is your physical health? Are you eating nutritious food and giving your body sufficient rest? Are you avoiding toxic substances, or are you eating highly processed foods that can have negative long-term consequences for your health?

    d.   What are your spiritual health needs?

    e.   How are you taking care of your financial health? Do you know how to budget to make sure that your basic needs are met? Do you use your budget to avoid spending money you don't have to avoid the stress of being in debt?

    f.   How are your social health needs met? Do the people around you support your life goals and encourage your success? Do you have at least one person you can count on when you need support?

    g.   How are you managing your resources and time to include sufficient rest, exercise, appropriate nutrition, and social interaction?

2. What are your professional self-care needs? Most practicums are unpaid, but the reward is the ability to develop professional skills. Does your practicum provide you with opportunities to learn and grow?

3. How do you deal with the negative emotions related to knowing that your best efforts will not always be enough?

Reflective Writing Practice

In a few sentences, describe your self-care plan and describe how self-care will help you become a competent and ethical social work practitioner.

_____

_____

_____

_____

Note: If you search for reasons social workers lose their professional license, you will notice that most of them had personal issues that interfered with their ability to function professionally. Therefore, it will be to your advantage to identify your personal needs so that you can address them before those issues derail your professional goals. Use Table 1.1 to identify the well-being needs you must address for yourself as you work on your professional development.

TABLE 1.1 Checklist of Well-Being Needs

Well-Being	Critical Questions	The Impact of Personal Well-Being on Professional Social Work Practice
Physical	What steps are you taking to ensure your own physical wellness?	Are you aware of your physical health needs? What steps are you taking to take care of your health? Are you showing up to your social work practicum with sufficient physical energy and stamina to handle practicum-related challenges?
Mental (Emotional)	What steps are you taking to take care of your own emotional needs?	Are you prepared to work with people who are experiencing emotional pain? Do you have a support system to make sure that you don't seek your client's approval?
Mental (Intellectual)	What steps are you taking to increase your intellectual capacity?	Are you a self-guided learner? Working with people will present challenges you have not faced before; do you understand that you do not need to know everything, but you need to be willing to actively engage in the learning process as you encounter new situations?
Social (Relationships)	What steps are you taking to nurture positive social relationships?	Are you able to set clear boundaries with clients? Can you be friendly and personable without creating inappropriate relationships with clients? Do you have social supports outside the school and work environment?
Financial	What steps are you taking to ensure your own financial welfare?	Are you able to live within your means to avoid financial distress? Do you have a budget, and are you able to stick with it? If you manage money as part of your work or practicum, are you conscientious about keeping accurate records?
Occupational	What are you doing to develop appropriate occupational skills?	The social work practicum provides you an opportunity to develop occupational skills. Are you able to identify the specific skills necessary in the context of your social work practicum? Have you completed all required training? Are you able to explain how the required training relates to your overall occupational goal?
Spiritual	What role does spirituality play in your life?	Are you aware of your own spiritual needs? If you are not religious, can you accept that for some of your clients religion will be a critical aspect of their life? If you are religious, can you be careful not to impose your religious beliefs on clients? Note: There are some social work settings where spirituality is a central aspect of social work practice, and it is important to understand that difference.
Cultural	How is your cultural background helping you? How is it hindering you?	What are your cultural obstacles? Are you aware of the impact that culture has on your own life? Are you aware of the impact that culture has on the lives of your clients? Can you be culturally humble?
Environmental	What are the environmental factors that impact your overall well-being?	Do you live and work in a safe environment? Are you aware of the environmental factors that impact your clients? If your client's environment is unsafe, do you have the skills to appropriately interact with clients in their environment?

Application Follow-Up

Date you recognized the impact of your personal self-care on your practicum performance:
_____

In a few sentences, describe what you learned from the process of identifying your self-care needs and describe how your self-care will help you become a competent and ethical social worker.

_____

_____

_____

_____

Self-Evaluation

Successful	I can effectively demonstrate these competency requirements during practicum, and I can explain how these competency requirements contribute to effective social work practice.
Developing	I can identify the information I need and am able to apply it in some practicum situations, but I am also aware of some knowledge and skill gaps that I need to address.
Unsuccessful	Currently, I am not able to successfully demonstrate these competency requirements in practicum.

Competency 1

Demonstrate Ethical and Professional Behavior

Social workers use rights-based, antiracist, and anti-oppressive lenses to understand and critique the profession's history, mission, roles, and responsibilities and recognize historical and current contexts of oppression in shaping institutions and social work.

Identify Key Concepts, Search for the Meaning of Those Concepts, and Critically Examine the Requirements of the Competency

1. Conduct an internet search for anti-oppressive social work practices and analyze the information you find.
2. Conduct an internet search for rights-based and antiracist social work practices and analyze the information you find.
3. Using the information you found, identify the rights-based, antiracist, and anti-oppressive practices at your practicum.

4. If you cannot identify those practices, share what you learn from reading about antiracist and anti-oppressive practices with your field instructor during supervision and ask for help to connect theory to practice.

Reflective Writing Practice

In a few sentences, describe the specific steps you will take to engage in rights-based, antiracist, and anti-oppressive practices during your social work practicum.

_____

_____

_____

_____

Application Follow-Up

Date you were able to apply antiracist and anti-oppressive social work practices at your practicum: _____

In a few sentences, describe what you learned from the process of engaging in rights-based, antiracist, and anti-oppressive practices during your social work practicum.

_____

_____

_____

_____

Self-Evaluation

Successful	I can effectively demonstrate these competency requirements during practicum, and I can explain how these competency requirements contribute to effective social work practice.
Developing	I can identify the information I need and am able to apply it in some practicum situations, but I am also aware of some knowledge and skill gaps that I need to address.
Unsuccessful	Currently, I am not able to successfully demonstrate these competency requirements in practicum.

Competency 1

Demonstrate Ethical and Professional Behavior

Social workers understand the role of other professionals when engaged in interprofessional practice.

Identify Key Concepts, Search for the Meaning of Those Concepts, and Critically Examine the Requirements of the Competency

1. Identify the professions that intersect with social work practice in your field practicum. (For example, if you are in a school setting, teachers, administrators, and nurses are some of the professionals you will interact with.)
2. Identify how each one of those professionals contributes to the client's well-being. (For example, teachers play an important role in the life of a student. If you are placed at a school, how might your relationship with teachers help you be more effective in your work with students and their families?)

Reflective Writing Practice

In a few sentences, describe the interprofessional work practices used at your practicum and your efforts to work effectively as part of an interdisciplinary work team.

_____

_____

_____

_____

Application Follow-Up

Date you recognized the role of other professionals at your practicum and engaged in interprofessional social work practices: _____

In a few sentences, describe what you learned from the process of engaging in interprofessional social work practice.

_____

_____

_____

_____

Self-Evaluation

Successful	I can effectively demonstrate these competency requirements during practicum, and I can explain how these competency requirements contribute to effective social work practice.
Developing	I can identify the information I need and am able to apply it in some practicum situations, but I am also aware of some knowledge and skill gaps that I need to address.
Unsuccessful	Currently, I am not able to successfully demonstrate these competency requirements in practicum.

Competency 1

Demonstrate Ethical and Professional Behavior

Social workers recognize the importance of lifelong learning and are committed to continually updating their skills to ensure relevant and effective practice.

Identify Key Concepts, Search for the Meaning of Those Concepts, and Critically Examine the Requirements of the Competency

1. Identify the role of the social worker at your practicum setting.
2. Identify the knowledge and skills necessary to be an effective social worker in that role.
3. Identify one way the knowledge and skills needed today might change in the future.
4. Identify at least one professional journal that might be useful to a social worker who wants to access innovations in social work practice or stay informed about social changes that might impact social work practice.
5. Identify the professional organizations that might be useful in helping you keep up with your professional growth as you enter the social work profession.

Reflective Writing Practice

In a few sentences, outline a plan for continuous professional growth and describe how you would use research and professional affiliations to ensure you remain competent.

_____

_____

_____

_____

Application Follow-Up

Date you identified a professional organization or journal that you can use to engage in continuous learning after graduation: _____

In a few sentences, describe what you learned from the process of outlining a plan for continuous professional growth.

_____

_____

_____

_____

Self-Evaluation

Successful	I can effectively demonstrate these competency requirements during practicum, and I can explain how these competency requirements contribute to effective social work practice.
Developing	I can identify the information I need and am able to apply it in some practicum situations, but I am also aware of some knowledge and skill gaps that I need to address.
Unsuccessful	Currently, I am not able to successfully demonstrate these competency requirements in practicum.

Competency 1

Demonstrate Ethical and Professional Behavior

Social workers understand digital technology and the ethical use of technology in social work practice.

Identify Key Concepts, Search for the Meaning of Those Concepts, and Critically Examine the Requirements of the Competency

1. Identify the types of technology being used in your practicum setting.
2. Identify the ethical issues that might come up as you use technology in the practice setting.
3. Identify the ethical issues that might come up as you use technology in your personal life. (For example, do you evaluate your social media presence using an ethical decision-making tool? How would a client or potential employer judge your social media presence?)

Reflective Writing Practice

In a few sentences, describe your plan to use digital technology ethically. For example, consider your use of personal electronic devices during practicum hours. Do you put your electronic devices away as soon as you arrive at your practicum? Are you distracted by phone messages during your meetings with clients or during supervision? Explore your reasoning behind your answer to these questions and explain how your reasoning is in line with the NASW Code of Ethics.

_____

_____

_____

_____

Application Follow-Up

Date you identified an ethical issue related to technology use at your practicum: _____

In a few sentences, describe what you learned from the process of describing your plan to use digital technology ethically.

_____

_____

_____

_____

Self-Evaluation

Successful	I can effectively demonstrate these competency requirements during practicum, and I can explain how these competency requirements contribute to effective social work practice.
Developing	I can identify the information I need and am able to apply it in some practicum situations, but I am also aware of some knowledge and skill gaps that I need to address.
Unsuccessful	Currently, I am not able to successfully demonstrate these competency requirements in practicum.

Demonstrating Ethical and Professional Behavior

There are many settings where social work students can do their social work internship. If your practice does not have a direct client contact component, it is important that you connect the competency requirements to the requirements of your practicum. Ask your social work field instructor or liaison for guidance if you cannot connect the following competency behaviors with your practicum experience.

Make ethical decisions by applying the standards of the National Association of Social Workers Code of Ethics, relevant laws and regulations, models for ethical decision making, ethical conduct of research, and additional codes of ethics within the profession as appropriate to the context.

Demonstrating Competency 1 With the Smith and Johnson Family	Demonstrating Competency 1 During Your Practicum
1. If you are in a school setting, your main clients are Daniel and Alyssa Johnson. They are minors, so they are clients who lack decision-making capacity. Therefore, your first ethical responsibility is to take reasonable steps to safeguard their interests and rights. You will also need to work with their grandparents. 2. In addition to your ethical responsibilities to clients, you will have ethical responsibilities to your colleagues, the school, the community, the social work profession, and society. You will need to make sure that you work ethically with all the people involved in this case and consider the role of the institutions involved. 3. You will need to become familiar with the policy manual of the school as well as school district policies and have a working understanding of national educational policies such as Individuals with Disabilities Education Act (IDEA), Every Student Succeeds Act (ESSA), Family Educational Rights and Privacy Act (FERPA) and Title II, IX, and IV and be aware of their relevance to this case. 4. Dolgoff et al.'s general decision-making model might be useful in this case, since the first step will be to identify the issues that might hinder the educational success of Daniel and Alyssa Johnson and the people who should be involved in addressing those issues. 5. Since bullying might be an issue in this case, you need to identify research relevant to this issue and make sure that it addresses the issue ethically before you use the information in this case. 6. You need to get familiar with the code of ethics for educators to be aware of the ethical point of view of other professionals involved in the case.	1. Who are your clients at your practicum? How can you use the standards in the NASW Code of Ethics when you work with clients? 2. Can you describe how you demonstrate your ethical responsibilities to your colleagues, your practice setting, the community, the social work profession, and society as you engage in social work practice in your practicum? 3. Have you identified the policies, laws, and regulations that guide your work in your practicum setting? How do federal laws guide client services in your practicum? 4. Can you describe how you can use an ethical decision-making model to address ethical issues during practicum? 5. Can you provide an example of how you have been able to use research ethically to learn about the issues that are relevant to your client or client population? 6. What are the other professional codes of ethics that are relevant in your practicum setting? How will understanding their ethical perspective help your interactions with other professionals in your practicum?

Demonstrate professional behavior; appearance; and oral, written, and electronic communication.

Demonstrating Competency 1 With the Smith and Johnson Family	Demonstrating Competency 1 During Your Practicum
1. How can you prepare to work with the Smith and Johnson family? Can you review Daniel's file and make notes of any questions you should ask your supervisors? 2. Do you have a working knowledge of your role and what you need to do to help the Smith Johnson family? 3. What steps do you take to make sure that you are professionally dressed and groomed?	1. How do you prepare to work with clients at your practicum? Do you review client's records? Do you discuss with your social work instructor the cases assigned to you before meeting with clients? 2. Describe your role at your practicum and what you need to do to help clients during your practicum. 3. Do you always show up to practicum professionally dressed and groomed?

4. Do you speak in a professional manner, without using terminology that clients might not understand? 5. What steps can you take to ensure that you use professional language appropriate to your work setting in written communications? Are your written and electronic messages appropriate and grammatically correct?	4. Can you describe a situation when you were able to explain social work services to clients professionally without using terminology that clients might not understand? 5. Can you describe the steps you take to ensure that your written and electronic communications are appropriate and grammatically correct?

Use technology ethically and appropriately to facilitate practice outcomes.

Demonstrating Competency 1 With the Smith and Johnson Family	Demonstrating Competency 1 During Your Practicum
1. How might technology help facilitate social work practice outcomes with the Smith and Johnson family? 2. Daniel and Alyssa had to use technology to engage in distance learning during the COVID-19 pandemic. How would you know if they benefited from the use of technology? If they struggled to keep up, what can be done to help students who were not able to successfully use technology during the pandemic? 3. In most school settings, technology is used to keep electronic student records. If Daniel and Alyssa are your clients, do you know who has access to their student records? How is access granted? 4. What steps can you take to use technology ethically? What steps can be taken to secure client information? What can you do to safeguard this family's information?	1. Give an example of how technology helps facilitate social work practice outcomes in your work with clients at your social work practicum. 2. If clients must use technology to engage in social work services, how do you know if all clients benefit from the use of technology? Can you provide an example of what can be done to help those who are not able to successfully use technology? 3. If technology is used to keep electronic client records at your practicum, can you describe the steps you take to ensure that you are using that technology appropriately? Can you describe who has access to client records and how access is granted? 4. Can you provide an example of how you are using technology ethically? What steps are you taking to secure client information?

Use supervision and consultation to guide professional judgment and behavior.

Demonstrating Competency 1 With the Smith and Johnson Family	Demonstrating Competency 1 During Your Practicum
1. What are the professional judgments that need to be made as you work with the Smith and Johnson family? 2. How might you use supervision and consultation to guide your behavior as you interact with this family? 3. Is there a specific issue related to the Smith and Johnson family that you should consult with your supervisor about? For example, as you interviewed Alyssa, she said that she believes "her grandma wants to get rid of her." If you don't know if that is something that needs to be addressed, you will need to consult your social work instructor. 4. Daniel stated that he had been bullied and got in trouble after defending himself. How can the teachers, school administrators, and social workers contribute to provide a safe environment for him?	1. Can you identify the professional judgments that need to be made in your practicum setting? 2. How are you using supervision and consultation during your social work practicum? 3. Can you describe a specific practicum case that you reviewed with your social work instructor to identify the best strategy to work with a client? 4. What are the specific issues that you bring to your instructional meetings to consult with your social work instructor? 5. Have you identified specific issues that might hinder your relationship with clients? Have you used consultation and supervision to explore those issues?

(Continued)

Demonstrating Competency 1 With the Smith and Johnson Family	Demonstrating Competency 1 During Your Practicum
5. What can you do to show Daniel that you are a trustworthy professional and care about his safety? 6. How can you develop an effective working relationship with the children's teachers, if the children need accommodations due to their mental or emotional health needs?	6. Can you describe a specific professional relationship you need to cultivate in your practicum setting? Do you work with doctors, attorneys, or other professionals? How do you cultivate a positive professional relationship with people at your practicum?

Competency Development Topics for the Social Work Practicum Seminar

▶ Competency 1 Field Seminar Topics

- Ethical social work practice and the ethical decision-making process
- The use of instructional supervision to address competency development needs
- Factors that contribute to professional behavior during social work practicum
- The skills needed to use technology appropriately during the social work practicum

▼ Prior Planning

- If you completed all reading and writing exercises in this chapter, you can review your notes and identify the key concepts related to each of the seminar discussion topics.
- Identify the parts of the competency that you have not been able to successfully demonstrate and formulate specific discussion questions you can bring to seminar to explore how your peers are dealing with those issues.
- Review your work with clients at your practicum setting and consider any ethical and professional questions you might have.

◀ During Seminar

- Listen to your peers and your seminar instructor.
- Seek to understand and ask clarifying questions to help you comprehend the requirements related to competency 1. Can you provide an example of how you are using technology ethically? What steps are you taking to secure client information?
- Be ready to contribute by sharing your struggles as well as your successes in addressing competency 1 requirements.
- Find the joy of professional growth. Do you want to become the best social worker you can be? If so, identify the successes along the way. Even the smallest gains are still part of your overall progress in your journey to become an ethical and professional social worker.

Competency Development Topics for the Educational Supervision Meeting

▶ **Competency 1 Social Work Practicum Instructional Supervision Meeting Topics**

- Identify the most common ethical decision-making opportunities in this social work practicum setting.
- List the specific professional behavior expectations you should demonstrate during your social work practicum.
- Describe the specific skills needed to appropriately use technology during social work practicum.
- Establish a regular instructional supervision schedule and discuss the instructional supervision agenda.

▼ **Prior Planning**

- Review your field practicum work and identify any issues you are unsure about regarding each of the supervision topics above.
- Identify the parts of the competency that you have not been able to successfully demonstrate and come up with possible tasks you can volunteer to perform to create a learning opportunity for yourself.

◀ **During the Instructional Supervision Meeting**

- Be prepared to ask questions that will help you develop and practice competency 1.
- Listen attentively to your social work instructor.
- Prepare mentally for the fact that part of the learning-by-doing process includes a need to understand that our best efforts at demonstrating effective performance usually need improvement.

Summary

As you can see in Figure 1.3, continuous learning is required to demonstrate ethical and professional behavior in social work practice.

In this chapter, you had the opportunity to explore the meaning of each sentence of the description of competency 1. You had several opportunities to think about the requirements of the competency as you identified key concepts, searched for the meaning of those concepts, and critically examined the requirements of the competency. If you made notes in this workbook, you could use those notes when you get ready for your final field performance evaluation, and you will be able to cite specific examples of how you are demonstrating your ability to demonstrate competency requirements related to ethical and professional social work practice. If you

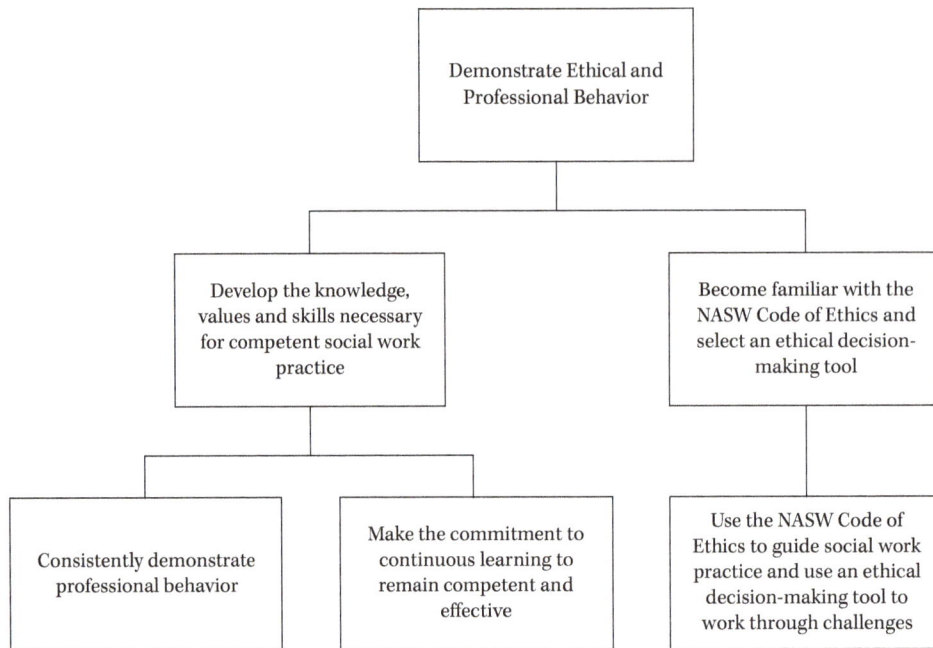

FIGURE 1.3   Requirements of ethical and professional behavior.

make the commitment to spend the time and energy necessary to become a competent, ethical social work professional, you will become a valued member of the social work profession.

Recommended Reading Materials

Books	Descriptions
Dolgoff, R., Harrington, D., & Loewenberg, F. M. (2012). *Ethical Decisions for Social Work Practice (Ethics & Legal Issues)*. Cengage Learning.	Competency 1 requires an understanding of social work ethics and the ability to use ethical decision-making frameworks. This book offers both.
Paul, R., & Elder, L. (2019). *The miniature guide to critical thinking concepts and tools*. Rowman & Littlefield.	Critical thinking skills are essential. This short guide provides user-friendly tools for analyzing the information required to develop the competencies.
Goleman, D. (1996). Emotional intelligence. Why it can matter more than IQ. *Learning, 24*(6), 49–50.	Social work is about working with people, and people are emotional beings. Developing emotional intelligence can be very useful.
Goleman D. (1998). *Working With Emotional Intelligence*. Bantam.	This book explains the role of emotional intelligence in workplace success.
Leal, B. C., III (2017). *4 Essential Keys to Effective Communication in Love, Life, Work–Anywhere! A How-to Guide for Practicing the Empathic Listening, Speaking, and Dialogue Skills to Achieve Relationship Success With the Important People in Your Life*. Self-Published.	Communication skills are essential in social work practice.

Brown, B. (2012). *The Power of Vulnerability: Teachings on Authenticity, Connection and Courage [Audiobook].* Sounds True.	Authenticity, connection, and courage are indispensable in social work practice. The author's research is centered on social work practice.
Harari, Y. N. (2018). *21 Lessons for the 21st Century.* Random House.	This collection of provocative essays deals with globalization, ethics, technology, and other social issues.
Grise-Owens, E. (Ed.). (2016). *The A-to-Z Self-Care Handbook for Social Workers and Other Helping Professionals.* New Social Worker Press.	If you want to effectively help others, start by taking care of yourself. This book will provide you with ideas to create your own self-care plan.

References

Council on Social Work Education. (2022, May 23). *2022 EPAS.* https://www.cswe.org/accreditation/info/2022-epas/

Dolgoff, R., Harrington, D., & Loewenberg, F. M. (2012). *Ethical decisions for social work practice.* Cengage Learning.

National Association of Social Workers. (2022, May 23). *NASW code of ethics.* https://www.socialworkers.org/About/Ethics/Code-of-Ethics/Code-of-Ethics-English

Paul, R., & Elder, L. (2019). *The miniature guide to critical thinking concepts and tools.* Rowman & Littlefield.

CREDIT

Competency 2

Advance Human Rights and Social, Racial, Economic, and Environmental Justice

In this chapter, you will explore the second of the nine social work competencies provided by the CSWE. Competency 2 is at the core of social work ethics and the role of the profession in society. To develop this competency, you need knowledge about human rights, social justice issues, racial justice issues, and the economic and environmental issues that affect social work clients. Advocating for social change requires an understanding of the advocacy process and the ability to interact with politicians and other power brokers.

However, the essential step to advance human rights and social, racial, economic, and environmental justice is to accept the premise that every person in society has fundamental human rights. Therefore, coming to terms with our own social, racial, and economic status is necessary when we approach human rights issues.

If we grew up marginalized and oppressed, we might be more aware of social injustices because we know that not everything that happened to us was our choice. However, if we grew up in affluence, we might not be fully aware that not everyone in society has access to drinkable water, safe neighborhoods, the best educational opportunities, excellent medical care, proper nutrition, and powerful attorneys who will protect our civil liberties if we get into legal trouble.

To fully embrace the requirements in competency 2, we need self-awareness to identify the way we see people who are socially, racially, and economically different from us. We must be willing to examine the role of power and privilege at every level of society, from the home to the community to the entire society. Social work as a profession has made the commitment to advance the human rights and social, racial, economic, and environmental justice due to all members in society. To live up to the profession's code of ethics, we need to make the commitment to become knowledgeable about these issues and be willing to develop the necessary skills to address them.

Competency 2 Description as Provided by CSWE: Advance Human Rights and Social, Racial, Economic, and Environmental Justice

As you read the following description, consider the meaning of each sentence and your ability to demonstrate the requirements of this competency as you work with clients during your social work practicum.

Competency 2

Advance Human Rights and Social, Racial, Economic, and Environmental Justice

Social workers understand that every person regardless of position in society has fundamental human rights. Social workers are knowledgeable about the global intersecting and ongoing injustices throughout history that result in oppression and racism, including social work's role and response. Social workers critically evaluate the distribution of power and privilege in society in order to promote social, racial, economic, and environmental justice by reducing inequities and ensuring dignity and respect for all. Social workers advocate for and engage in strategies to eliminate oppressive structural barriers to ensure that social resources, rights, and responsibilities are distributed equitably and that civil, political, economic, social, and cultural human rights are protected.

Social workers:

a. advocate for human rights at the individual, family, group, organizational, and community system levels; and
b. engage in practices that advance human rights to promote social, racial, economic, and environmental justice.

As you can see in Figure 2.1, The ability to advance human rights and social, racial, economic, and environmental justice, encompasses every aspect of social work practice. It is in the process of engaging, assessing, and intervening with clients that social workers need to demonstrate their ability to advance human rights and social, racial, economic, and environmental justice for clients.

Applying Competency 2

As you consider the case of the Smith and Johnson family, the human rights and the social, racial, economic, and environmental justice issues that affect them will become essential to your understanding of their needs. For example, in a school setting, we might focus on the fact that children have a human right to an education. However, we also know that social factors such as school funding, social policies regarding minorities' access to educational opportunities, and even teacher education and experience and overall community resources will influence their educational opportunities. Think about how the requirements of competency 2 might relate to your work with clients during your social work practicum experience.

Competency 1:

Advance the human rights, social, racial, economic and environmental justice of clients as we as we demonstrate ethical and professional behavior

Competency 2:

What are the knowledge, values, and skills necessary to advance human rights and social, racial, economic, and environmental justice in my role as a social worker?

Competency 9:

Advance the human rights, social, racial, economic and environmental justice of clients as we evaluate social work practice

Competency 3:

Advance the human rights, social, racial, economic and environmental justice of clients as we as we engage in anti-racism, diversity, equity and inclusion

Competency 8:

Advance the human rights, social, racial, economic and environmental justice of clients as we intervene with clients

**Competency 2
Advance Human Rights and Social, Racial, Economic, and Environmental Justice**

Competency 4:

Advance the human rights, social, racial, economic and environmental justice of clients as we engage in research

Competency 7:

Advance the human rights, social, racial, economic and environmental justice of clients as we assess clients

Competency 6:

Advance the human rights, social, racial, economic and environmental justice of clients as we engage with clients

Competency 5:

Advance the human rights, social, racial, economic and environmental justice of clients as we engage in policy practice

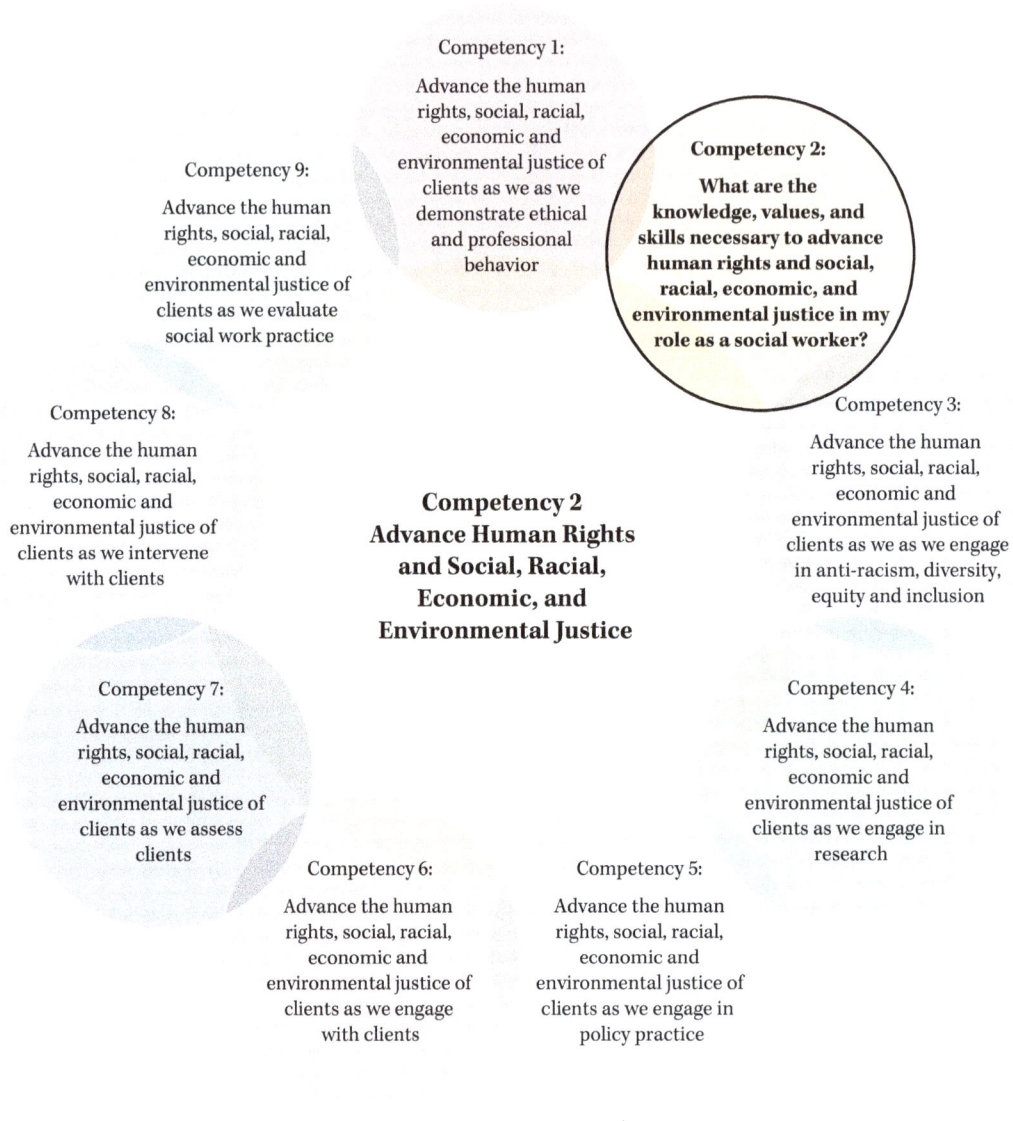

FIGURE 2.1   The relationship of competency 2 to the rest of the competencies.

Reflective Questions on Competency Application

Carefully read the following questions and reflect on the need to advance the human rights and social, racial, economic, and environmental justice issues relevant to the Smith and Johnson family. You do not need to answer these questions since they are only meant to help you consider some aspects of the competency and their application in practice. However, you might want to explore the answers to those questions that directly relate to your practicum setting.

What do you need to know and be able to do to advance the human rights and social, racial, economic, and environmental justice for clients like the Smith and Johnson family?

If your clients are Alyssa and Daniel, they have a human right to an education. What other human rights apply to children?

If your client is Mr. Johnson, he has a human right to not be tortured. Is isolation a kind of torture? How often do prisons use isolation as a punishment? Would that be a violation of his human rights? Does he have a human right to have contact with his children?

Is health care a human right? Mrs. Smith and her son are going through medical issues; do they have access to the medical care they need?

What are the specific social, racial, economic, and environmental justice issues that impact the life of each member of the Smith and Johnson family?

Is there a difference in the kinds of services available to this family if this family is White, Black, Hispanic, Native American, or recent immigrants? How would you identify those differences? Do you have the knowledge and skills to effectively work across cultures? How will your own ethnic identity influence how you work with a family that is culturally different from yours?

Are you aware of the structural barriers to provide needed services when working with undocumented families or families with mixed immigration status?

What is the impact of the economic status of this family on the kinds of services they can receive? Does it make a difference if this family is poor or middle class? Do social workers provide social work services to wealthy families? Is there a difference between the services provided to wealthy clients from those provided to low-income or middle-class clients?

One member of this family belongs to the LGBTQIA2S+ community; his parents do not accept the fact that he is gay, and the family has made "peace" with the situation by ignoring the issue. What are the problems and benefits with that kind of arrangement? He can now get married in the United States, but there are still people who will disrespect him, mistreat him, or exclude him. How could social workers protect the human rights of LGBTQIA2S+ clients? Do you have personal biases around these issues? If so, what steps can you take to ensure that you engage in ethical social work practice?

Is this family safe in their community? If this family belongs to a racial minority, do you know the rate of hate crimes against that minority group in your community? How are minority families impacted by the hate-motivated mass shootings that are so prevalent these days?

Daniel is being bullied in school; can you investigate if the bullying is related to social, racial, or economic factors? What can the school do to address those kinds of issues?

If Daniel and Alyssa are members of a Native American tribe and do not speak English at home, how would you investigate their cultural norms? How would that fact impact their access to appropriate educational opportunities?

How would you identify the environmental justice issues that affect this family? Do they have access to drinkable water? Is the air they breathe clean or polluted? Do they have access to clean nutritious food, or do they live in a food desert and only have access to highly processed food that can exacerbate Mrs. Smith's diabetes?

Think about the clients at your practicum setting. Are these questions relevant to your work with them? What other questions related to competency 2 would you explore?

Investigating Each Sentence in the Competency Description

In this section, you will explore the meaning and application of the concepts relevant to competency 2. You will use your basic research skills to explore the knowledge base of the competency, finding and studying research articles and other relevant sources such as the Universal Declaration of Human Rights, along with your textbooks and course notes. While the exercises in this chapter call for you to do some independent learning, you need to also explore your university library and consult with a librarian and your instructors to ensure that you access scientific sources of knowledge.

Competency 2

Advance Human Rights and Social, Racial, Economic, and Environmental Justice

Social workers understand that every person regardless of position in society has fundamental human rights.

Identify Key Concepts, Search for the Meaning of Those Concepts, and Critically Examine the Requirements of the Competency

1. Read and analyze the Universal Declaration of Human Rights (https://www.un.org/en/about-us/universal-declaration-of-human-rights).

   a. Critically analyze each of the 30 articles. Can you identify one human right that you are willing to give up? Have you enjoyed every one of those rights? If not, has the issue been rectified? If not, how should that issue be addressed?

   b. Consider the 30 human rights and think of the client population in your practicum setting. Can you identify the human rights that are most pertinent to your client population?

2. Identify the human rights that directly relate to your practicum setting. For example, if you are placed in a criminal justice setting, how might articles 5 through 11 relate to your clients?

3. Make a list of specific actions you can take to advance the fundamental human rights of your clients.

Reflective Writing Practice

In a few sentences, describe what you learned by examining the Universal Declaration of Human Rights and how you might be able to safeguard the fundamental human rights of clients at your practicum.

_____

_____

_____

_____

Application Follow-Up

Date you identified the specific human rights relevant to your practicum setting: _____

In a few sentences, describe what you learned from the process of identifying the fundamental human rights relevant to your clients and taking steps to protect those human rights in your work with clients.

_____

_____

_____

_____

Self-Evaluation

Successful	I can effectively demonstrate these competency requirements during practicum, and I can explain how these competency requirements contribute to effective social work practice.
Developing	I can identify the information I need and am able to apply it in some practicum situations, but I am also aware of some knowledge and skill gaps that I need to address.
Unsuccessful	Currently, I am not able to successfully demonstrate these competency requirements in practicum.

Competency 2

Advance Human Rights and Social, Racial, Economic, and Environmental Justice

Social workers are knowledgeable about the global intersecting and ongoing injustices throughout history that result in oppression and racism, including social work's role and response.

Identify Key Concepts, Search for the Meaning of Those Concepts, and Critically Examine the Requirements of the Competency

1. Use the phrase "global injustices" to search the internet, and carefully read and analyze at least two scholarly articles about this topic.

    a. What did you learn about global injustices from the articles?

2. Use the phrase "historical oppression in the United States" to search the internet, and carefully read and analyze at least two scholarly articles about this topic.

    a. What did you learn about historical oppression from your analysis of the articles?

3. Use the phrase "oppression and racism in the United States" to search the internet, and carefully read and analyze at least two scholarly articles about this topic.

   a. What did you learn about oppression and racism from the articles?

4. Use the phrase "injustices against Native Americans" to search the internet, and carefully read and analyze at least two scholarly articles about this topic.

   a. What did you learn about injustices against Native Americans from your analysis of the articles?

5. Use the phrase "social work response to social problems" to search the internet, and carefully read and analyze at least two scholarly articles about this topic.

   a. What did you learn about the role of social work in addressing social problems from your analysis of the articles?

Reflective Writing Practice

In a few sentences, describe the specific steps you can take to increase your knowledge and awareness of the global injustices that you might encounter in your role as social work intern.

_____

_____

_____

_____

Application Follow-Up

Date you were able to identify a connection between global injustice and the needs of the clients at your practicum: _____

In a few sentences, describe what you learned about ongoing injustices throughout history to consider the needs of clients at your practicum.

_____

_____

_____

_____

Self-Evaluation

Successful	I can effectively demonstrate these competency requirements during practicum, and I can explain how these competency requirements contribute to effective social work practice.
Developing	I can identify the information I need and am able to apply it in some practicum situations, but I am also aware of some knowledge and skill gaps that I need to address.
Unsuccessful	Currently, I am not able to successfully demonstrate these competency requirements in practicum.

Competency 2

Advance Human Rights and Social, Racial, Economic, and Environmental Justice

Social workers critically evaluate the distribution of power and privilege in society in order to promote social, racial, economic, and environmental justice by reducing inequities and ensuring dignity and respect for all.

Identify Key Concepts, Search for the Meaning of Those Concepts, and Critically Examine the Requirements of the Competency

1. Use the phrase "distribution of power and privilege in society" to search the internet, and carefully read and analyze at least two scholarly articles about this topic.

   a. What did you learn about power and privilege from your analysis of the articles?

2. Use the phrase "social justice and social work" to search the internet, and carefully read and analyze at least two scholarly articles about this topic.

   a. What did you learn about social justice and social work from the articles?

3. Use the phrase "racial justice and social work" to search the internet, and carefully read and analyze at least two scholarly articles about this topic.

   a. What did you learn about racial justice and social work from the articles?

4. Use the phrase "economic justice and social work" to search the internet, and carefully read and analyze at least two scholarly articles about this topic.

   a. What did you learn about economic justice and social work from the articles?

5. Use the phrase "environmental justice and social work" to search the internet, and carefully read and analyze at least two scholarly articles about this topic.

   a. What did you learn about environmental justice and social work from the articles?

6. Use the phrase "reducing inequities in social work practice" to search the internet, and carefully read and analyze at least two scholarly articles about this topic.

   a. What did you learn about the role of social workers in reducing inequities?

7. Use the phrase "ensuring dignity and respect in social work practice" to search the internet, and carefully read and analyze at least two scholarly articles about this topic.

   a. What did you learn about how you can demonstrate dignity and respect from your analysis of the articles?

Reflective Writing Practice

In a few sentences, describe what you learned about the distribution of power and privilege in society and how social workers can promote social, racial, economic, and environmental justice.

_____

_____

_____

_____

Application Follow-Up

Date you identify a specific step you can take to reduce social inequities as you work with clients during your practicum: _____

In a few sentences, describe what you learned from the process of implementing what you learned about inequities to inform your work with clients.

_____

_____

_____

_____

Self-Evaluation

Successful	I can effectively demonstrate these competency requirements during practicum, and I can explain how these competency requirements contribute to effective social work practice.
Developing	I can identify the information I need and am able to apply it in some practicum situations, but I am also aware of some knowledge and skill gaps that I need to address.
Unsuccessful	Currently, I am not able to successfully demonstrate these competency requirements in practicum.

Competency 2

Advance Human Rights and Social, Racial, Economic, and Environmental Justice

Social workers advocate for and engage in strategies to eliminate oppressive structural barriers to ensure that social resources, rights, and responsibilities are distributed equitably, and that civil, political, economic, social, and cultural human rights are protected.

Identify Key Concepts, Search for the Meaning of Those Concepts, and Critically Examine the Requirements of the Competency

1. Use the phrase "social workers advocate" to search the internet, and carefully read and analyze at least two scholarly articles about this topic.

   a. What did you learn about the advocacy process?

2. Use the phrase "strategies to eliminate oppressive structural barriers" to search the internet, and carefully read and analyze at least two scholarly articles about this topic.

   a. What did you learn about oppressive structural barriers from your analysis of the articles?

3. Use the phrase "equitable distribution of social resources, rights, and responsibilities" to search the internet, and carefully read and analyze at least two scholarly articles about this topic.

   a. What did you learn about the distribution of social resources from your analysis of the articles?

4. Use the phrase "civil, political, economic, social, and cultural human rights" to search the internet, and carefully read and analyze at least two scholarly articles about this topic.

   a. What did you learn about civil, political, economic, social, and cultural human rights from your analysis of the articles?

Reflective Writing Practice

In a few sentences, describe what you learned about the advocacy process in addressing structural barriers and how you plan on using that information as a future social worker.

_____

_____

_____

_____

Application Follow-Up

Date you identified the specific steps you can take to advocate to eliminate oppressive structural barriers in your work with clients as a social work intern: _____

In a few sentences, describe what you learned about the advocacy process during your practicum.

_____

_____

_____

_____

Self-Evaluation

Successful	I can effectively demonstrate these competency requirements during practicum, and I can explain how these competency requirements contribute to effective social work practice.
Developing	I can identify the information I need and am able to apply it in some practicum situations, but I am also aware of some knowledge and skill gaps that I need to address.
Unsuccessful	Currently, I am not able to successfully demonstrate these competency requirements in practicum.

Demonstrating the Ability to Advance Human Rights and Social, Racial, Economic, and Environmental Justice

Advocating for the human rights of clients might start with helping clients identify their human rights, such as education, and the benefits of holding on to them. This could be the case in school dropout prevention programs, for example, but you should also be conscious of the way students who drop out experience the educational system and what led them to believe there is no value in the system or that they don't belong there. In other settings, consider the human rights you identified as relevant to the services provided at your practicum setting and try to identify structural barriers relevant to your specific client population.

Advocate for human rights at the individual, family, group, organizational, and community system levels.

Demonstrating Competency 2 With the Smith and Johnson Family	Demonstrating Competency 2 During Your Practicum
1. What are the human rights relevant to the Smith and Johnson family?	1. What are the human rights relevant to the clients at your social work practicum setting?
2. If Daniel Johnson is being bullied in school, how is his right to education being affected?	2. Can you identify how the denial of human rights might negatively impact your client's ability to grow and become a full participant in society?
3. How would you advocate for his human right to safety and to an education?	3. Can you identify how the denial of human rights might negatively impact your client's well-being?
4. If Mrs. Smith is your client, does she have a right to health care? Does she have access to nutritious healthy food?	4. Can you identify how the denial of human rights might negatively impact your client's family system?
5. If Mr. Johnson is your client, does he have a right to maintain a family relationship? How would you advocate for his human rights?	5. Can you provide an example of how you can advocate for the human rights of clients at your practicum?

Engage in practices that advance human rights to promote social, racial, economic, and environmental justice.

Demonstrating Competency 2 With the Smith and Johnson Family	Demonstrating Competency 2 During Your Practicum
1. What are the practices that will advance the human rights of the Smith and Johnson family?	1. What are the practices that advance the human rights of the clients at your social work practicum setting?
2. Identify the human rights relevant to each family member.	2. Identify the human rights relevant to your clients. Are you able to provide services that advance those human rights?
3. Do you have the skills and ability to provide services that advance those human rights?	3. Can you give an example of how you are able to provide appropriate services to ensure that the human rights of your clients are not hindered?
4. What could you do to provide Daniel a safe learning environment and the appropriate instruction to ensure that his human right to an education is not hindered?	4. How do social workers promote the social, racial, economic, and environmental justice of clients at your practicum setting?
5. How might social workers promote the social, racial, economic, and environmental justice of the Smith and Johnson family?	5. Identify the social factors that might negatively impact your clients.
6. Identify the social factors that might negatively impact this family.	6. If you work with clients who are racially different than you, describe the steps you can take to address any racial issues that might interfere with your ability to successfully work with clients.
7. If the Smith and Johnson family have a different racial identity from you, what steps can you take to develop the knowledge and skills needed to successfully work with this family? How would you find out if the racial identity of this family marginalized them in the community?	7. What steps can you take to gain the knowledge and skills needed to work with marginalized communities?
8. What are the economic issues that might negatively impact this family? How might those issues be addressed in this case?	8. What are the economic issues that might negatively impact your clients?
9. How would you identify any physical, social, or environmental justice issues that might negatively impact this family?	9. What are the physical and social environmental justice issues that might negatively impact your clients?
10. How would you identify any physical, social, or environmental justice issues that might negatively impact this family?	10. Describe the steps you are taking to gain the knowledge, values, and skills necessary to engage in social work practices that advance human rights to promote social, racial, economic, and environmental justice.

Competency Development Topics for the Social Work Practicum Seminar

▶ **Competency 2 Field Seminar Topics**

- Social work practice and human rights
- Equality and advocacy knowledge, values, and skills
- Historical oppression and discrimination and social work's role and response
- Social, racial, economic, and environmental justice issues and social work strategies to address those issues
- Strategies to identify and address oppressive structural barriers

▼ **Prior Planning**

- Completing the reading and writing exercises in this chapter will give you the opportunity to identify the key concepts related to each of the seminar discussion topics.
- Identify the parts of the competency that you have not been able to successfully implement in your practicum and formulate specific questions you can bring to seminar to explore your knowledge and skills gaps.

◀ **During Seminar**

- Listen carefully to your peers and seminar instructor.
- Consider the utility of the different perspectives your peers bring to the topic.
- Be ready to contribute by sharing your struggles as well as your successes in addressing competency 2 requirements.
- Identify something you learned through the process of completing the exercises in this chapter and consider how that knowledge contributes to your professional development and competence.

Competency Development Topics for the Educational Supervision Meeting

▶ **Competency 2 Social Work Practicum Instructional Supervision Meeting Topics**

- Human rights issues relevant to the services provided at your social work practicum setting
- Skills needed to address historical oppression and discrimination in the practicum setting
- Social, racial, economic, and environmental justice issues that concern the clients served at your practicum setting
- What you need to know and be able to do to integrate equality and advocacy into the social work practicum

▼ **Prior Planning**

- Consider the client population served at your practicum setting. Can you identify the social, racial, economic, and environmental justice issues relevant to your client population?
- Examine your work with clients during your practicum. Have you been able to use what you are learning about social, racial, economic, and environmental justice issues during your practicum? If not, can you identify tasks you can volunteer for that will provide you with the opportunity?
- Make a list of questions you want to address during your instructional supervision meeting with your social work instructor.

◀ **During the Instructional Supervision Meeting**

- Listen attentively to your social work instructor.
- Let your instructor know that you have questions related to competency development and use the questions you prepared to guide the conversation.
- Prepare mentally for the fact that oppression and racism are difficult issues and that we are usually blinded to our own prejudice. Learning to become antiracist social workers will require the ability to critically examine the social structures we have taken for granted and might have benefit us to the detriment of others.

Summary

Figure 2.2 illustrates a three-step process for identifying the information you need to seek, the advocacy role you need to take as a social worker, and the commitment you need to make to engage in the advocacy process.

   In this chapter, you had the opportunity to identify the key concepts relevant to human rights and social, racial, economic, and environmental justice, and to consider the requirements of competency 2. You also had the opportunity to reflect on the process of utilizing the information you examined as you worked with clients during your social work practicum experience, and hopefully you had the opportunity to discuss the requirements of competency 2 with peers and social work faculty. Competency 2 cannot be separated from the other eight competencies

Advance Human Rights and Social, Racial, Economic, and Environmental Justice	Identify the human rights social, racial, economic, and environmental justice issues relevant to clients.
	Identify the role of social workers in addressing the human rights, social, racial, economic, and environmental justice issues that have a significant impact on the life of clients.
	Make the commitment to develop the knowledge, values, and skills necessary to work with clients in a way that advances human rights and social, racial, economic, and environmental justice for the clients we serve.

FIGURE 2.2   A three-step process for advancing human rights and social justice.

because it is when you engage in everyday social work tasks that competency 2 can be put into practice and its absence can be detrimental not only to the clients we serve, but to the social work profession.

Recommended Reading Materials

Books	Description
Knox, J. H., & Pejan, R. (Eds.). (2018). *The Human Right to a Healthy Environment*. Cambridge University Press.	This book defines the relationship between human rights and the environment.
Stevenson, B. (2014). *Just Mercy A Story of Justice and Redemption*. Spiegel & Grau.	This book is written by an attorney who has worked to release wrongly convicted prisoners on death row.
Usual Cruelty: The Complicity of Lawyers in the Criminal Injustice System Karakatsanis, A. (2019). United States: New Press.	This book is written by an attorney who has challenged everyday brutality inflicted disproportionately on the bodies and minds of low-income people and people of color.
Moyn, S. (2018). *Not Enough Human Rights in an Unequal World*. Harvard University Press.	The author provides an analysis of human rights ideals as inequality persists.
DiAngelo, D. R. (2018). *White Fragility: Why It's So Hard for White People to Talk About Racism*. Beacon Press.	The author examines how White fragility develops and how it protects racial inequality.
Martinez, M. M. (2018). *The Injustice Never Leaves You: Anti-Mexican Violence in Texas*. Harvard University Press.	The author provides an account of how vigilantes and law enforcement officials killed Mexican residents with impunity during the decade between 1910 and 1920.

References

Council on Social Work Education. (2022, May 23). *2022 EPAS*. https://www.cswe.org/accreditation/info/2022-epas/

National Association of Social Workers. (2022, May 23). *NASW Code of Ethics*. https://www.socialworkers.org/About/Ethics/Code-of-Ethics/Code-of-Ethics-English

CREDIT

CHAPTER 3

Competency 3

Engage Anti-Racism, Diversity, Equity, and Inclusion (ADEI) in Practice

In this chapter, you will explore the third of the nine social work competencies as provided by the CSWE. Competency 3 requires us to situate our own life experiences and critically examine our own privilege and power as well as our own experience with oppression, poverty, marginalization, and alienation. As social work practitioners we will bring who we are into the helping process, and we need to be aware of how we have been shaped by our social environment, as well as our personal agency, to overcome difficulties given the resources available to us. If we have mostly experienced privilege and power, we will have difficulty understanding the life experience of marginalized clients, and we need to develop the humility to listen and learn from our clients because we do not know anything about their life.

As a developing social work practitioner, you are learning different human development and social environment theories but remember that all those theories are incomplete and tentative and that the life experience of each of your clients will be unique. Some clients may not be ready or might not have the ability to overcome their situation, and we need to be careful not to think that if we were able to rise above our circumstances, others should do the same. Once again, humility will be needed to listen and learn from our clients, because different people experience negative circumstances differently.

To engage antiracism, diversity, equity, and inclusion in our social work practice, we need to be willing to learn not just about the meaning of each one of these concepts, but also their impact on people's lives, including ourselves, because we cannot function if separated from who we are and our life experiences.

Competency 3 Description as Provided by CSWE: Engage Anti-Racism, Diversity, Equity, and Inclusion (ADEI) in Practice

As you read the following description, consider the meaning of each sentence and your ability to demonstrate the requirements of this competency as you work with clients during your social work practicum.

Competency 3

Engage Anti-Racism, Diversity, Equity, and Inclusion (ADEI) in Practice

Social workers understand how racism and oppression shape human experiences and how these two constructs influence practice at the individual, family, group, organizational, and community levels and policy and research. Social workers understand the pervasive impact of White supremacy and privilege and use their knowledge, awareness, and skills to engage in anti-racist practice. Social workers understand how diversity and intersectionality shape human experiences and identity development and affect equity and inclusion. The dimensions of diversity are understood as the intersectionality of factors including but not limited to age, caste, class, color, culture, disability and ability, ethnicity, gender, gender identity and expression, generational status, immigration status, legal status, marital status, political ideology, race, nationality, religion and spirituality, sex, sexual orientation, and tribal sovereign status. Social workers understand that this intersectionality means that a person's life experiences may include oppression, poverty, marginalization, and alienation as well as privilege and power. Social workers understand the societal and historical roots of social and racial injustices and the forms and mechanisms of oppression and discrimination. Social workers understand cultural humility and recognize the extent to which a culture's structures and values, including social, economic, political, racial, technological, and cultural exclusions, may create privilege and power resulting in systemic oppression.
Social workers:

a. demonstrate anti-racist and anti-oppressive social work practice at the individual, family, group, organizational, community, research, and policy levels

b. demonstrate cultural humility by applying critical reflection, self-awareness, and self-regulation to manage the influence of bias, power, privilege, and values in working with clients and constituencies, acknowledging them as experts of their own lived experiences

As you can see in Figure 3.1, Competency 3 must be an integral part of every aspect of social work practice. We cannot effectively engage, assess, intervene, and evaluate diverse client populations without considering the issues that shape the lived experience of clients. If we do not make sure that social work practices are inclusive and carefully develop the skills to engage antiracism, diversity, equity, and inclusion in practice, we can easily perpetuate the marginalizing practices of the past.

Applying Competency 3

Our possession of the knowledge, values, and skills necessary to engage antiracism, diversity, equity, and inclusion will affect the helping process whether we are aware of it or not. In the case of the Smith and Johnson family, if we belong to a significantly different cultural group, we need to learn about these clients' cultural norms and make an effort to not do or say something that will be offensive to them. There is a long history of racism in the United States, and we need to be aware that if our group has been the oppressor, we need to earn clients' trust because they have every reason not to trust us. However, even if we belong to the same racial group, we need to understand that we might have experienced more social privileges due to socioeconomic factors or different educational opportunities. Competency 3 requires us to be cognizant of social issues and their impact on social work practice.

Competency 1:

Engage Anti-Racism, Diversity, Equity, and Inclusion as we demonstrate ethical and professional behavior

Competency 9:

Engage Anti-Racism, Diversity, Equity, and Inclusion as we evaluate social work practice

Competency 2:

Engage Anti-Racism, Diversity, Equity, and Inclusion as we advance the human rights and social, racial, economic and environmental justice of clients

Competency 3:

What are the knowledge, values and skills necessary to engage anti-racism, diversity, equity and inclusion in social work practice?

Competency 8:

Engage Anti-Racism, Diversity, Equity, and Inclusion as we intervene with clients

Competency 3
Engage Anti-Racism, Diversity, Equity, and Inclusion (ADEI) in Practice

Competency 7:

Engage Anti-Racism, Diversity, Equity, and Inclusion as we assess clients

Competency 4:

Engage Anti-Racism, Diversity, Equity, and Inclusion as we use scientific research

Competency 6:

Engage Anti-Racism, Diversity, Equity, and Inclusion as we engage with clients

Competency 5:

Engage Anti-Racism, Diversity, Equity, and Inclusion as we engage in policy practice

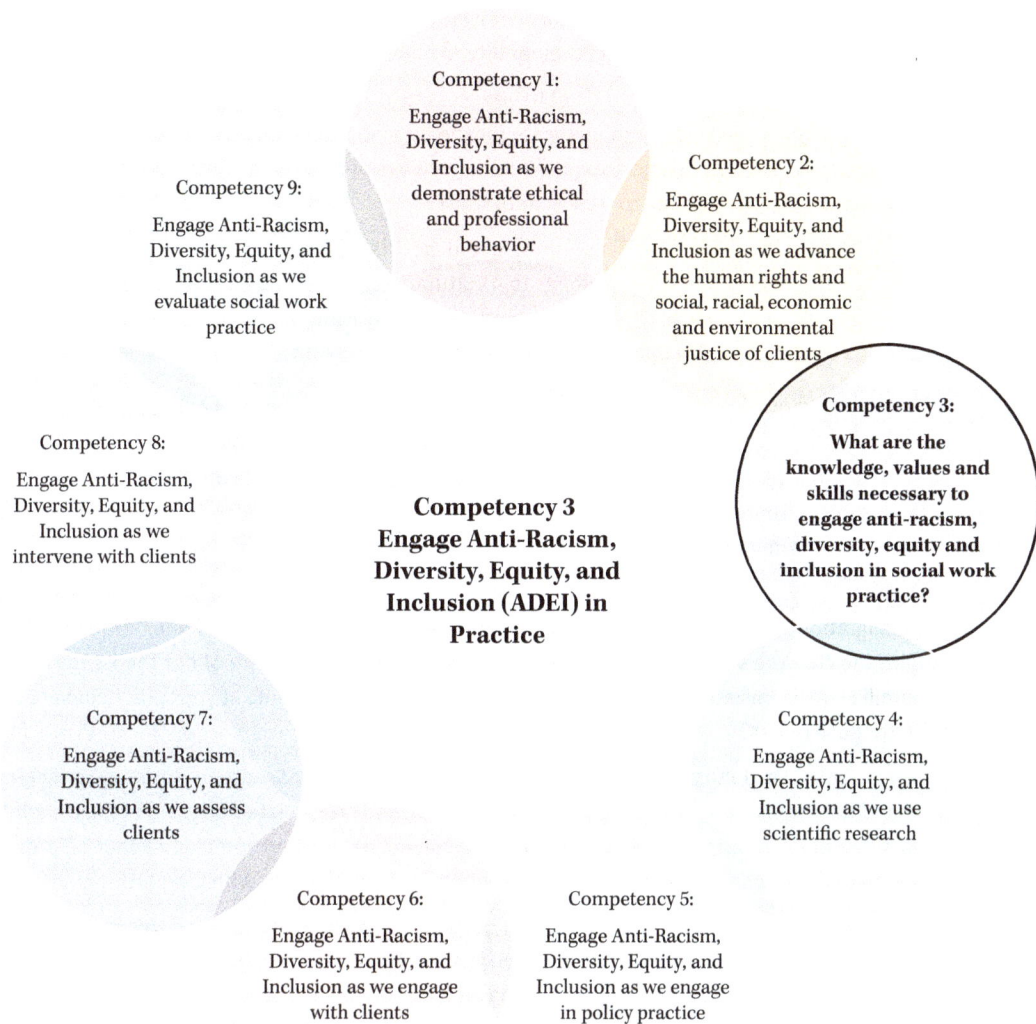

FIGURE 3.1   The relationship of competency 3 to the rest of the competencies.

Reflective Questions on Competency Application

Carefully reflect on the following questions to consider some of the requirements of competency 3 and its role in your work with clients. Although you do not need to answer these questions, you might want to explore the answer to those questions that directly relate to your practicum setting.

> What do you need to know and be able to do to engage antiracism, diversity, equity, and inclusion if the Smith and Johnson family belongs to a racial group different from you?

> Consider some of the intersectionality factors that might be relevant to the Smith and Johnson family:

> > Age: Mr. and Mrs. Smith are elderly, and Alyssa and Daniel are minor children.

> > Minority status: The grandparents grew up in the 1950s and 1960s; if they belong to a minority population, how were they treated in their community? If they were discriminated and oppresses, how will that influence their trust in social institutions?

(Continued)

Class: The socioeconomic status of this family is low income. How will the economic status of the Smith and Johnson family impact their ability to meet basic needs?

Education: If the grandparents did not have access to formal schooling when they grew up, how will that fact impact their ability to advocate for the educational needs of their grandchildren? If the grandparents are Native American and had negative experiences in boarding schools, how would that fact impact their ability to trust school staff?

Cultural and racial identity: This family could be Black, Hispanic, Native American, White, or another ethnicity. If this family belongs to a cultural group that you have not interacted with, what do you need to do to learn about their cultural norms? How would you go about learning about their cultural norms? Are minorities accepted in your community?

Disability: Mrs. Smith is unable to work due to her diabetes. What can you do to learn about the impact of disability on quality of life and life expectancy?

Gender identity: James, the children's uncle, is gay, and until 2015 he could not get married in most states in the United States. Additionally, the legal right to marry does not prevent many people from considering homosexuality wrong and treat the LGBTQIA2S+ community badly. Is the social work practice setting welcoming to all people?

Immigration status: This family could have a mixed immigration status if one of the grandparents or if the children's father is undocumented. What can you do to learn about the issues that affect families with a mixed immigration status? Do you know if the clients at your practicum are dealing with those issues?

Legal status: Mr. Johnson is incarcerated. He is serving a 20-year sentence for drug trafficking. Are mandatory minimum sentencing provisions for drug and drug-related offenses in the United States fair? Are minorities more likely to receive long convictions? Alfred Johnson cannot be present for his children, but do the children have a right to have a relationship with their father?

Religion and spirituality: This family could belong to a minority church, or if this is a Native American family, they might practice Native American spiritual rituals. If this family belongs to a minority, does the school honor their religious holidays?

Tribal sovereign status: If this family belongs to a Native American tribe, what steps can you take to learn about the process to coordinate social work services with the tribe?

If this is a Native American family and the grandparents were victimized in boarding schools, what can you do to gain the knowledge and skills necessary to work with this family in a manner that will not retraumatize them?

Think about how these intersectionality factors relate to the clients at your practicum setting. Are there additional questions relevant to your work with clients?

Investigating Each Sentence in the Competency Description

Competency 3 requires a commitment to engage antiracism, diversity, equity, and inclusion in social work practice. Consider the intersectional factors that influence your own life and how those factors affect your ability to consider the needs of diverse client populations. It might be helpful to review your textbooks and consult with social work faculty if you find the concepts in this competency difficult to understand and implement. Racism, oppression, and discrimination all provoke strong feelings in both the victims and the oppressors. Some victims refuse to see themselves as victims, and that can be an effective coping mechanism, but it can also prolong the structures that maintain social inequality. Some oppressors are oblivious to their role and the benefits they reap from maintaining marginalized groups oppression.

As you develop the knowledge and skills required in this competency, you might recognize situations in your past when you were oppressed or discriminated against, or you might feel angry at having to think about issues that have caused you and your loved one's pain. On the other hand, you might recognize situations when you conducted yourself with an attitude of entitlement and behaved in ways that were offensive or even abusive to others, and that can also cause you distress. Seek the help of a counselor or mentor from among your social work field instructors if the concepts related to this competency cause you any emotional distress.

Competency 3

Engage Anti-Racism, Diversity, Equity, and Inclusion (ADEI) in Practice

Social workers understand how racism and oppression shape human experiences and how these two constructs influence practice at the individual, family, group, organizational, and community levels and policy and research.

Identify Key Concepts, Search for the Meaning of Those Concepts, and Critically Examine the Requirements of the Competency

1. Use the phrase "the impact of racism and oppression" to search the internet, and carefully read and analyze at least two scholarly articles about this topic.

   a. What did you learn about racism and oppression from the articles?

2. Use the phrase "racism and oppression in social work practice" to search the internet, and carefully read and analyze at least two scholarly articles about this topic.

   a. What did you learn about racism and oppression in social work practice from the articles?

3. Use the phrase "racism and oppression in social work policy" to search the internet, and carefully read and analyze at least two scholarly articles about this topic.

   a. What did you learn about racism and oppression in social work policy from the articles?

4. Use the phrase "racism and oppression in the United States" to search the internet, and carefully read and analyze at least two scholarly articles about this topic.

   a. What did you learn about racism and oppression in the United States from the articles?

Reflective Writing Practice

In a few sentences, describe your plan use your knowledge of racism and oppression in your social work practicum.

_____

_____

_____

_____

Application Follow-Up

Date you identified and addressed a situation that was oppressive or racist during your social work practicum: _____

In a few sentences, describe what you learned from the process of using your knowledge of oppression and racism to inform your work during your social work practicum.

_____

_____

_____

_____

Self-Evaluation

Successful	I can effectively demonstrate these competency requirements during practicum, and I can explain how these competency requirements contribute to effective social work practice.
Developing	I can identify the information I need and am able to apply it in some practicum situations, but I am also aware of some knowledge and skill gaps that I need to address.
Unsuccessful	Currently, I am not able to successfully demonstrate these competency requirements in practicum.

Competency 3

Engage Anti-Racism, Diversity, Equity, and Inclusion (ADEI) in Practice

Social workers understand the pervasive impact of White supremacy and privilege and use their knowledge, awareness, and skills to engage in anti-racist practice.

Identify Key Concepts, Search for the Meaning of Those Concepts, and Critically Examine the Requirements of the Competency

1. Use the phrase "White supremacy and privilege" to search the internet, and carefully read and analyze at least two scholarly articles about this topic.

    a. What did you learn about White supremacy and privilege from the articles?

2. Use the phrase "anti-racist practice in social work" to search the internet, and carefully read and analyze at least two scholarly articles about this topic.

    a. What did you learn about White supremacy and privilege from the articles?

Reflective Writing Practice

In a few sentences, describe your plan to engage in antiracist social work practice.

_____

_____

_____

_____

Application Follow-Up

Date you identified an opportunity to engage in anti-racist social work practice: _____

In a few sentences, describe what you learned about anti-racist social work practice to inform your work as a social work practicum student.

_____

_____

_____

_____

Self-Evaluation

Successful	I can effectively demonstrate these competency requirements during practicum, and I can explain how these competency requirements contribute to effective social work practice.
Developing	I can identify the information I need and am able to apply it in some practicum situations, but I am also aware of some knowledge and skill gaps that I need to address.
Unsuccessful	Currently, I am not able to successfully demonstrate these competency requirements in practicum.

Competency 3

Engage Anti-Racism, Diversity, Equity, and Inclusion (ADEI) in Practice

Social workers understand how diversity and intersectionality shape human experiences and identity development and affect equity and inclusion. The dimensions of diversity are understood as the intersectionality of factors including but not limited to age, caste, class, color, culture, disability and ability, ethnicity, gender, gender identity and expression, generational status, immigration status, legal status, marital status, political ideology, race, nationality, religion and spirituality, sex, sexual orientation, and tribal sovereign status.

Identify Key Concepts, Search for the Meaning of Those Concepts, and Critically Examine the Requirements of the Competency

1. Use the phrase "diversity and social work" to search the internet, and carefully read and analyze at least two scholarly articles about this topic.

    a. What did you learn about diversity and social work from the articles?

2. Use the phrase "intersectionality and social work" to search the internet, and carefully read and analyze at least two scholarly articles about this topic.

    a. What did you learn about intersectionality and social work from the articles?

3. Use the phrase "diversity and social work" to search the internet, and carefully read and analyze at least two scholarly articles about this topic.

    a. What did you learn about diversity and social work from the articles?

4. Use the phrase "equity and inclusion in social work" to search the internet, and carefully read and analyze at least two scholarly articles about this topic.

    a. What did you learn about equity and inclusion in social work from the articles?

5. Use the phrase "intersectionality of factors in social work" to search the internet, and carefully read and analyze at least two scholarly articles about this topic.

    a. What did you learn about intersectionality of factors in social work from the articles?

Reflective Writing Practice

In a few sentences, describe your plan to use your knowledge of diversity and intersectionality in your work with clients during your social work practicum.

_____

_____

_____

_____

Application Follow-Up

Date you identified an opportunity to use your knowledge of diversity and intersectionality in your work with a client during practicum: _____

In a few sentences, describe what you learned from the process of using your knowledge of diversity and intersectionality in your work with a client during practicum.

_____

_____

_____

_____

Self-Evaluation

Successful	I can effectively demonstrate these competency requirements during practicum, and I can explain how these competency requirements contribute to effective social work practice.
Developing	I can identify the information I need and am able to apply it in some practicum situations, but I am also aware of some knowledge and skill gaps that I need to address.
Unsuccessful	Currently, I am not able to successfully demonstrate these competency requirements in practicum.

Competency 3

Engage Anti-Racism, Diversity, Equity, and Inclusion (ADEI) in Practice

Social workers understand that this intersectionality means that a person's life experiences may include oppression, poverty, marginalization, and alienation as well as privilege and power.

Identify Key Concepts, Search for the Meaning of Those Concepts, and Critically Examine the Requirements of the Competency

1. Use the phrase "social work clients and oppression, poverty, marginalization, and alienation" to search the internet, and carefully read and analyze at least two scholarly articles about this topic.

    a. What did you learn about social work clients and oppression, poverty, marginalization, and alienation from the articles?

2. Use the phrase "social work and privilege and power" to search the internet, and carefully read and analyze at least two scholarly articles about this topic.

    a. What did you learn about social work and privilege and power from the articles?

Reflective Writing Practice

In a few sentences, describe your plan to increase your awareness of the intersectional factors that impact your client population.

_____

_____

_____

_____

Application Follow-Up

Date you identified an opportunity to use your knowledge of intersectional factors during your social work practicum: _____

In a few sentences, describe what you learned from the process of using your knowledge of intersectional factors during your social work practicum.

_____

_____

_____

_____

Self-Evaluation

Successful	I can effectively demonstrate these competency requirements during practicum, and I can explain how these competency requirements contribute to effective social work practice.
Developing	I can identify the information I need and am able to apply it in some practicum situations, but I am also aware of some knowledge and skill gaps that I need to address.
Unsuccessful	Currently, I am not able to successfully demonstrate these competency requirements in practicum.

Competency 3

Engage Anti-Racism, Diversity, Equity, and Inclusion (ADEI) in Practice

Social workers understand the societal and historical roots of social and racial injustices and the forms and mechanisms of oppression and discrimination.

Identify Key Concepts, Search for the Meaning of Those Concepts, and Critically Examine the Requirements of the Competency

1. Use the phrase "societal and historical roots of social and racial injustices in the United States" to search the internet, and carefully read and analyze at least two scholarly articles about this topic.

    a. What did you learn about societal and historical roots of social and racial injustices in the United States from the articles?

2. Use the phrase "forms and mechanisms of oppression and discrimination in the United States" to search the internet, and carefully read and analyze at least two scholarly articles about this topic.

    a. What did you learn about forms and mechanisms of oppression and discrimination in the United States from the articles?

Reflective Writing Practice

In a few sentences, describe your plan to increase your knowledge and skills to address racial injustices.

_____

_____

_____

_____

Application Follow-Up

Date you had the opportunity to use what you learned about racial injustice during your social work practicum: _____

In a few sentences, describe what you learned about racial injustice during your social work practicum.

_____

_____

_____

_____

Self-Evaluation

Successful	I can effectively demonstrate these competency requirements during practicum, and I can explain how these competency requirements contribute to effective social work practice.
Developing	I can identify the information I need and am able to apply it in some practicum situations, but I am also aware of some knowledge and skill gaps that I need to address.
Unsuccessful	Currently, I am not able to successfully demonstrate these competency requirements in practicum.

Competency 3

Engage Anti-Racism, Diversity, Equity, and Inclusion (ADEI) in Practice

Social workers understand cultural humility and recognize the extent to which a culture's structures and values, including social, economic, political, racial, technological, and cultural exclusions, may create privilege and power resulting in systemic oppression.

Identify Key Concepts, Search for the Meaning of Those Concepts, and Critically Examine the Requirements of the Competency

1. Use the phrase "cultural humility in social work" to search the internet, and carefully read and analyze at least two scholarly articles about this topic.

   a. What did you learn about cultural humility in social work from the articles?

2. Use the phrase "culture's structures and values" to search the internet, and carefully read and analyze at least two scholarly articles about this topic.

   a. What did you learn about culture's structures and values from the articles?

3. Use the phrase "cultural exclusions" to search the internet, and carefully read and analyze at least two scholarly articles about this topic.

   a. What did you learn about cultural exclusions from the articles?

4. Use the phrase "privilege and power" to search the internet, and carefully read and analyze at least two scholarly articles about this topic.

   a. What did you learn about privilege and power from the articles?

Reflective Writing Practice

In a few sentences, describe your plan to use what you learned about cultural humility, culture privilege, and power to inform your social work practice.

_____

_____

_____

_____

Application Follow-Up

Date you identified an opportunity to use what you learned about cultural humility, as well as power and privilege to inform your social work practice: _____

In a few sentences, describe what you learned about cultural humility as well as power and privilege during your social work practicum.

_____

_____

_____

_____

Self-Evaluation

Successful	I can effectively demonstrate these competency requirements during practicum, and I can explain how these competency requirements contribute to effective social work practice.
Developing	I can identify the information I need and am able to apply it in some practicum situations, but I am also aware of some knowledge and skill gaps that I need to address.
Unsuccessful	Currently, I am not able to successfully demonstrate these competency requirements in practicum.

Intersectional Factors and the Smith and Johnson Family

Consider the influence of intersectionality factors on the Smith and Johnson family and the clients you serve during your social work practicum. Use Figure 3.2 as a guide.

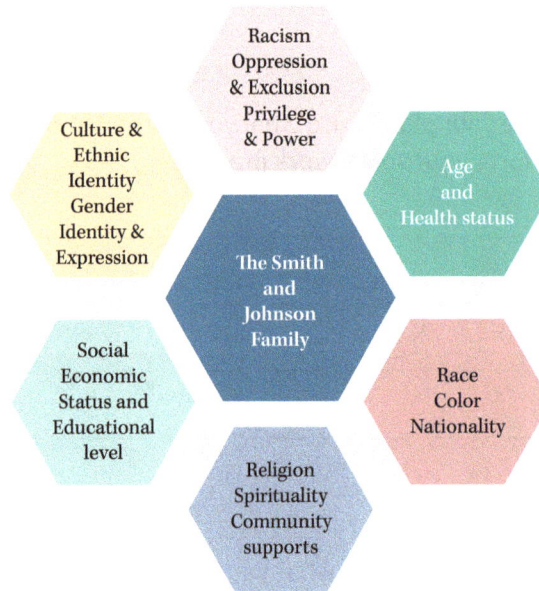

FIGURE 3.2 Intersectionality factors relevant to competency 3.

Demonstrate anti-racist and anti-oppressive social work practice at the individual, family, group, organizational, community, research, and policy levels.

Demonstrating Competency 3 With the Smith and Johnson Family	Demonstrating Competency 3 During Your Practicum
1. If the Smith and Johnson family has a cultural and racial identity that is different from your cultural and racial identity, what steps can you take to demonstrate antiracist and anti-oppressive social work practice as you work with this family? 2. For example, are you aware that calling Mrs. Smith by her first name is disrespectful in several minority cultures? 3. If the bullying Daniel was experiencing is racially motivated, what are the anti-oppressive measures that should be taken by the school system? As a social work student, how might you contribute to addressing this issue? 4. If the Smith and Johnson family belongs to a marginalized racial group, do you know if your community is safe for this family? 5. Have you reviewed research studies that will help you understand the racial and cultural needs of this family? 6. How might agency policies guide your work with this family? Do those policies support antiracist and anti-oppressive social work practices?	1. What is the racial identity of the clients at your social work practicum? 2. Can you provide an example of how you can demonstrate antiracist and anti-oppressive social work practice as you work with diverse clients? 3. Can you describe the differences in social norms that might impact your work with diverse clients? 4. Identify a form of racial oppression your clients might experience in your community. If your clients belong to a marginalized racial group, do you know if your community is safe for your clients? 5. Describe what you have learned from a research study that will help you understand the racial and cultural needs of your clients. 6. Have you reviewed the agency policies to make sure that the policies that guide your social work practicum support antiracist and anti-oppressive social work practices? If so, can you explain how those policies support diverse clients?

Demonstrate cultural humility by applying critical reflection, self-awareness, and self-regulation to manage the influence of bias, power, privilege, and values in working with clients and constituencies, acknowledging them as experts of their own lived experiences.

Demonstrating Competency 3 With the Smith and Johnson Family	Demonstrating Competency 3 During Your Practicum
1. If the Smith and Johnson family belongs to a different cultural group than you do, can you demonstrate cultural humility?	1. If the clients at your practicum belong to a different cultural identity than you, can you provide an example of your ability to demonstrate cultural humility?
2. What steps can you take to learn about the history of oppression and discrimination that has formed the lived experience of this family? How might your understanding of their experience with oppression impact how you relate to them?	2. Are you aware of the history of oppression and discrimination that has formed the lived experience of your client population? Describe how your understanding of their experience with oppression might impact how you relate to them.
3. Do you have the knowledge and skills to use critical reflection to identify the bias, power, privilege, and values that influence your role in the social work helping process?	3. Can you give an example of how you are using your knowledge and skills to critically reflect on your own identity and the bias, power, privilege, and values that influence your role in the social work helping process?
4. What steps can you take to become self-aware and able to identify how your bias, power, privilege, and values influence your role in the social work helping process?	4. Can you give an example of something you have learned about yourself through self-reflection and how that will influence your role as a social worker?
5. Can you demonstrate the self-regulation to manage the bias, power, privilege, and values that influence your role in the social work helping process?	5. Can you provide an example of how you have demonstrated self-regulation to manage the bias, power, privilege, and values that influence your role in the social work helping process?
6. How can you demonstrate that you recognize the Smith and Johnson family as experts of their own lived experiences?	6. Can you provide an example of how you have been able to demonstrate your ability to recognize your clients as experts of their own lived experiences?

Competency Development Topics for the Social Work Practicum Seminar

▶ **Competency 3 Field Seminar Topics**

- Antiracist social work practice and the pervasive impact of White supremacy and privilege
- Intersectionality theory and its relevance to social work practice
- The societal and historical roots of social and racial injustices and social work practice
- Cultural humility concepts and skills

▼ **Prior Planning**

- Completing the reading and writing exercises in this chapter will give you the opportunity to identify the key concepts related to each of the seminar discussion topics.
- Identify the parts of the competency that you have not been able to successfully implement in your practicum.
- Formulate specific questions you can take to seminar to address your knowledge and skills gaps.

◀ **During Seminar**

- Listen carefully to your peers and seminar instructor.
- Consider the utility of the different perspectives your peers bring to the topic.
- Be ready to contribute by sharing your struggles as well as your successes in addressing competency 3 requirements.
- Celebrate every step toward competence. Identify something you learned through the process of completing the exercises in this chapter as well as through your work with clients, and consider how the knowledge and skills you have gained contributes to your professional development and competence.

Competency Development Topics for the Educational Supervision Meeting

▶ **Competency 3 Social Work Practicum Instructional Supervision Meeting Topics**

- Can you identify antiracist social work practices in your social work practicum? If not, ask your social work field instructor to help you explore the issue.
- Can you identify the intersectionality factors that you can use to identify the needs and strengths of clients in the practicum setting?
- What are the societal and historical racial injustices that are relevant to the practicum setting?
- Have you been able to demonstrate cultural humility during your social work practicum?

▼ **Prior Planning**

- Use your chapter notes to formulate questions that will help you address knowledge and skills gaps related to competency 3 during your supervision meeting.
- Consider the client populations served at your social work practicum and review your notes in this chapter to reflect on the following questions:
  - What are the intersectionality factors that might help you understand the client's perspective?
  - How are racial minorities served at your social work practicum setting?
  - How do you demonstrate cultural humility as you work with clients during your practicum?

◀ **During the Instructional Supervision Meeting**

- Be prepared to ask questions that will help you develop and practice competency 3.
- Listen attentively to your social work instructor.
- Prepare mentally for the fact that competency 3 requirements are difficult to discuss and integrate into social work practice. Culture is invisible to those who live in it, and none of us is comfortable with the idea that we might exhibit racist and prejudiced behaviors.

Summary

Figure 3.3 provides a summary of the main requirements of competency 3.

In this chapter, you had the opportunity to identify key concepts, search for the meaning of those concepts, and critically examine the requirements of competency 3. By completing the reflective writing exercises and evaluating your ability to demonstrate competency 3 requirements during practicum, you should have developed a working knowledge of competency 3 requirements. Like competency 1 and 2, competency 3 cannot be separated from the other eight competencies because it is when you establish a working relationship with clients and assess their needs to identify appropriate interventions that the need to demonstrate cultural humility and use critical reflection and self-evaluation emerges, as does the importance of becoming aware of personal biases and practicing self-regulation to manage the influence of prejudice, power, privilege, and personal values. If you are hoping to become a leader in the social work profession, accepting the challenge to become an antiracist and anti-oppressive social worker is a good start.

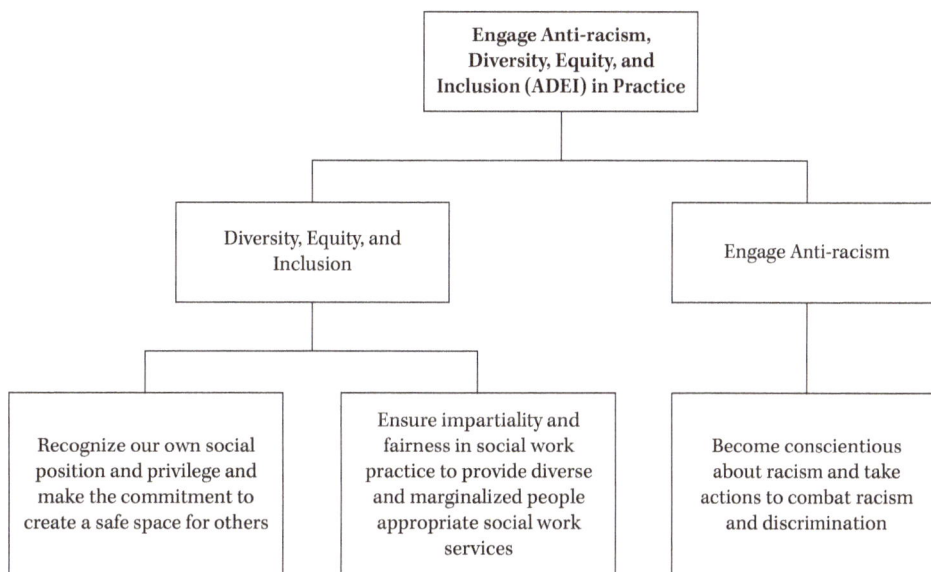

FIGURE 3.3. The main requirements of competency 3.

Recommended Reading Materials

Books	Description
Alexie, S. (2009). *The Absolutely True Diary of a Part-Time Indian*. Little Brown Books for Young Readers.	This novel provides a humorous account of racism, oppression, and discrimination as a young Indian attempt to leave the reservation.
Jiménez, F. (1997). *The Circuit*. University of New Mexico Press.	This novel provides an account a migrant family in constant movement to follow agricultural jobs and the struggle to survive.
Zamora, J. (2022). *Solito: A Memoir*. Random House.	This novel provides an account of a 9-year-old boy who travels from his small town in El Salvador through Guatemala and Mexico, and across the U.S. border to reunite with his parents.
Walls, J. (2007). *The Glass Castle: A Memoir*. Pocket Books.	This novel provides an account of a White family who struggles with mental illness and poverty.
Houston, J. W., & Houston, J. D. (2002). *Farewell to Manzanar*. Houghton Mifflin.	This novel provides an account of life in a Japanese American internment camp during World War II
Rawles, N. (2006). *My Jim: A Novel*. Crown.	This story is told in the voice of an ex-slave who shares her experience of slavery with a granddaughter.
Ditto, B., Jones, O., & Alexander, O. (2022). *We Can Do Better Than This: 35 Voices on the Future of LGBTQ+ Rights*. Random House UK.	This book includes the voices of actors, musicians, writers, artists, and activists to report the discrimination and extreme violence experienced by the LGBTQ community.

Note: Although academic studies on oppression and discrimination are useful, there is no better way to understand the impact of oppression and discrimination on people than reading a personal story of struggle in a society that does not value the possibilities of diversity and inclusion.

References

Council on Social Work Education. (2022, May 23). *2022 EPAS*. https://www.cswe.org/accreditation/info/2022-epas/

National Association of Social Workers. (2022, May 23). *NASW Code of Ethics*. https://www.socialworkers.org/About/Ethics/Code-of-Ethics/Code-of-Ethics-English

CREDIT

CHAPTER 4

Competency 4

Engage in Practice-Informed Research and
Research-Informed Practice

I n this chapter, you will examine the requirements of the fourth of the nine social work competencies provided by the CSWE. Competency 4 requires an ability to identify social work practice
needs and to identify current, empirically sound research studies that examine the issues that
are relevant to social work practice. Additionally, social workers need to be able to critically
analyze research studies to determine their relevance, reliability, and applicability; the ethical
and cultural aspects of the research methods used to study the issue; as well as the ethical and
cultural implications of utilizing research study results with different client populations. At the
foundation level of social work practice, the focus of research is to increase our knowledge base
about those issues as well as the methods of intervention that other professionals have used to
address them. At an advanced level, we might need to engage in original research to explore our
own social work practice modalities and the results of those practices.

If you have already taken a social work research course, you should review your research
textbooks and course notes to refresh your understanding of the research process. If you are
taking the research course concurrently with your field course, you can use the research course
assignments to focus your research efforts on topics relevant to your practicum. If you have not
taken the course and are not currently taking it, you will need to use your independent learning
skills to become familiar with the scientific research process. At a minimum, you need to know
the difference between qualitative and quantitative research methods as well as the role of
bias in research. You also need to consider the limitations of your current knowledge about the
social issues that affect your client population. For example, if you have a relative who struggles
with mental health issues, drug addiction, or any other issue your clients face, you are bringing
some knowledge about what these challenges are like, but to develop the knowledge and skills
necessary to become a professional, you need to know more than just your personal experience.

The fundamental benefit of research is that it provides a space to recognize that sometimes
what we think we know about an issue is incorrect. For example, for many years it was assumed
that once you got type II diabetes, you had it for life and all you could do was manage your chronic
condition. Yet now we are learning that type II diabetes can be reversed and that the impact of
lifestyle changes on overall health is life changing (Fung, 2018).

However, we also know that changing our behavior, even when we know it's for our own benefit,
is very difficult. That is another reason as social workers we need to use research to gain a better
understanding of human behavior. Social work is fundamentally a profession that aims at helping
people make changes in their life. Therefore, we need to learn as much as possible about how people
change, what the barriers to change are, and how to approach setbacks and encourage clients to set
and achieve their well-being goals. A good first step on your path to research practice is to identify a
personal lifestyle change that you know would improve your own well-being so that you can investigate its benefits and attempt to use that information to make a difference in your life. Putting yourself
through this process can give you the opportunity to understand how difficult it is to change a behavior.

Competency 4 Description as Provided by CSWE: Engage in Practice-Informed Research and Research-Informed Practice

As you read the description of competency four, consider the meaning of each sentence and your ability to engage in practice-informed research and research-informed practice during your social work practicum.

Competency 4

Engage in Practice-Informed Research and Research-Informed Practice

Social workers use ethical, culturally informed, and anti-racist and anti-oppressive approaches in conducting research and building knowledge. Social workers use research to inform their practice decision making and articulate how their practice experience informs research and evaluation decisions. Social workers critically evaluate and critique current, empirically sound research to inform decisions pertaining to practice, policy, and programs. Social workers understand the inherent bias in research and evaluate design, analysis, and interpretation using an anti-racist and anti-oppressive perspective. Social workers know how to access, critique, and synthesize the current literature to develop appropriate research questions and hypotheses. Social workers demonstrate knowledge and skills regarding qualitative and quantitative research methods and analysis, and they interpret data derived from these methods. Social workers demonstrate knowledge about methods to assess reliability and validity in social work research. Social workers can articulate and share research findings in ways that are usable to a variety of clients and constituencies. Social workers understand the value of evidence derived from interprofessional and diverse research methods, approaches, and sources.

Social workers:

a. apply research findings to inform and improve practice, policy, and programs; and
b. identify ethical, culturally informed, anti-racist, and anti-oppressive strategies that address inherent biases for use in quantitative and qualitative research methods to advance the purposes of social work.

As you can see in Figure 4.1, competency 4 plays an essential role in the development of the other eight competencies. The knowledge base of the social work profession is derived from research, and as social work practitioners we need to be able to identify research studies that are relevant to our client population; this is practice-informed research. We also need to be able to analyze research findings from a social work perspective. As we analyze research studies that explore human behavior and the social conditions that foster or hinder human growth, development, and achievement, we need to critically select intervention practices that are helpful to diverse client populations, which is research-informed practice.

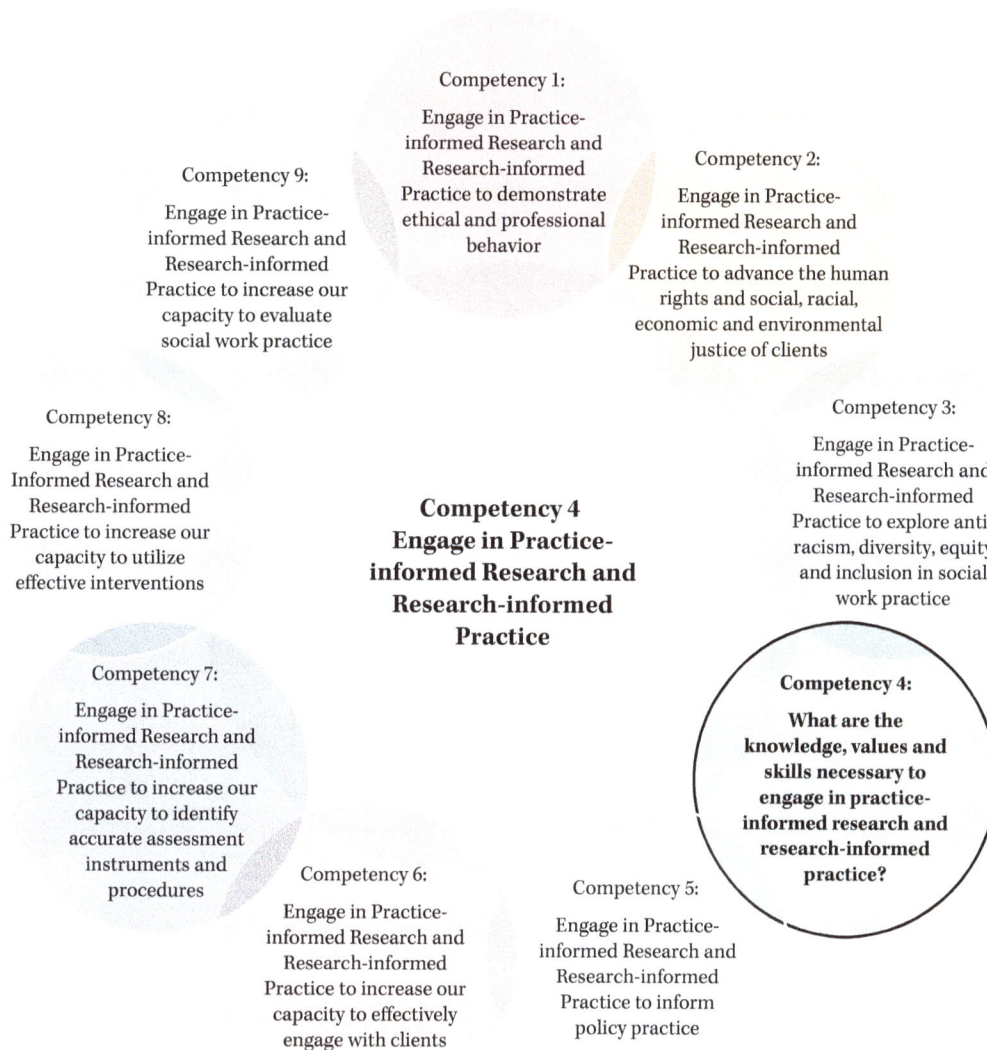

Competency 1:
Engage in Practice-informed Research and Research-informed Practice to demonstrate ethical and professional behavior

Competency 2:
Engage in Practice-informed Research and Research-informed Practice to advance the human rights and social, racial, economic and environmental justice of clients

Competency 9:
Engage in Practice-informed Research and Research-informed Practice to increase our capacity to evaluate social work practice

Competency 3:
Engage in Practice-informed Research and Research-informed Practice to explore anti-racism, diversity, equity and inclusion in social work practice

Competency 8:
Engage in Practice-Informed Research and Research-informed Practice to increase our capacity to utilize effective interventions

Competency 4
Engage in Practice-informed Research and Research-informed Practice

Competency 7:
Engage in Practice-informed Research and Research-informed Practice to increase our capacity to identify accurate assessment instruments and procedures

Competency 4:
What are the knowledge, values and skills necessary to engage in practice-informed research and research-informed practice?

Competency 6:
Engage in Practice-informed Research and Research-informed Practice to increase our capacity to effectively engage with clients

Competency 5:
Engage in Practice-informed Research and Research-informed Practice to inform policy practice

FIGURE 4.1 The relationship of competency 4 with the rest of the competencies.

Applying Competency 4

Competency 4 is a process we use to increase our professional knowledge and skills. As we work with the Smith and Johnson family, we will encounter a variety of issues that might require us to conduct a literature review to improve our understanding. Every practicum setting will require you to focus on specific issues to study. For example, if your social work practicum is in a school setting, you might benefit from reading the *Children & Schools* journal. If your practicum is at a prison and Mr. Johnson is your main client, you might learn from the *Journal of Law and Social Policy*. If Mrs. Smith is your main client, it could be helpful to become familiar with the *Journal of Family Social Work*, the *Journal of Gerontological Social Work*, or *Health & Social Work*. Several journals provide a forum for social work researchers to share their research findings. A good way to start exploring them is by joining NASW, which will give you access to research articles on a variety of issues relevant to social work practice, such as aging, behavioral health, child welfare, clinical social work, ethnicity and race, health, LGBTQIA2S+, and school social work.

Reflective Questions on Competency Application

These reflective questions are meant to help you consider some of the requirements of competency 4 and its role in your work with clients. You do not have to answer the questions, but if a question arouses your interest, you should explore it.

What do you need to know and be able to do to identify research studies that will increase your knowledge of the issues that affect the Smith and Johnson family?

What do you need to know and be able to do to integrate and implement research findings to inform your work with the Smith and Johnson family?

How can you use research to become a more effective social work practicum student? What kinds of issues do you need to learn about to become a knowledgeable social worker?

If your clients are Alyssa and Daniel, you might want to learn about the following:

- What is the impact of grief and loss on student learning outcomes?
- What are the needs of children with incarcerated parents?
- How does incarceration affect parent–child relationships?
- What are needs of children being raised by grandparents?
- What is the impact of bullying victimization on academic outcomes?
- How prevalent is bullying and school violence?
- Are there effective strategies to address bullying and school violence?
- What is the impact of adverse childhood experiences?
- How can resilience be fostered in children?
- What is the role of social workers in school settings?

If Alyssa and Daniel belong to a minority population and are English learners, you might want to learn about the following:

- What are educational needs of diverse student populations?
- What is the role of culture and language in learning?
- What do minority students need to feel safe in public schools?

If Mrs. Smith is your client, you might want to learn about the following:

- How many grandparents are raising their grandchildren in the United States?
- What are some ways that society can support grandparents raising grandchildren?
- What are the challenges for grandparents raising their grandchildren?
- What is the impact of caring for grandchildren on the health of grandparents?
- What is the impact of chronic illness on family relationships?
- Are depressive symptoms elevated among caregiving grandparents?
- What are the strengths of grandparents raising grandchildren?
- How does type 2 diabetes affect the elderly?
- How does socioeconomic status affect health outcomes?
- What can social workers do to assist the elderly?

If Mrs. Smith belongs to a minority population and she experienced oppression and discrimination, you might want to learn about the following:

- What is the impact of historical trauma on the helping process?
- What is culturally informed social work practice?
- What is antiracist and anti-oppressive social work practice?
- How does type 2 diabetes affect minority populations?
- How do adverse childhood experiences affect the elderly?

If Mr. Johnson is your client, you might want to learn about the following:

- What are the benefits of family connection with incarcerated parents?
- What are the most common problems that the families of prisoners have?
- What are the most effective strategies to maintain family connections during incarceration?
- What is the role of social workers in criminal justice and correctional settings?

James Smith is a gay male who has tried to be a father figure for Alyssa and Daniel, but his sexual orientation is an issue that is not spoken about with his parents because his parents belong to a religion that considers homosexuality a sin. James tested positive for COVID-19 on March 15, 2020, If James is your client, you might want to learn about the following:

- When was COVID-19 identified?
- What was known about COVID-19 in March 2020?
- Who's at higher risk of serious COVID-19 symptoms?
- What are racial and ethnic disparities in COVID-19 outcomes?
- What are the conflicts between religious identify and LGBTQIA2S+ identity?
- What is the prevalence of negative parental reactions to their son's disclosure of a gay identity?
- Why do LGBTQ adults keep ties with parents who reject them?
- What is the prevalence of the LGBTQIA2S+ identification by racial and ethnic groups in the United States?
- What are effective social work practices with sexual and gender minority clients?

Social workers deal with difficult client situations, so you might want to learn about the following:

- What is vicarious trauma and how can its risk be reduced?
- Why is self-care essential for social work professionals?
- How can you achieve work-life balance?

Think about the clients you work with in your social work practicum. Are some of these questions relevant to them? What other issues would you need to explore to effectively work with your clients?

Investigating Each Sentence in the Competency Description

Competency 4 requires active participation. You cannot just read when your goal is to gain the knowledge and skills necessary to accurately assist clients. You will need to critically evaluate research studies for accuracy, validity, relevance, trustworthiness, and usefulness. You can use the internet to explore the meaning of key terms and find relevant journals, but nothing is better than a good relationship with your university librarian.

There are three steps you should take before you start dissecting each phrase of this competency. First, check with your professors to identify the requirements for human subjects' research training at your university and complete them. Although the exercises in this book will only require you to examine research conducted by others, human subjects training will provide you with essential information regarding research ethics when studying human subjects and behavior. You will notice that the principles of ethical research are in line with ethical requirements of the social work profession.

Second, identify and explore the research foundation of the social work theories relevant to your social work practicum. Competencies 6, 7, 8, and 9 will require you to use theoretical frameworks, and understanding the research foundation of these theories will be useful.

Table 4.1 provides a short summary of some of the most used theories in social work practice. Each of these theories has strengths and limitations, but even theories that we might not use with clients provide a framework to explore some aspect of the world and how people behave in society.

TABLE 4.1 Short Summary of Theories and Models Useful to Social Work Practice

Theories	Scholars	Emphasis
Human development	Erik Erikson John Bowlby	Child development Attachment
Humanistic	Abraham Maslow Carl Rogers James F.T. Bugental Viktor Frankl	Motivation Personality development Humanistic psychology Logotherapy
Psychodynamic	Sigmund Freud Carl Jung Anna Freud Melanie Klein Alfred Adler	Psychosexual developmental Personality and motivation Child psychoanalysis Children's unconscious motivations Humans as social beings
Learning theories	Albert Bandura Jean Piaget Lev Vygotsky	Social learning Cognitive development Sociocultural development
Behavior	Ivan Pavlov B.F. Skinner John Watson	Physiology Behavior analysis Child development
Systems	Ludwig von Bertalanffy	Biology
Family systems	Murray Bowen	Families as an emotional unit
Critical race theory	Derrick Bell Kimberlé Crenshaw Richard Delgado Alan Freeman Cheryl Harris Charles R. Lawrence III Mari Matsuda Patricia J. Williams	Civil rights Race, racism, and the law Racial inequalities in the law Antidiscrimination jurisprudence Civil rights and civil liberties Assaultive speech and the First Amendment Hate speech Race, gender, literature, and law
Feminist	Betty Friedan Julia Kristeva Judith Butler Elaine Showalter Carol Gilligan Adrienne Rich	Career-oriented independence Intertextual relationships Normative heterosexuality Stereotypes of feminism Women's morality Poetic discourse

Change theory, Prochaska and DiClemente's stages of change model	James O. Prochaska Carlo DiClemente	Prevention of cancer and other chronic diseases Behavioral health care
The 5 A's behavior change model	U.S. Department of Health and Human Services	Improving chronic illness care
Motivational interviewing	William R. Miller Stephen Rollnick	Psychology of change Clinical psychology
Genograms in family assessment	Monica McGoldrick	The importance of culture, gender, and diversity

Third, you need to be able to conduct a literature review and read, analyze, and critique research studies to increase your social work knowledge and skills. If you are taking a research course with the social work practicum course, you can consult your research instructor. If you have already taken the research course, you can reference the textbook and course notes to review the literature review process, because you will need to use a similar process to complete the exercises in this section. However, there is a difference between a literature review conducted as an academic exercise and a literature review conducted to put research findings in practice. Review Figure 4.2 to explore the function of the literature review process as a learning tool for increasing your social work practice skills.

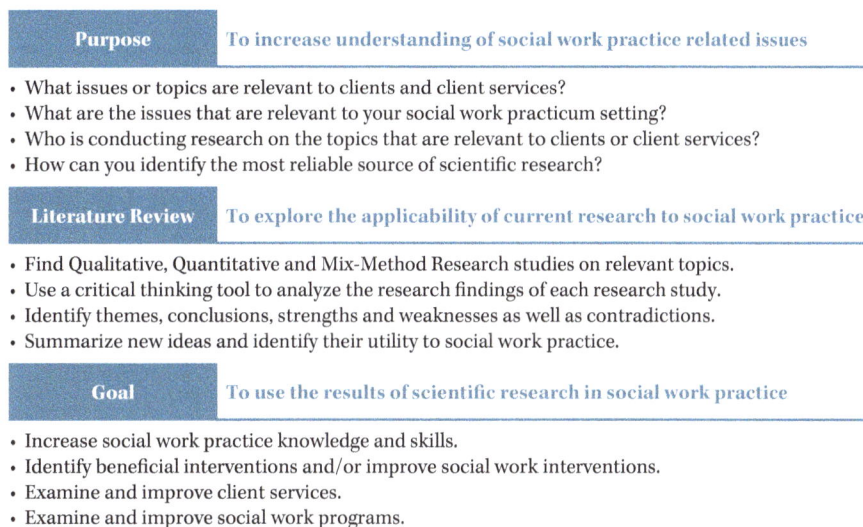

Purpose	**To increase understanding of social work practice related issues**

- What issues or topics are relevant to clients and client services?
- What are the issues that are relevant to your social work practicum setting?
- Who is conducting research on the topics that are relevant to clients or client services?
- How can you identify the most reliable source of scientific research?

Literature Review	**To explore the applicability of current research to social work practice**

- Find Qualitative, Quantitative and Mix-Method Research studies on relevant topics.
- Use a critical thinking tool to analyze the research findings of each research study.
- Identify themes, conclusions, strengths and weaknesses as well as contradictions.
- Summarize new ideas and identify their utility to social work practice.

Goal	**To use the results of scientific research in social work practice**

- Increase social work practice knowledge and skills.
- Identify beneficial interventions and/or improve social work interventions.
- Examine and improve client services.
- Examine and improve social work programs.

FIGURE 4.2   The function of a literature review in the social work practicum.

Competency 4

Engage in Practice-Informed Research and Research-Informed Practice

Social workers use ethical, culturally informed, and anti-racist and anti-oppressive approaches in conducting research and building knowledge.

Identify Key Concepts, Search for the Meaning of Those Concepts, and Critically Examine the Requirements of the Competency

1. Review your research textbook or conduct an internet search with the phrase "ethical approaches to conducting scientific research."

    a. What did you learn about ethical approaches to conducting scientific research, and how might that inform your research-informed practice?

2. Review your research textbook or conduct an internet search with the phrase "culturally informed approaches to conducting scientific research."

    a. What did you learn about culturally informed approaches to conducting scientific research, and how might that inform your research-informed practice?

3. Review your research textbook or conduct an internet search with the phrase "antiracist and anti-oppressive approaches to conducting scientific research."

    a. What did you learn about antiracist and anti-oppressive approaches to conducting scientific research, and how might that inform your research-informed practice?

4. Select an issue that is relevant to your client population and use what you learned about ethical, culturally informed, and anti-oppressive research approaches to search for a scientific study on that topic.

    a. What did you learn by using your knowledge about ethical, culturally informed, and antiracist and anti-oppressive approaches to conduct research to review research studies that are relevant to your client population?

Reflective Writing Practice

In a few sentences, outline your plan to use ethical, culturally informed, and antiracist and anti-oppressive approaches to conduct research and develop your social work professional knowledge base.

_____

_____

_____

_____

Application Follow-Up

Date you used ethical, culturally informed, and antiracist and anti-oppressive approaches in conducting research to learn about an issue relevant to the client population at your practicum:

_____

In a few sentences, describe what you learned from the process of exploring the meaning and application of ethical, culturally informed, and antiracist and anti-oppressive approaches in conducting research.

_____

_____

_____

_____

Self-Evaluation

Successful	I can effectively demonstrate these competency requirements during practicum, and I can explain how these competency requirements contribute to effective social work practice.
Developing	I can identify the information I need and am able to apply it in some practicum situations, but I am also aware of some knowledge and skill gaps that I need to address.
Unsuccessful	Currently, I am not able to successfully demonstrate these competency requirements in practicum.

Competency 4

Engage in Practice-Informed Research and Research-Informed Practice

Social workers use research to inform their practice decision making and articulate how their practice experience informs research and evaluation decisions.

Identify Key Concepts, Search for the Meaning of Those Concepts, and Critically Examine the Requirements of the Competency

1. Identify the main intervention provided by social workers in your practicum, and conduct an internet search to identify a scientific research article that explores the intervention.
2. Identify the main issues that affect the client population at your practicum, and conduct an internet search to identify at least two different approaches to address that issue.
3. As you read the available research on the intervention used at your practicum, compare what the studies report with what you are observing among clients at your practicum.
4. Compare the approach used at your practicum with the approaches proposed in the studies you are reading. Are they similar or different? Are their outcomes similar or different?
5. What kinds of questions come up for you as you compare the results of research and what you are observing during your practicum experience?

Reflective Writing Practice

In a few sentences, outline a plan to integrate what you are learning from research into your social work practicum experience.

_____

_____

_____

_____

Application Follow-Up

Date you were able to use research to inform your approach to address an issue at your practicum:
_____

In a few sentences, describe what you learned by using the scientific research process to learn about an issue that is relevant to clients at your practicum.

_____

_____

_____

_____

Self-Evaluation

Successful	I can effectively demonstrate these competency requirements during practicum, and I can explain how these competency requirements contribute to effective social work practice.
Developing	I can identify the information I need and am able to apply it in some practicum situations, but I am also aware of some knowledge and skill gaps that I need to address.
Unsuccessful	Currently, I am not able to successfully demonstrate these competency requirements in practicum.

Competency 4

Engage in Practice-Informed Research and Research-Informed Practice

Social workers critically evaluate and critique current, empirically sound research to inform decisions pertaining to practice, policy, and programs.

Identify Key Concepts, Search for the Meaning of Those Concepts, and Critically Examine the Requirements of the Competency

1. Identify the main social work practice modality being used at your practicum setting and find at least a couple of scientific research articles that investigate that modality.
2. Identify the main policy that guides client services and find at least a couple of scientific research articles that investigate that policy. For example, if your practicum is at a school setting, you might want to conduct a search with the following phrase "social workers and the Elementary and Secondary Education Act."
3. Identify the main program offered at your practicum and find at least a couple of scientific research articles that investigate similar programs.
4. Use a critical thinking tool to analyze the articles you found and compare what you learned from them with what you are observing in your practicum.

Reflective Writing Practice

In a few sentences, outline a plan to use empirically sound research to inform social work practicum decisions.

_____

_____

_____

_____

_____

Application Follow-Up

Date you were able to use current empirically sound research to inform social work practicum decisions: _____

In a few sentences, describe what you learned by using current empirically sound research to inform social work practicum decisions.

_____

_____

_____

_____

Self-Evaluation

Successful	I can effectively demonstrate these competency requirements during practicum, and I can explain how these competency requirements contribute to effective social work practice.
Developing	I can identify the information I need and am able to apply it in some practicum situations, but I am also aware of some knowledge and skill gaps that I need to address.
Unsuccessful	Currently, I am not able to successfully demonstrate these competency requirements in practicum.

Competency 4

Engage in Practice-Informed Research and Research-Informed Practice

Social workers understand the inherent bias in research and evaluate design, analysis, and interpretation using an anti-racist and anti-oppressive perspective.

Identify Key Concepts, Search for the Meaning of Those Concepts, and Critically Examine the Requirements of the Competency

1. Review your research textbook or conduct an internet search with the phrase "scientific research and inherent bias examples" and see if you can answer the following questions:

   ○ Is there a way to avoid leading question bias in research studies?
   ○ What is the halo effect?
   ○ Is there a way to recognize acquiescence bias in research studies?
   ○ How does social desirability bias affect research results?
   ○ What is the danger of sponsor bias?
   ○ Is there a way to avoid confirmation bias?
   ○ How can you spot culture bias in research studies?
   ○ How does question-order bias influence research?

2. Review your research textbook or conduct an internet search to find information about "research design methods."

3. Review your research textbook or conduct an internet search to study the "research analysis process."

4. Conduct an internet search with the phrase "antiracist and anti-oppressive research perspectives."

5. Use a critical thinking tool to analyze the information you found and summarize what you learned from reading about bias in research and research design and analysis.

Reflective Writing Practice

In a few sentences, outline a plan to use what you learned about research bias and increasing your ability to use antiracist and anti-oppressive research relevant to the client population served at your practicum.

_____

_____

_____

_____

Application Follow-Up

Date you used an antiracist and anti-oppressive perspective to analyze a research study relevant to the client population served at your practicum: _____

In a few sentences, describe what you learned from the process of applying an antiracist and anti-oppressive perspective to analyze a research study that you used in your practicum.

_____

_____

_____

_____

Self-Evaluation

Successful	I can effectively demonstrate these competency requirements during practicum, and I can explain how these competency requirements contribute to effective social work practice.
Developing	I can identify the information I need and am able to apply it in some practicum situations, but I am also aware of some knowledge and skill gaps that I need to address.
Unsuccessful	Currently, I am not able to successfully demonstrate these competency requirements in practicum.

Competency 4

Engage in Practice-Informed Research and Research-Informed Practice

Social workers know how to access, critique, and synthesize the current literature to develop appropriate research questions and hypotheses.

Identify Key Concepts, Search for the Meaning of Those Concepts, and Critically Examine the Requirements of the Competency

1. Identify at least one reliable source of scientific information relevant to your client population. For example, if you are interested in learning about substance abuse and mental health issues, samhsa.gov might be a good place to start.
2. Conduct an internet search with the phrase "how to critique a research study" to identify a guide to critique research articles.
3. Find at least three scientific research articles that are less than 5 years old on a subject relevant to your client population and analyze them.
4. Use the guide to critique research articles that you found to synthesize the key findings of the articles and consider their application to your client population.
5. Identify a research gap relevant to the issues that affect your client population and develop a research question to address that gap.

Reflective Writing Practice

In a few sentences, outline a plan to access, critique, and synthesize current literature and to develop research questions relevant to your client population.

_____

_____

_____

_____

Application Follow-Up

Date you were able to use your synthesis of relevant research to address an issue during practicum: _____

In a few sentences, describe what you learned from the process of synthesizing research studies and identifying their utility in practice.

_____

_____

_____

_____

Self-Evaluation

Successful	I can effectively demonstrate these competency requirements during practicum, and I can explain how these competency requirements contribute to effective social work practice.
Developing	I can identify the information I need and am able to apply it in some practicum situations, but I am also aware of some knowledge and skill gaps that I need to address.
Unsuccessful	Currently, I am not able to successfully demonstrate these competency requirements in practicum.

Competency 4

Engage in Practice-Informed Research and Research-Informed Practice

Social workers demonstrate knowledge and skills regarding qualitative and quantitative research methods and analysis, and they interpret data derived from these methods.

Identify Key Concepts, Search for the Meaning of Those Concepts, and Critically Examine the Requirements of the Competency

1. Conduct an internet search with the phrase "qualitative research methods" or use your research textbook to review the definition and other information.
2. Conduct an internet search with the phrase "quantitative research methods" or use your research textbook to review the definition and other information.
3. Conduct an internet search with the phrase "research analysis" or review your research textbook to see whether it provides a research analysis tool.
4. Identify a topic relevant to your client population and find at least one qualitative scientific research article that is less than 5 years old. Then answer the following questions:

    a. How did the researchers identify the main topic or idea?
    b. Who were the study participants?
    c. How did the setting affect the study?
    d. What insights were identified?
    e. What tools were used to conduct the content analysis, thematic analysis, or discourse analysis?
    f. Are the researcher's interpretations supported by the input of participants?
    g. How can qualitative research findings be used in social work practice?

5. Find at least one quantitative scientific research article on the same topic and answer the following questions:

    a. What kind of statistics were used? Was the scope of the problem well defined?
    b. Was a theory tested? Was the hypothesis supported or disproved?
    c. How did the researchers use numbers, graphs, and tables?
    d. How was the statistical analysis reported?
    e. Can the study be replicated?
    f. How can quantitative research findings be used in social work practice?

6. Explain the differences in the kind of information you gained from each of the two research methods.

Reflective Writing Practice

In a few sentences, describe a plan to use both qualitative and quantitative research methods to inform your work with clients.

_____

_____

_____

_____

Application Follow-Up

Date you were able to use the information you gained from qualitative and quantitative research methods and analysis to explore an issue relevant to the client population served at your practicum: _____

In a few sentences, describe what you learned from the process of utilizing qualitative and quantitative research methods to inform your work with clients.

_____

_____

_____

_____

Self-Evaluation

Successful	I can effectively demonstrate these competency requirements during practicum, and I can explain how these competency requirements contribute to effective social work practice.
Developing	I can identify the information I need and am able to apply it in some practicum situations, but I am also aware of some knowledge and skill gaps that I need to address.
Unsuccessful	Currently, I am not able to successfully demonstrate these competency requirements in practicum.

Competency 4

Engage in Practice-Informed Research and Research-Informed Practice

Social workers demonstrate knowledge about methods to assess reliability and validity in social work research.

Identify Key Concepts, Search for the Meaning of Those Concepts, and Critically Examine the Requirements of the Competency

1. Conduct an internet search with the phrase "how is research reliability and validity assessed" or use your social work research text to review the process.
2. Select a couple of social work research articles and use what you learned about the assessment of reliability and validity to examine them.

Reflective Writing Practice

In a few sentences, outline a plan to systematically assess the reliability and validity of research relevant to your client population.

_____

_____

_____

_____

Application Follow-Up

Date you were able to identify the steps researchers took to ensure validity and reliability in a research study that is relevant to your practicum: _____

In a few sentences, describe what you learned from the process of utilizing a method to assess the reliability and validity of research studies relevant to social work practice.

_____

_____

_____

_____

Self-Evaluation

Successful	I can effectively demonstrate these competency requirements during practicum, and I can explain how these competency requirements contribute to effective social work practice.
Developing	I can identify the information I need and am able to apply it in some practicum situations, but I am also aware of some knowledge and skill gaps that I need to address.
Unsuccessful	Currently, I am not able to successfully demonstrate these competency requirements in practicum.

Competency 4

Engage in Practice-Informed Research and Research-Informed Practice

Social workers can articulate and share research findings in ways that are usable to a variety of clients and constituencies.

Identify Key Concepts, Search for the Meaning of Those Concepts, and Critically Examine the Requirements of the Competency

1. Review the research articles you found in the previous sections and identify the findings you want to share with your social work field instructor or peers in seminar or study group.
2. Create a short presentation or outline to highlight the main findings in a way that a non-expert on the subject could understand and use.

Reflective Writing Practice

In a few sentences, outline the main findings of at least three articles on the same topic and explain how those findings can be used to improve client services.

_____

_____

_____

_____

Application Follow-Up

Date you were able to articulate and share research findings in ways that was useful to clients or colleagues: _____

In a few sentences, describe what you learned from the process of sharing research findings that are useful to the client population served at your practicum:

_____

_____

_____

_____

Self-Evaluation

Successful	I can effectively demonstrate these competency requirements during practicum, and I can explain how these competency requirements contribute to effective social work practice.
Developing	I can identify the information I need and am able to apply it in some practicum situations, but I am also aware of some knowledge and skill gaps that I need to address.
Unsuccessful	Currently, I am not able to successfully demonstrate these competency requirements in practicum.

Competency 4

Engage in Practice-Informed Research and Research-Informed Practice

Social workers understand the value of evidence derived from interprofessional and diverse research methods, approaches, and sources.

Identify Key Concepts, Search for the Meaning of Those Concepts, and Critically Examine the Requirements of the Competency

1. Conduct an internet search with the phrase "interprofessional collaboration in research," or find an article that has at least three authors from different professional disciplines, and identify the advantages of studies that include different perspectives.
2. Conduct an internet search with the phrase "diversity in research methods," or find an article that uses a mixed-methods approach and identify the advantages of combining research methods.
3. Conduct an internet search with the phrase "diverse views in scientific research," or find a scientific study that was conducted by an ethnically diverse team, and identify the contribution of diverse views to social work practice.
4. Synthesize the main insights you gained from exploring these issues.

Reflective Writing Practice

In a few sentences, describe the utility of using interprofessional and diverse research methods to learn about issues that impact your client population.

_____

_____

_____

_____

Application Follow-Up

Date you were able to use what you learned from interprofessional and diverse research studies at your practicum: _____

In a few sentences, describe what you learned from the process of identifying and using research findings derived from interprofessional collaboration.

_____

_____

_____

_____

Self-Evaluation

Successful	I can effectively demonstrate these competency requirements during practicum, and I can explain how these competency requirements contribute to effective social work practice.
Developing	I can identify the information I need and am able to apply it in some practicum situations, but I am also aware of some knowledge and skill gaps that I need to address.
Unsuccessful	Currently, I am not able to successfully demonstrate these competency requirements in practicum.

Demonstrating the Ability to Engage in Practice-Informed Research and Research-Informed Practice

Through the process of reading and analyzing scientific research studies relevant to your client population and attempting to use their findings to inform your social work practicum decisions, you are developing the ability to engage in practice-informed research and research-informed practice. As you identify the issues that affect your client population and search for research studies that explore them, you will notice that each researcher will focus on different aspects of those issues. You might also identify an aspect of the problem that research has not yet addressed, and you can then develop research questions that may lead you to become a scientific researcher if conducting original research is your interest. However, if you work in a social work setting that receives federal grants, you might still have the opportunity to participate in some aspects of research, since most grants require a process to examine the usefulness of the funded activities. Furthermore, if you recognize the value of scientific studies in the daily practice of social work, you will want to have access to current research studies you can use to increase your professional competence.

Apply research findings to inform and improve practice, policy, and programs.

Demonstrating Competency 4 With the Smith and Johnson Family	Demonstrating Competency 4 During Your Practicum
1. If your clients are Alyssa and Daniel, you might be better able to assist them if you use research to learn about the impact of grief and loss on student learning. 2. How would knowing about the needs of children who have an incarcerated parent influence your work with Alyssa and Daniel? 3. How might you be able to advocate for policies that account for the impact of bullying on student success? 4. If Alyssa and Daniel are English language learners, can you use research to learn more about the needs of bilingual students? How would you know whether the bilingual program at our school is effective? 5. If you feel overwhelmed by the demands of the social work profession, are there research studies that can help you maintain a balance between personal and professional life to avoid burnout?	1. What issues do you need to research to become a well-informed social work practicum student at your agency? 2. How can you use research to improve social work practices at your practicum? 3. How might you use research to advocate for policies that increase client well-being? 4. What issues are the social work programs at your practicum attempting to address? How do you know if those programs are effective? 5. Do you ever feel overwhelmed? Have you found research studies that might help you remain focused on your professional goals? What steps are you taking to avoid burnout?

Identify ethical, culturally informed, anti-racist, and anti-oppressive strategies that address inherent biases for use in quantitative and qualitative research methods to advance the purposes of social work.

Demonstrating Competency 4 With the Smith and Johnson Family	Demonstrating Competency 4 During Your Practicum
1. If the Smith and Johnson family are your clients, and they belong to a minority population, what steps can you take to identify research studies that are ethical and culturally informed and use anti-racist and anti-oppressive research strategies? 2. Have you used a critical thinking tool to evaluate quantitative and qualitative research studies relevant to the issues that affect the Smith and Johnson family? 3. Can you clearly describe how you can use the knowledge you gained by analyzing research studies to assist the Smith and Johnson family?	1. Does your agency serve marginalized populations? Have you found research studies that consider the role of culture in the helping process? Does your practicum agency serve clients who have experienced racism and oppression? What can you do to integrate antiracist and anti-oppressive social work practices? 2. Are you consistently using a critical thinking tool to analyze research? Are you able to identify the inherent biases in quantitative and qualitative research methods to avoid imposing research findings on populations that were not included in the research process? 3. When you find articles that address the needs of minority clients, can you identify whether the authors used ethical research methods? How would you know that clients' cultural identity was considered and respected?

Competency Development Topics for the Social Work Practicum Seminar

▶ **Competency 4 Field Seminar Topics**

- Critical thinking tools, the critical analysis of current and empirically sound research to inform practice, policy, and programs
- Ways to identify ethical, culturally informed, antiracist, and anti-oppressive research studies
- The process of evaluating research design and analysis
- The value of evidence derived from interprofessional and diverse research methods, approaches, and sources

▼ **Prior Planning**

- Use the reading and writing exercises in this chapter to identify the key concepts related to the seminar discussion topics.
- Identify the parts of the competency that you have not been able to successfully implement in your practicum.
- Formulate specific questions that you can bring to seminar to explore your knowledge and skills gaps.

◀ **During Seminar**

- Listen carefully to your peers and seminar instructor.
- Consider the utility of the different perspectives your peers bring to the topic.
- Be ready to contribute by sharing your struggles as well as your success in addressing competency 4 requirements.
- Find the satisfaction of professional growth. Identify a skill or insight you gained by completing the exercises in this chapter, and consider how that knowledge contributes to your ability to become the social work professional you want to be.

Competency Development Topics for the Educational Supervision Meeting

▶ **Competency 4 Social Work Practicum Instructional Supervision Meeting Topics**

- The most relevant practicum related issues or topics to study
- Relevant current empirically sound research to inform practice, policy, and programs
- The use of critical thinking tools to identify ethical, culturally informed, antiracist, and anti-oppressive research studies
- The process of implementing research finding in practice

▼   **Prior Planning**

- If you identified research studies relevant to your social work practicum and analyzed them, you can use your notes to formulate questions for your social work instructor prior to your instructional supervision meeting.
- Compare the service modalities and approaches used in the research studies you reviewed. Are there any differences you would like to discuss with your instructor?
- Consider the time and resource constraints in your practicum setting and think of ways you could help your social work instructor by analyzing and synthesizing research studies relevant to your practicum setting.

◄   **During the Instructional Supervision Meeting**

- Be prepared to ask questions that will help you develop and practice competency 4.
- Listen attentively to your social work instructor.
- Mentally prepare for the fact that you do not have the insight your instructor has about the service modalities and approaches used in your practicum setting and that your ideas about the utility of research studies might need further development.

Summary

Figure 4.3 summarizes the main steps in the process to engage in practice-informed research and research-informed practice. Competency 4 contributes to the professional standing of the social work profession. If you want to become an expert social worker, you need to make the

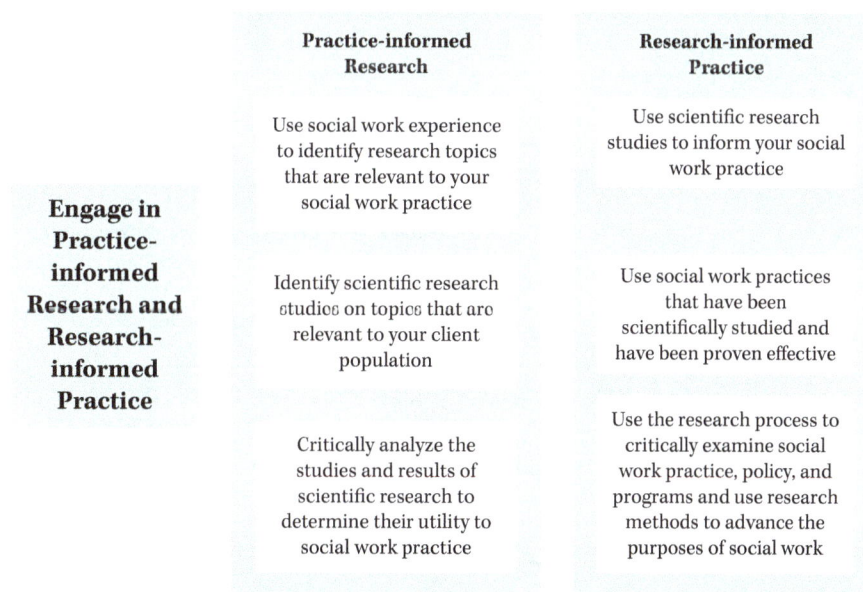

Engage in Practice-informed Research and Research-informed Practice	Practice-informed Research	Research-informed Practice
	Use social work experience to identify research topics that are relevant to your social work practice	Use scientific research studies to inform your social work practice
	Identify scientific research studies on topics that are relevant to your client population	Use social work practices that have been scientifically studied and have been proven effective
	Critically analyze the studies and results of scientific research to determine their utility to social work practice	Use the research process to critically examine social work practice, policy, and programs and use research methods to advance the purposes of social work

FIGURE 4.3   Main steps in the process to engage in practice-informed research and research-informed practice.

commitment to use scientific research not only to learn about the issues that affect your clients, but also to examine and improve your own social work practices.

By considering the requirements of competency 4, identifying research studies relevant to your client population, and using critical thinking tools to examine their relevance and utility in your social work practicum, you have already started to develop the skills necessary to develop your professional competence.

If you used each prompt to explore the issues that affect your clients, you are now more aware of the issues that face your client population, and you are better able to distinguish the difference between using qualitative and quantitative research methods. You should also be able to identify any topic you need to learn more about and have a good understanding of how to access scientific research articles to learn more about it. Like all the competencies, competency 4 will require a commitment to lifelong learning if your goal is to increase your competence and the quality of services you are able to provide your clients as a social work professional.

Recommended Reading Materials

Books	Description
Mauldin, R. L. (2020). *Foundations of Social Work Research*. Mavs Open Press.	This is an open-source textbook that introduces research methods to social work students.
Howe, D. (2009). *A Brief Introduction to Social Work Theory*. Bloomsbury.	The author explains how social work practice is influenced by various social work theories and shows how social work theories have evolved over time.
Teater, B. (2019). *An Introduction to Applying Social Work Theories and Methods*. McGraw-Hill Education.	The author explains the most prominent social work theories and how those approaches can be used in practice.
Van der Kolk, B. A. (2015). *The Body Keeps the Score: Brain, Mind, and Body in the Healing of Trauma*. Penguin.	This author integrates research to provide clear examples of how trauma impacts the mind, emotions, and our biology—fundamental knowledge for social work practitioners.
Burke Harris, N. (2018). *The Deepest Well: Healing the Long-Term Effects of Childhood Trauma and Adversity*. Houghton Mifflin.	This book explains how adverse childhood experiences such as abuse, neglect, parental addiction, mental illness, and divorce contributes to physical illness. Most social work clients seek help with these issues, and social workers benefit from understanding that alleviating these social issues has a long-term impact on clients' well-being.
Peterson, C. (2006). *A Primer in Positive Psychology*. Oxford University Press, USA.	This author provides a good description of positive psychology and its utility in practice.
Treleaven, D. A. (2018). *Trauma-Sensitive Mindfulness: Practices for Safe and Transformative Healing*. Norton.	This is a practical guide based on research. Mindfulness can be a useful practice for social work practitioners to prevent burnout.

The Diabetes Code: Prevent and Reverse Type 2 Diabetes Naturally Fung, J. (2018). United States: Greystone Books.	In this book, Dr. Fung explains how he used research to examine why people with people with Type 2 diabetes were not getting better with standard treatments. The same process can be used to examine social work practices when outcomes are not beneficial to clients.
Fuhrman, J., & Phillips, R. (2017). *Fast Food Genocide: How Processed Food Is Killing Us and What We Can Do About It*. HarperCollins.	This is a book is based on clinical experience and research and proposes that a nutrient dense, healthful diet can help us live a successful and fulfilling life. Social work is about helping people achieve wellness, and taking care of our own health is an essential step.
Brown, B. (2021). *Atlas of the Heart: Mapping Meaningful Connection and the Language of Human Experience*. Random House.	Social work requires a meaningful connection with clients. The author uses research to identify 87 human emotions and experiences that make us who we are.
Grant, A. (2021). *Think Again: The Power of Knowing What You Don't Know*. Penguin.	The author uses research and storytelling to encourage us to build the intellectual and emotional skills to stay curious enough about the world to change it.

References

Council on Social Work Education. (2022, September 29). *2022 EPAS*. https://www.cswe.org/accreditation/standards/2022-epas/

Fung, J. (2018). *The diabetes code: Prevent and reverse type 2 diabetes naturally* (Vol. 2). Greystone Books.

National Association of Social Workers. (2022, May 23). *NASW Code of Ethics*. https://www.socialworkers.org/About/Ethics/Code-of-Ethics/Code-of-Ethics-English

CREDIT

CHAPTER 5

Competency 5

The Requirement to Engage in Policy Practice

In this chapter, you will examine the requirements of the fifth of the nine social work competencies provided by the CSWE. Competency 5 requires an ability to understand the role of policy in social work practice as well as the ability to examine the social, racial, cultural, and economic impact of the policies that guide client services for diverse client populations.

If you have already taken a social work policy course, you should review your textbooks and course notes to review the social policy formulation and analysis process. If you are taking a policy course concurrently with your field course, you can use the course assignments to focus your policy research efforts on the policies that are relevant to your practicum. If you have not taken the course and are not currently taking it, you will need to use your independent learning skills to become familiar with the social policies that guide social work practice and the policy development, implementation, and evaluation process.

You will need to identify the specific policies that guide social work practice at your practicum setting and follow the step-by-step process provided in this guide so that you can develop your own ability to effectively engage in policy practice. Since social policy changes overtime and each social work practice setting is guided by specific social policies, a commitment to continuous learning is essential when it comes to social policy. You might also want to identify a social policy that affects your well-being directly and study it. For example, if you are taking student loans, you might want to examine how federal student aid works. Understanding the federal policies that guide student aid could be of great benefit to your future financial health and allow you to experience the power of knowing how social policies affect everyone who lives within a social environment.

Competency 5 Description as Provided by CSWE: Engage in Policy Practice

As you read the following description, consider your ability to identify and appropriately use the policies that guide client services during your social work practicum.

Competency 5

Engage in Policy Practice

Social workers identify social policies at the local, state, federal, and global level that affect well-being, human rights and justice, service delivery, and access to social services. Social workers recognize the historical, social, racial, cultural, economic, organizational, environmental, and global influences that affect social policy. Social workers understand and critique the history and current structures of social policies and services and the role of policy in service delivery through rights-based, anti-oppressive, and anti-racist lenses. Social workers influence policy formulation, analysis, implementation, and evaluation within their practice settings with individuals, families, groups, organizations, and communities. Social workers actively engage in and advocate for anti-racist and anti-oppressive policy practice to effect change in those settings.

Social workers:

a. use social justice, anti-racist, and anti-oppressive lenses to assess how social welfare policies affect the delivery of and access to social services; and

b. apply critical thinking to analyze, formulate, and advocate for policies that advance human rights and social, racial, economic, and environmental justice.

Figure 5.1 shows how competency 5 contributes to the other eight competencies. All social work practice settings develop and implement policies that set limits regarding the kinds of interventions clients are offered, the kinds of relationships we can develop with clients, and the kinds of assessment instruments and modalities we can use, and all those policies must be in alignment with federal and state laws and regulations. Not all policies are antiracist and anti-oppressive, and as social workers we need to analyze policies and advocate for those that advance the human rights and social justice of our diverse client populations.

Applying Competency 5

During your practicum, you might need to explain certain policies to clients as part of the intake process or before you start the evaluation and intervention process. At a minimum you will need to explain the limitations of the interventions offered and the process and availability of a referral for services available in the community. If the Smith and Johnson family are your clients, you need to develop a working knowledge of specific policies and procedures depending on the setting. Since the introduction to this fictitious case was in a school setting, it is easy to assume that only educational policies are relevant, but if we work with Mrs. Johnson at a health clinic or through a community agency, for instance, the relevant policies will change accordingly.

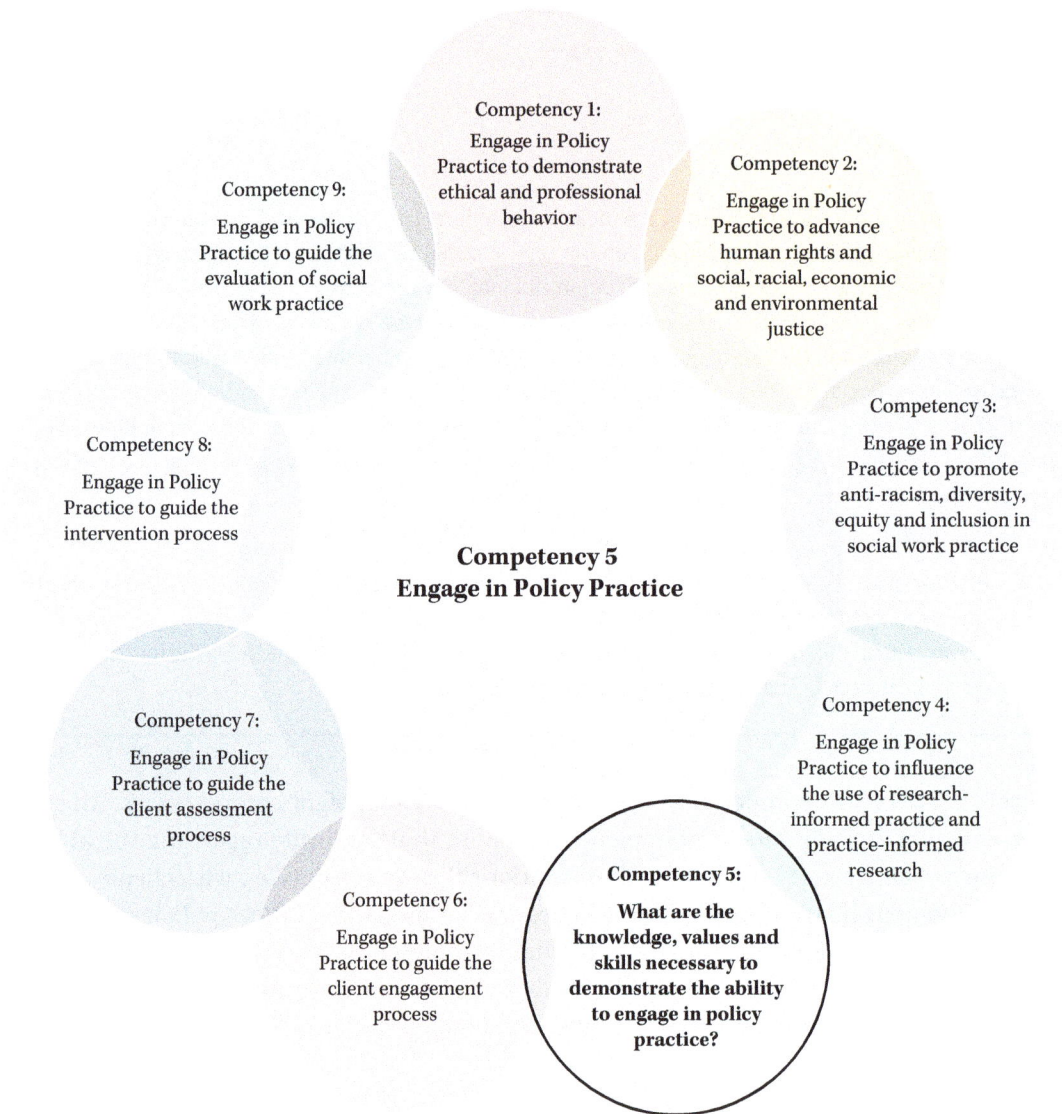

FIGURE 5.1   The relationship of competency 5 with the rest of the competencies.

Reflective Questions on Competency Application

These reflective questions are meant to help you consider some of the requirements of competency 5 and its role in your work with clients. You do not have to answer the questions, but if a question arouses your interest, you should explore it.

What are the policies that you need to be familiar with and be able to use and explain as you work with the Smith and Johnson Family?

If you are completing your social work practicum at a school and your clients are Alyssa and Daniel, you will need to learn about the following:

- How do school policies guide social work practice?
- How do school district policies shape school social work practice?
- What are the relevant state laws you need to know and follow?

For example:

Compulsory school attendance laws

Minimum and maximum age limits for required free education

- ○ What are the relevant federal educational policies you need to know and follow?

For example:

Every Student Succeeds Act (ESSA)

No Child Left Behind Act of 2001 (NCLB)

McKinney–Vento Homeless Assistance Act

Individuals With Disabilities Education Act (IDEA)

Elementary and Secondary Education Act (ESEA)

Higher Education Act of 1965

The problem that prompted the involvement of the social worker with this family was that Daniel hit another student, but after investigation, we learned that Daniel was defending himself after months of bullying.

What are the school policies regarding bullying?

Why did it take so long for school staff to become aware of the issue?

Are there any school policies that might protect the Daniel from further abuse from class-mates?

Most schools required in-home learning for a year or more. If Alyssa and Daniel got behind on their studies, are there any policies that could provide services to help them get back on track?

If you are completing your social work practicum at a health clinic and your client is Mrs. Smith, what are the policies you need to know and follow?

- ○ What are the policies that guide social work practice in the clinic?
- ○ Have you read the policies and procedures manual?
- ○ What are the state policies that you need to know and follow?

For example:

Patient care policies

Workplace health and safety policies

Information security policy

Data privacy and IT security practices

Drug-handling rules

Administrative and HR policies

Social media policies and guidelines for employee use of personally owned electronic devices for work-related purposes

- ○ What are the federal policies you need to know and follow?

For example:

The Health Insurance Portability and Accountability Act of 1996 (HIPAA)

The Medicare Access and CHIP Reauthorization Act (MACRA)

The Affordable Care Act (ACA)

(Continued)

The Health Information Technology for Economic and Clinical Health (HITECH) Act

Informed Consent of Human Subjects

If Mr. Johnson is your client, what are the policies you need to know and follow?

- How do prison policies and procedures shape social work practice?
- What are the state laws you need to know and follow?

For example:

Organization and administration

Fiscal management

Personnel and staff training

Information and records

Probation and parole management

Citizen involvement and volunteer services

Inmate discipline

Education programs

Special management

Inmate rights

Safety and sanitation

Health services

Mental health and addiction services

- What are the federal policies you need to know and follow?

For example:

First Step Act (FSA) of 2018

Federal Prison Bureau Nonviolent Offender Relief Act of 2021

The Sixth Amendment of the U.S. Constitution

The Eighth Amendment of the U.S. Constitution

If Mr. Johnson is your client, and he wants to maintain contact with his children, what steps can you take to advocate for his right to do so?

There were many policy changes made during the COVID-19 pandemic. Are you familiar with those changes? How have policy changes impacted social work services?

As you consider the different policies depending on social work practice setting, identify the local, state, and federal policies relevant to your social work practicum setting.

Investigating Each Sentence in the Competency Description

Competency 5 requirements include an ability to examine social policy to identify its impact on the diverse client populations we serve. If you are taking or have already taken a social work policy course, review your policy textbooks to examine the policy development process, the policy analysis process, and the policy advocacy process. The social work practicum is a place where you practice implementing the conceptual knowledge gained in the classroom, but it will often also require you to engage in independent learning to seek information you have not learned yet or have forgotten. An essential requirement in this section is a commitment to exploring unfamiliar terms to ensure you understand them and can integrate them into your social work practicum. The internet can be very useful in this process, if you are able to critically examine the source of the information you access and select government sites and reputable institutions of higher learning.

In Figure 5.2, you can see that social work practice policies have three main purposes. First, they guide client services and fees. In many settings, social work services are offered to clients free of charge, but those services are paid for by federal and state funds tied to regulations that must be followed to ensure the continuity of service availability.

Second, policies guide human behavior. What we can and cannot do as social workers is guided by policy, as is what clients can and cannot do. Some of those policies are very useful, but some can be limiting. For example, children in the child welfare system need nurturing, but social workers are discouraged from hugging children in care due to the possibility of further abuse.

The third purpose policies serve is to protect client and agency records. Confidentiality of client information is one reason records need to be protected, but the management of agency and client records is also an essential part in the evaluation of social work practices and procedures. In many social work settings, the audit of client records is the main quality management tool used to evaluate social work practices.

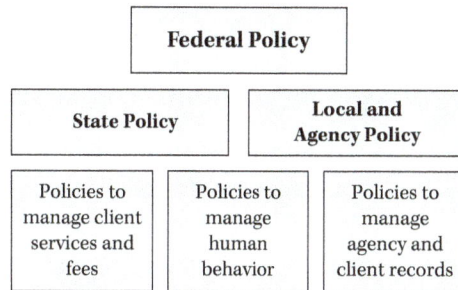

FIGURE 5.2   Social work practice policies and their alignment with state and federal policy.

Competency 5

Engage in Policy Practice

Social workers identify social policy at the local, state, federal, and global level that affects well-being, human rights and justice, service delivery, and access to social services.

Identify Key Concepts, Search for the Meaning of Those Concepts, and Critically Examine the Requirements of the Competency

1. Use the internet to find information about the Social Security Act of 1935 and the Social Security Amendments, and identify how the Social Security Act benefits the client population at your practicum agency.

   a. How does the Social Security Act promote social welfare?

2. Explore government benefits at https://www.usa.gov/benefits and identify the link between federal programs and the services offered at your agency.

   a. How do your clients benefit from government benefits?

3. Review the policies and procedures manual at your agency and identify the federal and state policies outlined in it.

    a. How do federal, state, and local policies impact the delivery of client services?

4. Use the internet to find at least two scholarly articles using the phrase "global social welfare," and identify an issue that might be relevant to your client population.

5. How are global issues related to the services provided in your practicum setting? For example, are you providing services to war refugees or immigrants who have come to this country escaping poverty or global unrest?

Reflective Writing Practice

In a few sentences, describe the relevance of the policies you reviewed to client services at your practicum and your role in ensuring that those policies are followed.

_____

_____

_____

_____

Application Follow-Up

Date you were able to identify how a policy guided client eligibility for services at your practicum:
_____

In a few sentences, describe what you learned by identifying a social policy at the local, state, and federal level that guides service delivery and access to social services at your practicum.

_____

_____

_____

_____

Self-Evaluation

Successful	I can effectively demonstrate these competency requirements during practicum, and I can explain how these competency requirements contribute to effective social work practice.
Developing	I can identify the information I need and am able to apply it in some practicum situations, but I am also aware of some knowledge and skill gaps that I need to address.
Unsuccessful	Currently, I am not able to successfully demonstrate these competency requirements in practicum.

> **Competency 5**
>
> **Engage in Policy Practice**
>
> Social workers recognize the historical, social, racial, cultural, economic, organizational, environmental, and global influences that affect social policy.

Identify Key Concepts, Search for the Meaning of Those Concepts, and Critically Examine the Requirements of the Competency

1. Select one of the federal policies that benefits the client population at your practicum and conduct an internet search for that policy's history and social impact. Consider the following questions as you research the policy:

   a. When was the policy proposed?
   b. What were the barriers to approving the policy?
   c. Who was in favor? What was their reasoning?
   d. Who was against it? What was their reasoning?
   e. What role did social, racial, and cultural factors play in getting the policy from proposal to implementation?
   f. If there is funding attached to the policy, how is it allocated?
   g. Can you identify the global influences that affect that policy? If not, are there similar policies in other countries?

Reflective Writing Practice

In a few sentences, describe the most important thing you learned about the policy's history and its impact on social welfare.

_____

_____

_____

_____

Application Follow-Up

Date you were able to identify the historical, social, racial, or cultural influences of a policy you use at your practicum: _____

In a few sentences, describe what you learned from the process of recognizing the historical, social, racial, cultural, economic, organizational, environmental, and global influences that affect a social policy that guides client services at your practicum.

_____

_____

_____

_____

Self-Evaluation

Successful	I can effectively demonstrate these competency requirements during practicum, and I can explain how these competency requirements contribute to effective social work practice.
Developing	I can identify the information I need and am able to apply it in some practicum situations, but I am also aware of some knowledge and skill gaps that I need to address.
Unsuccessful	Currently, I am not able to successfully demonstrate these competency requirements in practicum.

Competency 5

Engage in Policy Practice

Social workers understand and critique the history and current structures of social policies and services and the role of policy in service delivery through rights-based, anti-oppressive, and anti-racist lenses.

Identify Key Concepts, Search for the Meaning of Those Concepts, and Critically Examine the Requirements of the Competency

1. Select one of the federal policies that guides client services at your agency and that you have already researched to compare the social structures that facilitated its establishment with current social structures.

   a. Would the same policy be passed today?
   b. If not, how would social services be affected?

2. Use the internet to search for "rights-based social welfare policy."

   a. Is the policy in agreement with a human rights-based perspective?
   b. If not, how can the policy be improved?

3. Use the internet to search for "anti-oppressive social welfare policy."

   a. Can you identify anti-oppressive features in that policy?
   b. If not, how can the policy be improved?

4. Use the internet to search for "antiracist social welfare policy."

   a. Are antiracist aspects evident in the policy?
   b. If not, how can the policy be improved?

Reflective Writing Practice

In a few sentences, describe the most important thing you learned when a rights-based, anti-oppressive, and antiracist lens was used to evaluate federal policy.

_____

_____

_____

_____

Application Follow-Up

Date you were able to connect what you learned about a rights-based, anti-oppressive, and antiracist lens to evaluate a policy that guides client services at your agency: _____

In a few sentences, describe the most important thing you learned from the process of applying a policy that guides client services in your practicum.

_____

_____

_____

_____

Self-Evaluation

Successful	I can effectively demonstrate these competency requirements during practicum, and I can explain how these competency requirements contribute to effective social work practice.
Developing	I can identify the information I need and am able to apply it in some practicum situations, but I am also aware of some knowledge and skill gaps that I need to address.
Unsuccessful	Currently, I am not able to successfully demonstrate these competency requirements in practicum.

Competency 5

Engage in Policy Practice

Social workers influence policy formulation, analysis, implementation, and evaluation within their practice settings with individuals, families, groups, organizations, and communities.

Identify Key Concepts, Search for the Meaning of Those Concepts, and Critically Examine the Requirements of the Competency

1. Review the policies and procedures manual at your agency and identify an agency policy that you would like to analyze. If you have a social work policy textbook, review it to identify a policy analysis process and use it to analyze the policy. If you don't have a textbook, search the internet to find a policy analysis tool you can use and apply it to the policy you identified.

2. Identify a social issue that you believe should be addressed and consider possible policy actions to address it.

3. If you have a social work policy textbook, review it to examine the policy formulation process, and then formulate a policy to address the issue you identified. If you don't have a policy textbook, search the internet to find a policy formulation process.

4. Identify a policy that guides client services at your agency and answer the following questions:

   a. What issue or problem does the policy address?
   b. Is the policy effective in addressing the issue?
   c. What are the advantages and disadvantages of the policy?
   d. Are there any alternative options?
   e. What are the costs associated with the policy?
   f. What would the social costs be if the policy were not in place?
   g. Is the policy efficient?
   h. Is the policy fair?
   i. Is the policy accepted by the people affected by it?
   j. Are there any unintended negative consequences? If so, are they less detrimental than the original issue the policy addresses?
   k. How is the policy enforced?
   l. How are people affected by it?
   m. Are there any exemptions?
   n. Can the policy be improved? If so, how? What might be an unintended consequence of changing the policy?

5. Identify a policy that guides client services at your agency and use the internet to search for policy evaluation articles related to that policy. Try to find different perspectives, such as one in favor and one against it, and compare the authors' arguments.

Reflective Writing Practice

In a few sentences, describe what you learned about policy formulation, analysis, implementation, and evaluation by completing these tasks.

_____

_____

_____

_____

Application Follow-Up

Date you were able to discuss what you learned from your analysis of policies with your field instructor or in seminar: _____

In a few sentences, describe the most important thing you learned by identifying the policy formulation process, the policy analysis process, the policy implementation process, and the policy evaluation process.

_____

_____

_____

_____

Self-Evaluation

Successful	I can effectively demonstrate these competency requirements during practicum, and I can explain how these competency requirements contribute to effective social work practice.
Developing	I can identify the information I need and am able to apply it in some practicum situations, but I am also aware of some knowledge and skill gaps that I need to address.
Unsuccessful	Currently, I am not able to successfully demonstrate these competency requirements in practicum.

Competency 5

Engage in Policy Practice

Social workers actively engage in and advocate for anti-racist and anti-oppressive policy practice to effect change in those settings.

Identify Key Concepts, Search for the Meaning of Those Concepts, and Critically Examine the Requirements of the Competency

1. Conduct an internet search with the phrase "lobbyist organizations in the United States" and select an organization that advocates for social welfare issues.

   a. Look into the organization's practices and policy focus.
   b. Can you identify the role of race in its policy advocacy practices?
   c. Can you see any evidence of anti-oppressive goals?

2. Use what you learned about antiracist and anti-oppressive policy practice to evaluate a policy that guides social work services at your practicum agency.
3. Is there anything you would change in that policy to align it with an antiracist and anti-oppressive stance?

Reflective Writing Practice

In a few sentences, describe what you learned about the process to advocate for antiracist and anti-oppressive policy practice.

_____

_____

_____

_____

Application Follow-Up

Date on you were able to identify a policy that serves to promote antiracist and anti-oppressive social work practices: _____

In a few sentences, describe the most important thing you learned by investigating antiracist and anti-oppressive policy practices.

_____

_____

_____

_____

Self-Evaluation

Successful	I can effectively demonstrate these competency requirements during practicum, and I can explain how these competency requirements contribute to effective social work practice.
Developing	I can identify the information I need and am able to apply it in some practicum situations, but I am also aware of some knowledge and skill gaps that I need to address.
Unsuccessful	Currently, I am not able to successfully demonstrate these competency requirements in practicum.

Demonstrating the Ability to Engage in Policy Practice

In this section, you need to consider how you would demonstrate competency 5 with the Smith and Johnson family as well as your ability to engage in policy practice during your social work practicum. If you completed the exercises in this chapter, you have already reviewed many policies relevant to social work practice, and you can use your notes to provide examples of your ability to identify and use policies appropriately as you work with clients.

Use social justice, anti-racist, and anti-oppressive lenses to assess how social welfare policies affect the delivery of and access to social services.

Demonstrating Competency 5 With the Smith and Johnson Family	Demonstrating Competency 5 During Your Practicum
1. Identify a specific policy that facilitates the services the Smith and Johnson family can receive. 2. Explain how those policies guide client services. 3. If the Smith and Johnson family belongs to a minority population, describe how their racial identity affects their access to social work services. 4. If the Smith and Johnson family belongs to a minority population, describe how that fact might have made them vulnerable to social policies in the past. 5. If the Smith and Johnson family's ethnic group has been victimized in the past, describe how policies have changed to avoid further victimization. 6. Identify a current social policy that offers equal access to services for all clients. 7. Describe the steps you can take to acquire the knowledge and skills necessary to be an antiracist social worker.	1. Identify the specific policies that facilitate services to the clients at your practicum. 2. Describe how you would explain those policies to the clients you serve. 3. Do you serve clients who belong to a racial minority? If so, describe how their access to social work services is protected. 4. Describe how the racial identity of the clients at your practicum made them vulnerable to social policies in the past. 5. If your agency provides services to minority clients who have been victimized in the past, describe how policies have changed to avoid further victimization. 6. Describe how you would you analyze the policies that guide client services to ensure they are not oppressive to your clients. 7. What steps can you take to demonstrate your commitment to acquiring the knowledge and skills necessary to be an antiracist social worker?

Apply critical thinking to analyze, formulate, and advocate for policies that advance human rights and social, racial, economic, and environmental justice.

Demonstrating Competency 5 With the Smith and Johnson Family	Demonstrating Competency 5 During Your Practicum
1. Have you identified a critical thinking tool you can use to analyze the policies that guide your work with the Smith and Johnson family? 2. Describe the results of your analysis of a specific policy that affects your work with the Smith and Johnson family. 3. Explain how the policies that guide social work practice advance the human rights of the Smith and Johnson family. 4. Explain how the policies that guide social work practice promote social and racial justice for the Smith and Johnson family. 5. Explain how the policies that guide social work practice advance environmental justice. 6. Explain how the agency's policies contribute to economic justice for the Smith and Johnson family. 7. Describe the knowledge and skills necessary to engage in the policy advocacy process.	1. Identify a policy analysis tool you can use to analyze a policy that guides your work with clients at your practicum. 2. Use the policy analysis tool to critically analyze a specific federal policy that guides social work practice in your practicum. 3. Explain the results of your analysis. 4. Explain how the policies that guide social work practice advance the human rights of the clients at your practicum. 5. Explain how the agency's policies contribute to economic justice for the clients at your practicum. 6. Explain how the policies that guide social work practice promote social and racial justice for the clients at your practicum. 7. Explain how the policies that guide social work practice advance environmental justice.

Competency Development Topics for the Social Work Practicum Seminar

▶ **Competency 5 Field Seminar Topics**

- The use of critical thinking tools in policy practice
- The policy analysis process
- The policy advocacy process
- The way public policy advances or hinders human rights and social, racial, economic, and environmental justice
- The relationship between federal, state and agency policies
- Social justice and social policy
- The process to advocate for antiracist and anti-oppressive policies

▼ **Prior Planning**

- Complete the reading and writing exercises provided in this chapter.
- Review your notes and identify your competency development needs and learning gains.
- Prepare questions to address your competency development needs.
- Identify examples showing you were able to successfully demonstrate the requirements of competency

◀ **During Seminar and Supervision**

- Listen and seek to understand.
- Contribute.
- Find the joy in your own professional development and growth.
- Make the commitment to learn.

Competency Development Topics for the Educational Supervision Meeting

▶ **Competency 5 Social Work Practicum Instructional Supervision Meeting Topics**

- The policies and procedures manual
- The policy learning needs you identified prior to your supervision meeting
- The social justice, antiracist, and anti-oppressive policy practices relevant to your social work practicum
- The process to advocate for antiracist, and anti-oppressive policies in the real world

▼ **Prior Planning**

- Review the policies and procedures manual.
- Review the Self-Evaluation section for each competency description sentence and identify the items you marked as unsuccessful.
- Identify your learning needs and formulate questions to guide the supervision meeting to address them.
- Be ready to share with your social work field instructor your competency 5 learning gains. This will make the final social work practicum evaluation easier and faster since your social work field instructor will already be aware of your learning progress.

◄ **During Instructional Supervision Meeting**

- Ask the questions you prepared to address your competency development needs.
- Listen and seek to understand.
- Emotionally prepare to graciously receive constructive feedback. Remember you are in practicum to learn, so you are expected to need guidance.

Summary

Social work practice exists within a social environment, and it is guided by social policy. You might make policy practice the center of your social work career, but most social workers will engage in policy practice only as part of their main purpose, which is to provide direct client services. However, there are three occasions when it will be important to focus your attention on expanding your policy practice knowledge and skills.

First, every time you start a new social work position, you will need to go through the process of identifying the policies relevant to your job and be able to analyze their utility and alignment with social work professional ethics. Second, every time you notice a detrimental impact of a policy on clients or client services, you will need to apply your policy advocacy skills to address the problem.

Third, every time new policies are implemented, they can affect your work with clients. The COVID-19 pandemic required many adjustments to the normal operation of social work services, for example, and some policies facilitated the continuation of services while others fundamentally changed the way services are provided. It will take time to sort the positive from the negative outcomes, and it will be necessary to advocate for additional policy changes to ensure that the most vulnerable clients are able to receive the best possible social work services we can provide.

In this chapter, you had the opportunity to familiarize yourself with policies relevant to your social work practicum and to develop a better understanding of the way policy influences clients and social work practice. As you can see in Figure 5.3, social workers should be knowledgeable about the policies that affect your social work service delivery and access to services, and we also need to recognize the historical, racial, and cultural influences that affect social policy. Since we serve diverse client populations, we need to use a rights-based, anti-oppressive, and antiracist lens to critique the history and current structures of social policies. Additionally, to ensure that the policies that guide social work practice are antiracist and anti-oppressive, we must be committed to influence policy formulation, analysis, implementation, and evaluation.

Competency 5 Engage in Policy Practice		
Identify the social policies that affects service delivery, and access to social services		Recognize the historical, social, racial, and cultural influences that affect social policy
Use a rights-based, anti-oppressive, and anti-racist lens to critique the history and current structures of social policies	Influence policy formulation, analysis, implementation, and evaluation	Advocate for anti-racist and anti-oppressive policy practice

FIGURE 5.3   Main requirements of competency 5.

Recommended Materials

Books	Description
Ovington, M. W. (1996). *Black and White Sat Down Together: The Reminiscences of an NAACP Founder.* Feminist Press at the City University of New York.	This is a narrative account of the establishment of the NAACP. Their work strives to end racial discrimination and achieve full civil and legal rights for African Americans
Coates, T. (2015). *Between the World and Me.* Spiegel & Grau.	Written as a letter to his son, he clearly depicts what it is like to be Black in America.
Chavez, C. (2008). *An Organizer's Tale: Speeches.* Penguin.	Cesar Chavez organized farm laborers to demand policy changes to achieve fair wages, benefits, and humane working conditions for farm workers.
Strum, P. (2010). Mendez v. Westminster: *School Desegregation and Mexican American Rights.* University Press of Kansas.	*Mendez v. Westminster School District* was the first case in which school segregation was successfully challenged in federal court.
Green, J. R. (2016). *The Devil Is Here in These Hills: West Virginia's Coal Miners and Their Battle for Freedom.* Atlantic Monthly Press.	This book explores labor rights policies and the struggle to organize coal miners in West Virginia.
Prucha, F. P. (1997). *American Indian Treaties: The History of a Political Anomaly.* University of California Press.	The author argues that American Indian treaties are a political anomaly and continue to be problematic.
Hill N., & Ratteree K. (2017). *The Great Vanishing Act: Blood Quantum and the Future of Native Nations.* Fulcrum.	Tribes use blood quantum to manage tribal enrollment and social services. This rule was imposed on them by the U.S. government in part to minimize the growth of tribes, and many Native Americans are excluded from tribal enrollment.
Jackson, M. G. (2014). *Light, Bright and Damn Near White: Black Leaders Created by the One-Drop Rule.* Jackson Scribe.	In the United States, a person is considered Black if they have any African ancestry. This book explores the policy implications of the one-drop of blood rule.
Neuwirth, J. (2015). *Equal Means Equal: Why the Time for an Equal Rights Amendment Is Now.* The New Press.	This book covers topics ranging from pay equity and pregnancy discrimination to violence against women and the need for an Equal Rights Amendment to the U.S. Constitution.

Wilkerson, I. (2023). *Caste: The Origins of Our Discontents*. Random House.	This book provides examples of the dehumanization and brutality that oppressed and marginalized communities have endured around the world and how social policy has been used to keep people marginalized
PBS. (2011). *American Experience: A Class Apart* [Documentary]. https://www.pbs.org/video/american-experience-a-class-apart-preview/	This is the story of the Mexican American lawyers who took the *Hernandez v. Texas* case to the Supreme Court, challenging Jim Crow–style discrimination against Mexican American citizens.

Reference

Council on Social Work Education. (2022, May 23). *2022 EPAS*. https://www.cswe.org/accreditation/info/2022-epas/

CREDIT

CHAPTER 6

Competency 6

Engage with Individuals, Families, Groups, Organizations, and Communities

In this chapter you will examine the sixth of the nine social work competencies provided by the CSWE. Competency 6 outlines the essential engagement skills required to become an effective social worker. Forming effective professional relationships with clients, colleagues, other professionals, and the community is an essential component of social work practice. Without such relationships, effective assessments and interventions are unlikely to occur since the helping process depends on a foundation of trust between the social worker and the client. A client who is hesitant to trust a social worker is unlikely to share the sensitive personal information needed to complete an accurate assessment, and without an accurate assessment, an accurate intervention is not possible.

Human relationships are complex, and within our own family and social group we have developed patterns of interaction that work well enough, so we rarely stop to examine the way we interact with others. However, becoming a professional social worker will require you to be intentional in your interactions, because developing an effective social worker–client relationship takes effort and skill.

A modern-day barrier to effective face-to-face communication is the excessive use of social media. When people are constantly checking electronic devices for updates and posting only the best version of every aspect of their life, no one really knows the person behind the carefully chosen messages. Curated accounts of the "perfect" life are shared, but the need to connect with another human being is seldom fulfilled in that environment. Electronic communication is a great tool when used appropriately, but it cannot capture the shared human experience of being present for another human when human connection is what we need. If you want to become an effective social worker, you need to examine your ability to just sit and listen to others. Can you put all your electronics away and have a 1-hour conversation with a relative or friend? If you can do that, you already have some of the skills necessary to establish the human connection required in social work practice. If not, start practicing today.

Your interest in becoming a social work professional is likely rooted in a desire to help people, but helping a person in distress will require genuine compassion and the ability to be fully present during difficult situations, including times when clients express negative feelings and reactions such as anger and frustration. You might also have to deal with your own feelings of frustration and anger because real-life problems don't have easy solutions, and sometimes you will see solutions that clients are not ready to accept because every person has their own priorities and the free will to approach life in their own unique way. In other words, you will need the ability to establish a working relationship with clients that allows you to explore options with them instead of attempting to impose solutions that might not be in line with their abilities or timeline.

To develop the communication skills required to establish effective human relationships as a social work professional, you will need to consider the role of culture. Your cultural communication norms might be very different from those of your client population or even your work environment.

It takes humility to accept that if our goal is to effectively engage with others, imposing our own cultural norms is not the most effective strategy. And since social work requires collaboration with other professionals who have a different focus and training, having an open mind to explore different points of view on social issues will also be required. As you can see, competency 6 will require you to examine your own capacity to establish effective human relationships with clients, colleagues, and other professionals, and self-exploration and willingness to learn and grow are fundamental components of this competency.

Competency 6 Description as Provided by CSWE: Engage with Individuals, Families, Groups, Organizations, and Communities

As you read this description of professional engagement in social work practice, consider the knowledge and skills you need to develop during your social work practicum.

Competency 6

Engage with Individuals, Families, Groups, Organizations, and Communities

Social workers understand that engagement is an ongoing component of the dynamic and interactive process of social work practice with and on behalf of individuals, families, groups, organizations, and communities.

Social workers value the importance of human relationships. Social workers understand theories of human behavior and person-in-environment and critically evaluate and apply this knowledge to facilitate engagement with clients and constituencies, including individuals, families, groups, organizations, and communities. Social workers are self-reflective and understand how bias, power, and privilege as well as their personal values and personal experiences may affect their ability to engage effectively with diverse clients and constituencies. Social workers use the principles of interprofessional collaboration to facilitate engagement with clients, constituencies, and other professionals as appropriate.

Social workers:

a. Apply knowledge of human behavior and person-in-environment, as well as interprofessional conceptual frameworks to engage with clients and constituencies; and

b. Use empathy, reflection, and interpersonal skills to engage in culturally responsive practice with clients and constituencies

As you can see in Figure 6.1, engagement skills are necessary in every aspect of social work practice. Your ability to appropriately establish effective professional relationships with individuals, families, groups, organizations, and communities will require not only effective communication skills, but also integrity, reliability, and competence in all aspects of social work practice.

Competency 1:

Engage with with Individuals, Families, Groups, Organizations, and Communities in a way that demonstrates ethical and professional behavior.

Competency 9:

Engage with clients in ways that facilitate the evaluation of social work practice

Competency 2:

Engage with clients in ways that advance the human rights and social, racial, economic, and environmental justice of our clients

Competency 8:

Engage with clients in a way that facilitates the intervention process

Competency 6
Engage with Individuals, Families, Groups, Organizations, and Communities

Competency 3:

Engage with clients in ways that demonstrate anti-racism, diversity, equity and inclusion in our social work practice

Competency 7:

Engage with clients in a way that facilitates the client assessment process

Competency 4:

Engage with clients in a way that demonstrates our ability to use practice-informed research and research-informed practice

Competency 6:

What are the knowledge, values and skills necessary to effectively engage with individuals, families, groups, organizations, and communities?

Competency 5:

Engage with clients in a way that demonstrates our appropriate use of policy

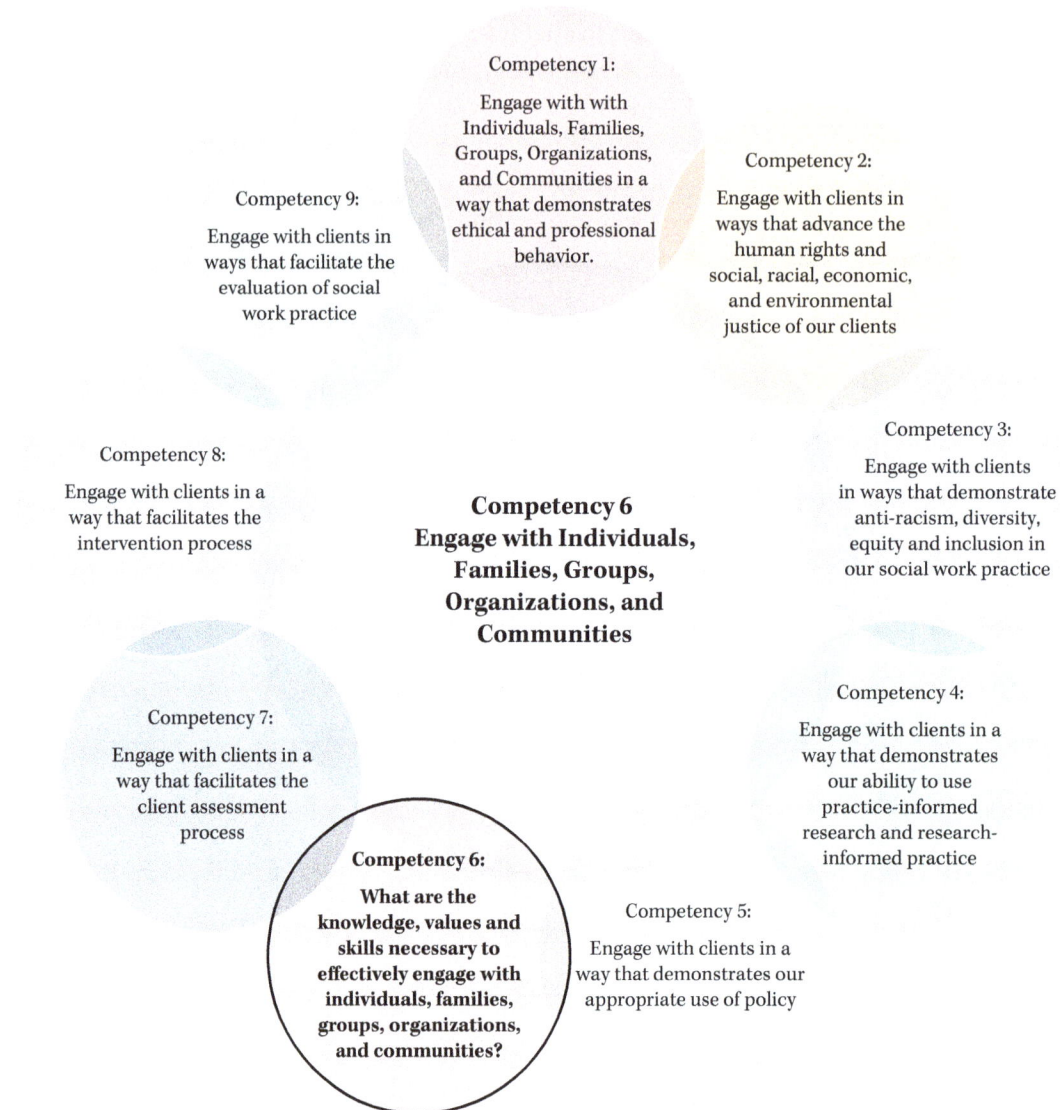

FIGURE 6.1   The relationship of competency 6 to the rest of the competencies.

Applying Competency 6

The knowledge, values, and skills necessary to demonstrate competency 6 become visible when you interact with clients in the real world. As you consider how you might interact with the Smith and Johnson family, think about your relationships with clients during your social work practicum. How do you earn your client's trust? How do you demonstrate empathy? How do you know whether your communication skills are effective in the work environment? How do you know that your clients feel respected and understood? What steps can you take to ensure that your relationship with clients is appropriate?

Reflective Questions on Competency Application

Since competency 6 is about engaging with the family, let's imagine you are in the room when Mrs. Smith meets with the social worker about Daniel's suspension.

Mrs. Smith sits quietly as the social worker attempts to address Daniel's violent behavior, and you notice a tear running down Mrs. Smith's face. The social worker hands her a tissue and asks if she would like some water. Mrs. Smith continues to cry silently, so the social worker gives her a few minutes to compose herself. When Mrs. Smith is able to talk, the social worker reassures her that the situation with Daniel can be addressed, and the important thing is to help him understand that violence is unacceptable.

Mrs. Smith says, "I am failing these kids. I want to take good care of them, but I just don't feel well, and I am worried about my son. I already lost my daughter, and I don't want to lose him."

The social worker asks, "What is going on with your son?"

Mrs. Smith replies, "He tested positive for COVID-19, and I can see in television reports that a lot of people are dying. He is such a good son, but he lives so far away from us; we only see him about once a month. God cannot take him away from us."

The social worker says, "I can see that you are very worried, and at this point you have reason to be. We don't know much about that virus yet, but surely, we can find a way to get it under control. What do you think we need to do to help Daniel?"

Mrs. Smith answers, "For one thing, you can protect him from those thugs instead of punishing him when he defends himself. Those kids are nasty, and they've been tormenting him for a long time. I don't blame Daniel for hitting back."

The social worker says, "There are no reports of bullying incidents against Daniel."

Mrs. Smith answers, "Well, now that you know, what are you going to do about it?

The social worker says, "We need to investigate, but in the meantime, we need to make sure that Daniel does not engage in violent behavior. Is there anything we can do to help you? You stated that you feel like you are failing the kids, but what makes you think that? As far as we can see from their school records, you've been taking good care of them for a few years."

Mrs. Smith answers, "My husband lost his sight because of diabetes, and he needs a lot of help just getting through the day. I'm afraid I might not be able to take care of my grandkids much longer because I'm always tired and in pain."

The social worker says, "It sounds like you would benefit from some community support. Would you like me to see whether I can find some resources for you?"

Mrs. Smith answers, "I don't know. We always take care of ourselves, and I don't like anyone feeling sorry for us. But if I can get help, maybe I can take better care of Alyssa and Daniel."

After investigating the claim that Daniel has been the victim of bullying, you find that in fact he has been victimized for at least a year by several peers. They insult, belittle, and demean him because they know his father is in prison, and they make fun of his attire and skin color. They do most of this bullying on the school bus or in the playground when adults are not present. Daniel keeps to himself and tries to ignore them, but he retaliated after the bullies escalated their tactics by pushing him and taking his homework to tear it up.

When Daniel was brough into the social worker's office, he sat quietly and didn't want to respond to any questions. He said only, "If you can't get them to leave me alone, I can't promise I won't hit back. Would you let someone hit you for no reason?"

Can you identify the engagement skills the social worker demonstrated in the vignette?

(Continued)

Carefully read the following questions and reflect on some of the engagement skills necessary to effectively engage with the Smith and Johnson family:

How would you demonstrate that you value the importance of human relationships as you interact with each member of the Smith and Johnson family?

If your clients are Alyssa and Daniel, what do you need to do to earn their trust? Are you able to communicate positive regard toward every member of this family?

What theories of human behavior and person in environment could you use to inform the engagement process with this family?

How would your awareness and understanding of your personal bias and privilege affect the client engagement process?

How would this family benefit from your ability to engage in interprofessional collaboration?

What steps can you take to learn about the racial and cultural identity of this family to effectively engage with them?

What steps can you take to demonstrate culturally responsive social work practice by using self-reflection, integrity, reliability, and empathy as you engage with clients during your practicum?

Investigating Each Sentence of the Competency Description

In this section, you will look at each sentence of the competency description to identify key concepts, explore the meaning of those concepts, and critically examine the requirements of competency 6. You have probably taken or are taking human behavior and social environment courses as well as generalist social work practice courses. Go through the indices of your textbooks from those courses to review social work practice principles such as acceptance, positive regard, self-awareness, cultural sensitivity, self-determination, accountability, empowerment, autonomy, collaboration, and the strengths perspective, as well as forming partnerships and creating alliances. Consider the steps you need to take to integrate those concepts into your social work practicum.

If you are outgoing and can easily engage in informal conversations, this competency will be somewhat easier for you, but there are also benefits for those who are reserved and take a slow approach to relationship building. You do not have to change who you are to effectively engage with clients; you just need to know how your own temperament and relationship style will influence the pace and rhythm of your professional relationships.

We all benefit from learning more about effective communication skills and putting them into practice in our everyday life. Consider the effect clarifying misunderstandings has on your personal relationships. If you love someone, you don't want to hurt them, yet we often offend people we love without realizing that what we do or say has had a negative impact on them. If you can apologize and make amends, your relationships with others can continue to grow, but if you don't have the ability to recognize the impact of your behavior on others, eventually people will start distancing themselves from you.

A similar process occurs in professional relationships. If you come across as uninterested, rude, aloof, critical, unprofessional, judgmental, or unsympathetic, clients and colleagues will not want to work with you. Therefore, a big step in developing competency 6 is to become aware of your ability to form and maintain positive relationships and take the steps necessary to increase your communication skills, especially listening and being present for others.

Figure 6.2 illustrates the engagement process necessary in generalist social work practice to highlight the fact that engagement skills need to be tailored to the social work practice level. Although the focus of client engagement in this book is at the individual and family levels, keep in mind that social work with groups, organizations, and communities will require the development of additional engagement skills and abilities.

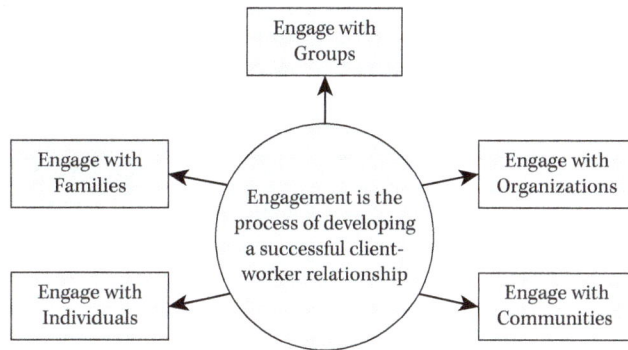

FIGURE 6.2   The client engagement process at different levels of practice.

Competency 6

Engage with Individuals, Families, Groups, Organizations, and Communities

Social workers understand that engagement is an ongoing component of the dynamic and interactive process of social work practice with and on behalf of individuals, families, groups, organizations, and communities.

Identify Key Concepts, Search for the Meaning of Those Concepts, and Critically Examine the Requirements of the Competency

1. Use the phrase "social work engagement process" to search the internet, and carefully read and analyze at least two scholarly articles about this topic.

   a. What did you learn about the social work engagement process from the articles?

2. Use the phrase "dynamic and interactive social work client engagement process" to search the internet, and carefully read and analyze at least two scholarly articles about this topic or explore your social work practice textbooks for a description of the dynamic and interactive social work client engagement process.

   a. What did you learn about the dynamic and interactive social work client engagement process from the articles?

3. Use the phrase "engagement with and on behalf of clients in social work practice" to search the internet, and carefully read and analyze at least two scholarly articles about this topic.

   a. What did you learn about engagement with and on behalf of clients in social work practice from the articles?

4. Use the phrases "family engagement in social work practice" "group engagement in social work practice," "community engagement in social work practice," and "engagement in social work practice with organizations" to search the internet, and select at least two articles that are relevant to your social work practicum. Carefully read and analyze those articles.

   a. What did you learn about the social work engagement process with families, groups, organizations, and communities from the articles?

Reflective Writing Practice

In a few sentences, outline a plan to engage with clients in a way that demonstrates your understanding of the dynamic and interactive process of social work practice with and on behalf of clients.

_____

_____

_____

_____

Application Follow-Up

Date you were able to demonstrate your understanding of the dynamic and interactive process of social work practice with and on behalf of clients: _____

In a few sentences, describe what you learned from the process of applying conceptual knowledge to engage with clients during practicum.

_____

_____

_____

_____

Self-Evaluation

Successful	I can effectively demonstrate these competency requirements during practicum, and I can explain how these competency requirements contribute to effective social work practice.
Developing	I can identify the information I need and am able to apply it in some practicum situations, but I am also aware of some knowledge and skill gaps that I need to address.
Unsuccessful	Currently, I am not able to successfully demonstrate these competency requirements in practicum.

> **Competency 6**
>
> ## Engage with Individuals, Families, Groups, Organizations, and Communities
>
> Social workers value the importance of human relationships.

Identify Key Concepts, Search for the Meaning of Those Concepts, and Critically Examine the Requirements of the Competency

1. Use the phrase "social workers value the importance of human relationships" to search the internet, and carefully read and analyze at least three scholarly articles about this topic.

   a. What did you learn about the way social workers demonstrate that they value the importance of human relationships?

Reflective Writing Practice

In a few sentences, outline a plan to demonstrate that you value the importance of human relationships during your social work practicum.

_____

_____

_____

_____

Application Follow-Up

Date you were able to demonstrate that you value the importance of human relationships during your social work practicum: _____

In a few sentences, describe what you learned from the process of applying the concept of valuing the importance of human relationships to engage with clients during practicum.

_____

_____

_____

_____

Self-Evaluation

Successful	I can effectively demonstrate these competency requirements during practicum, and I can explain how these competency requirements contribute to effective social work practice.
Developing	I can identify the information I need and am able to apply it in some practicum situations, but I am also aware of some knowledge and skill gaps that I need to address.
Unsuccessful	Currently, I am not able to successfully demonstrate these competency requirements in practicum.

Competency 6

Engage with Individuals, Families, Groups, Organizations, and Communities

Social workers understand theories of human behavior and person-in-environment and critically evaluate and apply this knowledge to facilitate engagement with clients and constituencies, including individuals, families, groups, organizations, and communities.

Identify Key Concepts, Search for the Meaning of Those Concepts, and Critically Examine the Requirements of the Competency

1. Use the phrase "theories of human behavior and person in environment and engagement skills" to search the internet, and carefully read and analyze at least two scholarly articles about this topic.

    a. What did you learn about the use of theories of human behavior and person in environment and the engagement process from the articles?

2. Use the phrase "social workers critically evaluate and apply knowledge" to search the internet, and carefully read and analyze at least two scholarly articles about this topic.

    a. What did you learn about the dynamic and interactive social work client engagement process from the articles?

3. Use the phrase "social work engagement with clients and constituencies" to search the internet, and carefully read and analyze at least two scholarly articles about this topic.

    a. What did you learn about engagement with and on behalf of clients in social work practice from the articles?

Reflective Writing Practice

In a few sentences, outline a plan to critically evaluate the human behavior theories you can use to facilitate the engagement process with clients during your practicum.

_____

_____

_____

_____

Application Follow-Up

Date you were able to demonstrate your ability to effectively use human behavior theories to facilitate the engagement process with clients: _____

In a few sentences, describe what you learned by using human behavior theories to facilitate the engagement process with clients during your practicum.

_____

_____

_____

_____

Self-Evaluation

Successful	I can effectively demonstrate these competency requirements during practicum, and I can explain how these competency requirements contribute to effective social work practice.
Developing	I can identify the information I need and am able to apply it in some practicum situations, but I am also aware of some knowledge and skill gaps that I need to address.
Unsuccessful	Currently, I am not able to successfully demonstrate these competency requirements in practicum.

Competency 6

Engage with Individuals, Families, Groups, Organizations, and Communities

Social workers are self-reflective and understand how bias, power, and privilege as well as their personal values and personal experiences may affect their ability to engage effectively with diverse clients and constituencies.

Identify Key Concepts, Search for the Meaning of Those Concepts, and Critically Examine the Requirements of the Competency

1. Use the phrase "becoming a self-reflective social worker" to search the internet, and carefully read and analyze at least two scholarly articles about this topic.

    a. What did you learn about becoming a self-reflective social worker from the articles?

2. Use the phrase "social work and bias, power, and privilege" to search the internet, and carefully read and analyze at least two scholarly articles about this topic.

    a. What did you learn about the dynamic and interactive social work client engagement process from the articles?

3. Use the phrase "personal values and social work practice" to search the internet, and carefully read and analyze at least two scholarly articles about this topic.

    a. What did you learn about personal values and social work practice from the articles?

4. Use the phrase "personal experiences and social work practice" to search the internet, and carefully read and analyze at least two scholarly articles about this topic.

    a. What did you learn about personal experiences and social work practice from the articles?

5. Use the phrase "engagement in social work practice with diverse clients and constituencies" to search the internet, and carefully read and analyze at least two scholarly articles about this topic.

    a. What did you learn about engagement in social work practice with diverse clients and constituencies from the articles?

Reflective Writing Practice

In a few sentences, outline a plan to demonstrate your ability to be self-reflective and understand how bias, power, and privilege as well as your personal values and personal experiences may affect your ability to engage effectively with diverse clients and constituencies.

_____

_____

_____

_____

Application Follow-Up

Date you were able to demonstrate your ability to be self-reflective and use your understanding of how bias, power, and privilege as well as personal values and experiences impact the client engagement process during practicum: _____

In a few sentences, describe what you learned from the process of using self-reflection and awareness of personal bias, power, and privilege to engage a client demonstrating positive regard.

_____

_____

_____

_____

Self-Evaluation

Successful	I can effectively demonstrate these competency requirements during practicum, and I can explain how these competency requirements contribute to effective social work practice.
Developing	I can identify the information I need and am able to apply it in some practicum situations, but I am also aware of some knowledge and skill gaps that I need to address.
Unsuccessful	Currently, I am not able to successfully demonstrate these competency requirements in practicum.

Competency 6

Engage with Individuals, Families, Groups, Organizations, and Communities

Social workers use the principles of interprofessional collaboration to facilitate engagement with clients, constituencies, and other professionals as appropriate.

Identify Key Concepts, Search for the Meaning of Those Concepts, and Critically Examine the Requirements of the Competency

1. Use the phrase "principles of interprofessional collaboration in social work" to search the internet, and carefully read and analyze at least two scholarly articles about this topic.

   a. What did you learn about the principles of interprofessional collaboration in social work practice from the articles?

2. Use the phrase "framework for understanding interprofessional collaboration" to search the internet, and carefully read and analyze at least two scholarly articles about this topic.

   a. What did you learn about the framework for understanding interprofessional collaboration from the articles?

3. Use the phrase "social work engagement with clients, constituencies, and other professionals" to search the internet, and carefully read and analyze at least two scholarly articles

about this topic or explore your social work practice textbooks for a description of the dynamic and interactive social work client engagement process.

a. What did you learn about social work engagement with clients, constituencies, and other professionals from the articles?

Reflective Writing Practice

In a few sentences, outline a plan to use the principles of interprofessional collaboration to facilitate engagement with clients, constituencies, and other professionals as appropriate during your social work practicum.

_____

_____

_____

_____

Application Follow-Up

Date you were able to demonstrate your ability to use the principles of interprofessional collaboration to facilitate engagement with clients, constituencies, and other professionals as appropriate during your practicum experience: _____

In a few sentences, describe what you learned from the process of exploring the principles of interprofessional collaboration to facilitate engagement with clients and using that knowledge to effectively engage with clients or other professionals during your social work practicum.

_____

_____

_____

_____

Self-Evaluation

Successful	I can effectively demonstrate these competency requirements during practicum, and I can explain how these competency requirements contribute to effective social work practice.
Developing	I can identify the information I need and am able to apply it in some practicum situations, but I am also aware of some knowledge and skill gaps that I need to address.
Unsuccessful	Currently, I am not able to successfully demonstrate these competency requirements in practicum.

Demonstrating the Ability to Engage with Individuals, Families, Groups, Organizations, and Communities

Having the knowledge, values, and skills necessary to effectively engaging with clients is an essential component of social work practice. Without this ability, social work interventions are unlikely to be appropriate or effective.

Apply knowledge of human behavior and person-in-environment, as well as interprofessional conceptual frameworks to engage with clients and constituencies.

Demonstrating Competency 6 With the Smith and Johnson Family	Demonstrating Competency 6 During Your Practicum
1. What human behavior and person-in-environment theories are relevant to the Smith and Johnson family?	1. What human behavior and person-in-environment theories are relevant to the client population served at your practicum?
2. If your clients are Alyssa and Daniel, how would having a good understanding of the five main educational learning theories help you relate to their teachers as you work in a school setting?	2. Describe at least one human development theory that is relevant to your client population and explain how you can use it to engage with clients at your practicum.
3. How would you use behaviorist, cognitive, constructivist, or humanist learning theories as you interact with Alyssa and Daniel?	3. How would you use behaviorist, cognitive, constructivist, or humanist learning theories as you interact with clients at your practicum?
4. How would you use your understanding of human development theories as you interact with each member of the Smith and Johnson family?	4. How would you use your understanding of human development theories as you interact with clients who are at different levels of intellectual development?
5. How relevant or useful are psychosocial theories of aging as you engage with the adults in this case?	5. How relevant or useful are psychosocial theories as you engage with diverse clients?
6. If your practicum is at a health clinic and your client is Mrs. Smith, how would you use health behavior theory as you engage with her?	6. If your practicum is at a health clinic, do you have a good understanding of health behavior theory?
7. Identify a framework for understanding interprofessional teamwork that you can use as you work with this family.	7. Identify a framework for understanding interprofessional teamwork that you can use as you interact with peers, colleagues, and other professionals during your practicum.

Use empathy, reflection, and interpersonal skills to engage in culturally responsive practice with clients and constituencies.

Demonstrating Competency 6 With the Smith and Johnson Family	Demonstrating Competency 6 During Your Practicum
1. How would you demonstrate empathy as you interact with the Smith and Johnson family?	1. How do you demonstrate empathy as you interact with clients during your practicum?
2. How would you demonstrate self-reflection as you interact with the Smith and Johnson family?	2. How do you demonstrate self-reflection as you interact with clients during your practicum?
3. How would you monitor your verbal and nonverbal communication as you interact with the Smith and Johnson family?	3. How do you monitor your verbal and nonverbal communication as you interact with clients?
4. How would you clarify both the verbal and nonverbal messages sent by Mrs. Smith?	4. What steps do you take to clarify both the verbal and nonverbal messages sent by your clients?
5. How would you demonstrate culturally appropriate practice as you interact with the Smith and Johnson family?	5. How would you demonstrate culturally appropriate practice as you interact with clients during your practicum?

Competency Development Topics for the Social Work Practicum Seminar

► Competency 6 Field Seminar Topics

- Theories of human behavior and person in environment and how they facilitate engagement with clients
- Self-reflection strategies and the influence of personal values and bias, power, and privilege on the client engagement process
- Effective engagement with diverse clients
- Principles of interprofessional collaboration

▼ Prior Planning

- Review your notes in this chapter and identify the key concepts related to each of the seminar discussion topics.
- Identify the parts of the competency that you have not been able to successfully demonstrate and formulate specific discussion questions that will help you explore your engagement skills during seminar.
- Consider the client population in your practicum setting. Are you mostly interacting with children? How would practicum interactions be different if you were interacting with another population?

◄ During Seminar

- Listen attentively to your peers because they will probably be interacting with different client populations during their practicum.
- Be ready to contribute by sharing your struggles as well as your success in establishing effective relationships with clients and colleagues during your practicum.
- Reflect on your professional growth. Think about the ways you have changed since starting your practicum. Are you more aware of your communication style? Have you increased your ability to pay attention during conversations?

Competency Development Topics for the Educational Supervision Meeting

▶ **Competency 6 Social Work Practicum Instructional Supervision Meeting Topics**

- The theories of human behavior and person in environment used in the practicum setting to facilitate engagement with clients
- Self-reflective strategies appropriate for your practicum setting
- The role of personal values and personal experience in the practicum setting
- Strategies to effectively engage with diverse clients during practicum
- The role of interprofessional collaboration in the practicum setting

▼ **Prior Planning**

- Review your interactions with clients, peers, and supervisors. Are there relationships you would like to improve?
- Review your notes in this chapter and identify the parts of the competency that you have not been able to successfully demonstrate.
- Formulate specific questions that will help you explore your engagement skills with your social work instructor during supervision.

◀ **During the Instructional Supervision Meeting**

- Be prepared to ask questions that will help you develop and practice competency 6.
- Ask the questions you prepared.
- Share your struggles as well as your successes in establishing effective relationships with clients and colleagues during your practicum. This will help your social work instructor understand your competency development needs.
- Discussing work-related human interactions with supervisors can be difficult, so mentally prepare for the fact that the only way to become better is to listen to feedback with an open mind and an open heart. If your social work instructor must give you negative feedback, consider the fact that it is not easy for anyone to do this, and if your social work instructor takes that risk, it is with the intention of helping you.

Summary

Competency 6 is about being able form professional relationships, and as you can see in Figure 6.3, although some skills remain relevant across the different levels of social work practice, there is a difference between relating to clients one-on-one and relating to larger groups of people. Most social workers will spend most of their career providing direct social work services to individuals, families, and groups, but some social workers contribute to the profession by consulting with organizations or organizing communities to create social change or change social policy.

The ability to effectively interact with others requires recognizing the way your own emotions affect your interactions. As a social worker, you will be expected to remain calm when clients are angry or sad, but you are entitled to have feelings and to take a minute when a situation is upsetting to you. With experience, you will learn to keep your feelings in check while you work with people who are dealing with difficult emotions. However, it is important that you find balance and take steps to take care of your emotional needs outside your work environment. Meditation, prayer, or a gratitude journal can be a good strategy to calm yourself after a stressful day at work. You can also schedule physical activity to work off stress or visit with a good friend or supportive family member. Remember that your work is only one part of your life and that you deserve a balanced life.

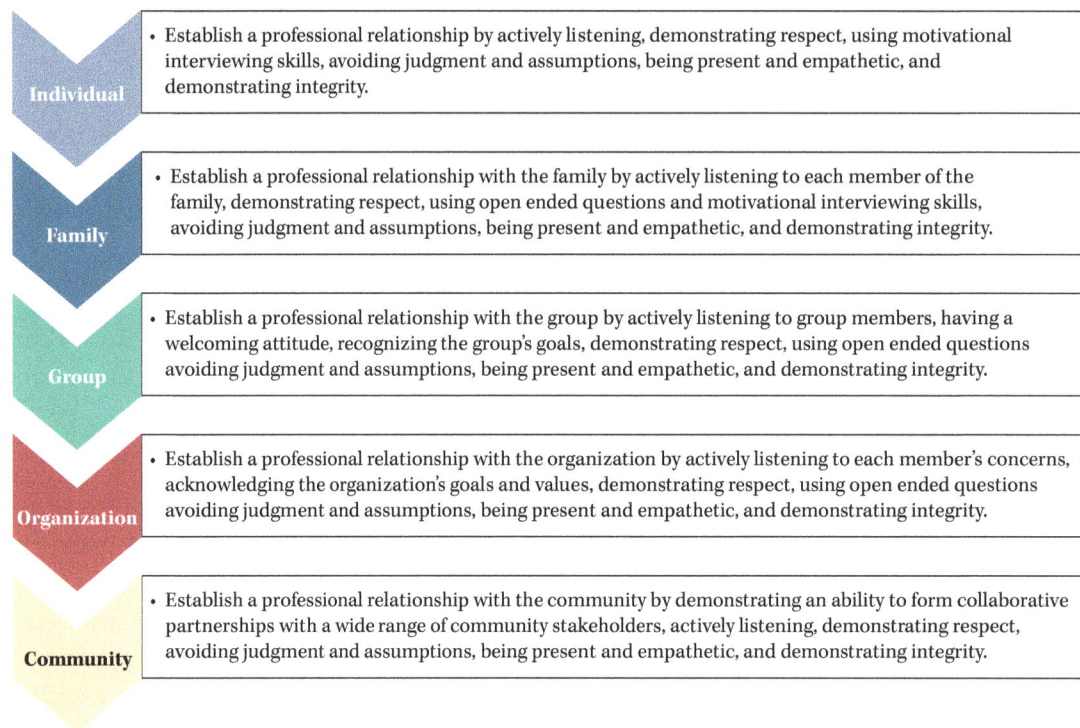

Individual
- Establish a professional relationship by actively listening, demonstrating respect, using motivational interviewing skills, avoiding judgment and assumptions, being present and empathetic, and demonstrating integrity.

Family
- Establish a professional relationship with the family by actively listening to each member of the family, demonstrating respect, using open ended questions and motivational interviewing skills, avoiding judgment and assumptions, being present and empathetic, and demonstrating integrity.

Group
- Establish a professional relationship with the group by actively listening to group members, having a welcoming attitude, recognizing the group's goals, demonstrating respect, using open ended questions avoiding judgment and assumptions, being present and empathetic, and demonstrating integrity.

Organization
- Establish a professional relationship with the organization by actively listening to each member's concerns, acknowledging the organization's goals and values, demonstrating respect, using open ended questions avoiding judgment and assumptions, being present and empathetic, and demonstrating integrity.

Community
- Establish a professional relationship with the community by demonstrating an ability to form collaborative partnerships with a wide range of community stakeholders, actively listening, demonstrating respect, avoiding judgment and assumptions, being present and empathetic, and demonstrating integrity.

FIGURE 6.3 Social work engagement skills at different levels of social work practice.

Recommended Reading Materials

Books	Descriptions
Mark, G. A. (2023). *Attention Span: A Groundbreaking Way to Restore Balance, Happiness and Productivity*. Hanover Square Press.	The author proposes that understanding how to pay attention will help us be more successful in our careers and increase our health and wellness.
Leonardo, N. (2020). *Active Listening Techniques: 30 Practical Tools to Hone Your Communication Skills*. Rockridge Press.	The author proposes that listening actively leads to people feeling respected, understood, and heard and provides 30 practical communication tools to acquire the skills you need to cultivate healthier relationships and greater career success.

Heen, S., & Stone, D. (2015). *Thanks for the Feedback: The Science and Art of Receiving Feedback Well*. United States: Penguin.	The authors explain why receiving feedback is difficult, and they blend neuroscience and psychology with practical advice.
Butler, C. C., Rollnick, S., & Miller, W. R. (2022). *Motivational Interviewing in Health Care: Helping Patients Change Behavior*. Guilford.	The authors propose that motivational interviewing is a process of building trust to help clients make healthier choices.
Eurich, T. (2017). *Insight: Why We're Not as Self-Aware as We Think, and How Seeing Ourselves Clearly Helps Us Succeed at Work and in Life*. Crown.	The author proposes that self-awareness can help us be more fulfilled, confident, and successful, but most people are not self-aware, so she offers techniques and strategies to develop self-awareness.
Freeman, M., & Jana, T. (2016). *Overcoming Bias: Building Authentic Relationships Across Differences*. Berrett-Koehler.	The authors provide exercises and activities to help us reflect on our personal biases, become self-aware, and approach relationships with an intent to enrich our lives and expand our perspective.
Winters, M. (2020). *Inclusive Conversations: Fostering Equity, Empathy, and Belonging Across Differences*. Berrett-Koehler.	The author explains how effective dialogue across different dimensions of diversity fosters a sense of belonging and inclusion, which in turn leads to greater productivity.
Gallo, A. (n.d.). *Getting Along: How to Work With Anyone (Even Difficult People)*. Harvard Business Review Press.	The author provides real-life examples and behavioral science research to offer practical advice about dealing with difficult people.
Markova, D., & McArthur, A. (2015). *Collaborative Intelligence: Thinking With People Who Think Differently*. Random House.	The authors propose that we need to recognize our own mind patterns and develop our ability to collaborate and inspire if we want to influence others.
Murthy, V. H. (2020). *Together: The Healing Power of Human Connection in a Sometimes Lonely World*. HarperCollins.	The author proposes that loneliness is a public health epidemic and offers four strategies to overcome it and become more connected to others.
Ruiz, D. M., & Mills, J. (1997). *The Four Agreements: A Practical Guide to Personal Freedom*. Amber-Allen.	The author proposes that self-limiting beliefs rob us of joy and create needless suffering. Four agreements are relevant to effective social work practice: Be impeccable with your word, don't take anything personally, don't make assumptions, always do your best.
Francis-Cheung, T. (2020). *100 Ways to Be Kind: Everyday Actions to Change Your Life and Save the World*. Thread.	The author proposes that the kinder you are, the more likely you are to experience happiness.

References

Council on Social Work Education. (2022, May 23). *2022 EPAS*. https://www.cswe.org/accreditation/info/2022-epas/

National Association of Social Workers. (2022, May 23). *NASW Code of Ethics*. https://www.socialworkers.org/About/Ethics/Code-of-Ethics/Code-of-Ethics-English

CREDIT

Fig. 6.1: Adapted from Educational Policy and Accreditation Standards. Copyright © 2022 by Council on Social Work Education.

CHAPTER 7

Competency 7

Assess Individuals, Families, Groups, Organizations, and Communities

In this chapter you will examine the seventh of the nine social work competencies provided by the CSWE. Competency 7 outlines the essential assessment skills required to become an effective social worker. You have probably taken or are currently taking a social work skills course and human behavior and social environment coursework. Those courses provide you with the theoretical knowledge you need to engage clients in the assessment process, and you should review your textbooks to identify the differences between assessment tools and procedures used with individuals, families, groups, organizations, and communities.

The evaluation tool used most often in social work practice with individuals is the biopsychosocial assessment. This provides a comprehensive view of biological, psychological, and social factors that may contribute to a problem, and it allows us to consider strengths and supports that we can use to help clients address their needs. An informal assessment process usually starts with the first client encounter and relies on open-ended questions to identify the issue that brought a client to seek services. Another useful assessment tool is the genogram, which provides a map of family relationships. Needs assessment inventories explore a client's safety needs, current situation, or survival needs. One-to-ten scales offer a quick assessment of a client's preferences, progress in attaining goals, or satisfaction level.

The client assessment process and evaluation instruments will change depending on the social work practice level and the role of the social worker. However, the knowledge, values, and skills necessary to complete accurate assessments are transferable. You will need analytical skills to select the appropriate assessment instruments as well as to interpret the results. The capacity to avoid judgments and assumptions, as well as to consider diverse cultural perspectives, will increase the probability that the assessment results will be culturally appropriate. And the ability to explain assessment results, including the strengths and limitations of the assessment process and instruments, is a necessary skill for increasing the integrity of the assessment process.

Competency 7 Description as Provided by CSWE: Assess Individuals, Families, Groups, Organizations, and Communities

Competency 7

Assess Individuals, Families, Groups, Organizations, and Communities

Social workers understand that assessment is an ongoing component of the dynamic and interactive process of social work practice. Social workers understand theories of human behavior and person-in-environment, as well as interprofessional conceptual frameworks, and they critically evaluate and apply this knowledge in culturally responsive assessment with clients and constituencies, including individuals, families, groups, organizations, and communities. Assessment involves a collaborative process of defining presenting challenges and identifying strengths with individuals, families, groups, organizations, and communities to develop a mutually agreed-upon plan. Social workers recognize the implications of the larger practice context in the assessment process and use interprofessional collaboration in this process. Social workers are self-reflective and understand how bias, power, privilege, and their personal values and experiences may affect their assessment and decision making.

Social workers:

a. apply theories of human behavior and person-in-environment, as well as other culturally responsive and interprofessional conceptual frameworks, when assessing clients and constituencies; and

b. demonstrate respect for client self-determination during the assessment process by collaborating with clients and constituencies in developing a mutually agreed-upon plan.

Figure 7.1 illustrates the relationship between the assessment process and the other eight competencies. Although the engagement, assessment, intervention, and evaluation processes are most strongly related, the ethical principles of the profession must be present during those processes, and issues of social justice and inclusion must be considered. Assessment instruments must also be evidence based and in line with social policy.

Competency 1:

Assess Individuals, Families, Groups, Organizations, and Communities in a manner that demonstrates ethical and professional behavior

Competency 9:

Assess clients in a way that contributes to the evaluation of social work practices

Competency 2:

Assess clients in ways that advance the human rights and social, racial, economic, and environmental justice of our clients

Competency 3:

Assess clients in ways that demonstrate anti-racism, diversity, equity and inclusion in our social work practice

Competency 8:

Assess clients in a way that contributes to a successful intervention

**Competency 7
Assess Individuals,
Families, Groups,
Organizations, and
Communities**

Competency 7:

What are the knowledge, values and skills necessary to effectively assess individuals, families, groups, organizations, and communities?

Competency 4:

Assess clients in a way that demonstrates our ability to use practice-informed research and research-informed practice

Competency 6:

Assess clients in a way that contributes to a positive client engagement process

Competency 5:

Assess clients in a way that demonstrates our ability to engage in policy practice

FIGURE 7.1   The relationship of competency 7 to the rest of the competencies.

Applying Competency 7

Competency 7 requires the ability to assess clients. As you consider how you might assess the needs of the Smith and Johnson family, think about the clients you serve at your social work practicum. How do you assess their needs? What assessment instruments are used in your practicum setting? Do you know whether they are culturally appropriate? What steps are you taking to gain the knowledge and skills necessary to accurately conduct client assessments?

Reflective Questions on Competency Application

Since Competency 7 is about the client assessment process, let's imagine a social worker completed a biopsychosocial assessment with the Smith and Johnson family. As you can see in Figure 7.2, the biopsychosocial assessment provides you with a profile of the family's biological, psychological, social, and spiritual needs and strengths.

Summary of biopsychosocial assessment:

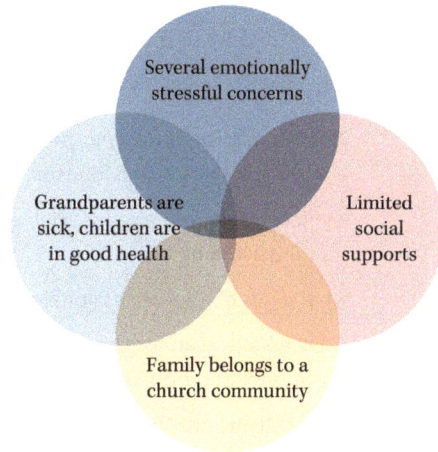

Biological: Mrs. and Mrs. Smith's ill health has had a negative impact on their ability to care for the children. Mr. Smith is blind due to diabetes, so his childcare contribution is limited.

Mrs. Smith gets tired easily and she reports that her temperament has changed, she does not seem to have the kind of patience she would like to have when dealing with the children. The grandparents' ability to socialize was greatly diminished once they became caregivers for their grandchildren. They used to be able to take a vacation once per year, but there is no money for

FIGURE 7.2 The biopsychosocial assessment of the Smith and Johnson family.

that now. Mrs. Smith is worried about Daniel because, since the bullying started, he has been less engaged in social activities. She believes witnessing Daniel being victimized has had a negative impact on Allyssa's health because Allyssa often complains of stomach aches, but the doctor says there is nothing wrong with her.

Psychological: Mrs. Smith reports that loss of vitality due to illness has diminished her ability to enjoy life. She feels stressed about having to take care of her grandchildren because she is often too tired to do everything that she would like to with them. The death of her daughter was devastating to her, and she feels the pain will never go away. She is aware that Allyssa and Daniel are also devastated about not having their parents around, so she tries to show them as much love as possible, but she is aware that it is impossible to fill the gap.

Mr. Smith feels bad that he cannot help his wife care for the children, but he tries to engage with them by asking them to teach him what they learned in school each day because he needs to keep learning. The children loved to play that game, but lately they have been less willing to talk about school.

Mr. and Mrs. Smith love their grandchildren and want them to do well in life, so they always encourage them to focus on working hard in school. Allyssa and Daniel know their grandparents love them, and when they visit their father, he always encourages them to obey their grandparents and do well in school. However, it has been difficult for Daniel and Allyssa to concentrate on their studies since the bullying of Daniel started.

Social: The main social supports for this family include Social Security, Medicare for the grandparents, and Medicaid for the grandchildren. A few families from their church community volunteer to help with childcare when the grandparents have medical appointments, but their basic needs would not be adequately met without the additional financial support they get from their son. The school is a key social support because education is important to the family, but the school system failed to provide a safe environment for Daniel and Allyssa, and that is an issue that needs to be addressed as soon as possible.

Spiritual: The family belongs to a church community, and that is a source of spiritual, psychological, and social support.

(Continued)

Completing a genogram helped the social worker explore the potential supports Daniel and Allyssa might have on their father's side of the family. However, Mrs. Smith reports that the children's father wants his children to remain in her care for as long as possible, in part because the only sister who might be able to care for them lives too far away, so his chances of seeing them would diminish.

Carefully read the following questions and reflect on the skills necessary to effectively assess clients:

What human behavior and person-in-environment theories could you use to inform the assessment process with Smith and Johnson family?

If you are completing your social work practicum in a school setting, how might you benefit from understanding learning theories?

What kinds of interprofessional collaboration might be required in a school setting?

Teachers will evaluate the educational participation and progress of Alyssa and Daniel. How valuable is the information from those assessments to social work practice in a school setting?

If your clients are Alyssa and Daniel, how might human development theories be useful?

How might understanding attachment theory be useful to understanding Alyssa and Daniel?

If you are completing your social work practicum in a health clinic and your client is Mrs. Smith, how might change theory help you understand her reluctance to change her diet and exercise behaviors? What kinds of interprofessional collaboration might be required in a health care setting?

If the Smith and Johnson family belongs to a different ethnic group than you do, what steps can you take to make sure the assessment process is culturally appropriate?

What steps can you take to ensure that the assessment process is collaborative to identify challenges as well as strengths as you work with Smith and Johnson family?

If you notice that your personal values are different from those of the Smith and Johnson family, what steps can you take to keep your feelings in check to avoid imposing them on your clients during the assessment process?

What are you learning about the assessment process during your practicum? What assessment instruments are used at your practicum?

Have you been able to complete an assessment during your practicum? If not, have you observed the assessment process, or have you reviewed a client's file to review the assessment process?

As you think about these questions, consider the diversity of the clients in your social work practicum. What steps can you take to increase your ability to be self-reflective and increase your understanding of the way bias, power, and privilege as well as your personal values and experiences may affect your assessment and decision-making?

Investigating Each Sentence in the Competency Description

In this section, you will scrutinize each sentence of the competency description to identify key concepts, explore the meaning of those concepts, and critically examine the requirements of competency 7. Figure 7.3 highlights the fact that assessment skills need to be tailored to the social work practice level. Although the focus of client assessment in this book is at the individual and family levels, keep in mind that social work with groups, organizations, and communities will require the development of additional assessment skills and abilities.

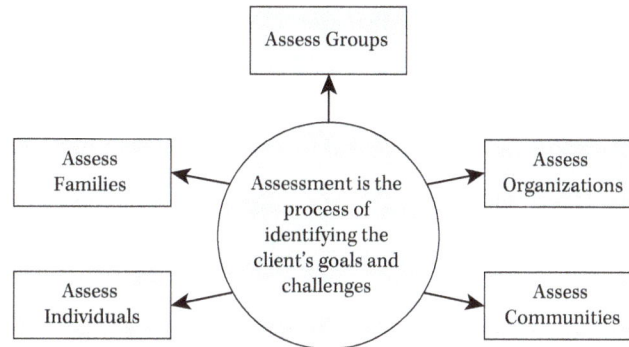

FIGURE 7.3 The client assessment process at different levels of social work practice.

Competency 7

Assess Individuals, Families, Groups, Organizations, and Communities

Social workers understand that assessment is an ongoing component of the dynamic and interactive process of social work practice.

Identify Key Concepts, Search for the Meaning of Those Concepts, and Critically Examine the Requirements of the Competency

1. Use the phrase "ongoing assessment in social work" to search the internet, and carefully read and analyze at least two scholarly articles about this topic.

   a. What did you learn about the ongoing assessment in social work practice from the articles?

2. Use the phrase "dynamic and interactive social work practice" to search the internet, and carefully read and analyze at least two scholarly articles about this topic. Or explore your social work practice textbooks for a description of the dynamic and interactive social work client engagement process.

   a. What did you learn about the dynamic and interactive social work process from the articles?

3. Use the phrase "interactive assessment in social work" to search the internet, and carefully read and analyze at least two scholarly articles about this topic.

   a. What did you learn about interactive assessment in social work practice from the articles?

Reflective Writing Practice

In a few sentences, describe how your understanding of assessment as an ongoing component of the dynamic and interactive process of social work practice might be used during your social work practicum.

_____

_____

_____

_____

Application Follow-Up

Date you were able to integrate your understanding of assessment as an ongoing component of the dynamic and interactive process of social work practice during your social work practicum:

_____

In a few sentences, describe what you learned from the process of integrating your understanding of assessment as an ongoing component of the dynamic and interactive process of social work practice during your social work practicum.

_____

_____

_____

_____

Self-Evaluation

Successful	I can effectively demonstrate these competency requirements during practicum, and I can explain how these competency requirements contribute to effective social work practice.
Developing	I can identify the information I need and am able to apply it in some practicum situations, but I am also aware of some knowledge and skill gaps that I need to address.
Unsuccessful	Currently, I am not able to successfully demonstrate these competency requirements in practicum.

Competency 7

Assess Individuals, Families, Groups, Organizations, and Communities

Social workers understand theories of human behavior and person-in-environment, as well as inter-professional conceptual frameworks, and they critically evaluate and apply this knowledge in culturally responsive assessment with clients and constituencies, including individuals, families, groups, organizations, and communities.

Identify Key Concepts, Search for the Meaning of Those Concepts, and Critically Examine the Requirements of the Competency

1. Use the phrase "theories of human behavior and person-in-environment and assessments" to search the internet, and carefully read and analyze at least two scholarly articles about this topic.

    a. What did you learn about theories of human behavior and person in environment and assessment skills from the articles?

2. Use the phrase "culturally responsive assessment with clients" to search the internet, and carefully read and analyze at least two scholarly articles about this topic.

    a. What did you learn about culturally responsive assessment in social work practice from the articles?

Reflective Writing Practice

In a few sentences, outline a plan to integrate your understanding of theories of human behavior and person in environment to critically evaluate and use culturally responsive assessments with clients during your social work practicum.

_____

_____

_____

_____

Application Follow-Up

Date you were able to integrate theories of human behavior and person in environment to critically evaluate and use culturally responsive assessments with clients during your social work practicum: _____

In a few sentences, describe what you learned from the process of integrating theories of human behavior and person in environment to critically evaluate and use culturally responsive assessments with clients during your social work practicum.

_____

_____

_____

_____

Self-Evaluation

Successful	I can effectively demonstrate these competency requirements during practicum, and I can explain how these competency requirements contribute to effective social work practice.
Developing	I can identify the information I need and am able to apply it in some practicum situations, but I am also aware of some knowledge and skill gaps that I need to address.
Unsuccessful	Currently, I am not able to successfully demonstrate these competency requirements in practicum.

Competency 7

Assess Individuals, Families, Groups, Organizations, and Communities

Assessment involves a collaborative process of defining presenting issues and identifying strengths with individuals, families, groups, organizations, and communities to develop a mutually agreed-upon plan.

Identify Key Concepts, Search for the Meaning of Those Concepts, and Critically Examine the Requirements of the Competency

1. Use the phrase "collaborative assessment process in social work practice" to search the internet, and carefully read and analyze at least two scholarly articles about this topic.

    a. What did you learn about the collaborative assessment process in social work practice from the articles?

2. Use the phrase "defining presenting issues and identifying strengths with individuals in social work practice" to search the internet, and carefully read and analyze at least two scholarly articles about this topic.

    a. What did you learn about defining presenting issues and identifying strengths with individuals in social work practice from the articles?

3. Use the phrase "mutually agreed-on plan in social work practice" to search the internet, and carefully read and analyze at least two scholarly articles about this topic.

   a. What did you learn about mutually agreed-on plan in social work practice from the articles?

Reflective Writing Practice

In a few sentences, outline a plan to implement a collaborative process of defining presenting issues and identifying strengths in the assessment process with clients during your social work practicum.

_____

_____

_____

_____

Application Follow-Up

Date you were able to implement a collaborative process of defining presenting issues and identifying strengths in the assessment process with clients during your social work practicum:

_____

In a few sentences, describe what you learned from the process of using a collaborative process of defining presenting issues and identifying strengths in the assessment process with clients during your social work practicum.

_____

_____

_____

_____

Self-Evaluation

Successful	I can effectively demonstrate these competency requirements during practicum, and I can explain how these competency requirements contribute to effective social work practice.
Developing	I can identify the information I need and am able to apply it in some practicum situations, but I am also aware of some knowledge and skill gaps that I need to address.
Unsuccessful	Currently, I am not able to successfully demonstrate these competency requirements in practicum.

> ### Competency 7
>
> ### Assess Individuals, Families, Groups, Organizations, and Communities
>
> Social workers recognize the implications of the larger practice context in the assessment process and use interprofessional collaboration in this process.

Identify Key Concepts, Search for the Meaning of Those Concepts, and Critically Examine the Requirements of the Competency

1. Use the phrase "implications of the larger practice context in the assessment process in social work practice" to search the internet, and carefully read and analyze at least two scholarly articles about this topic.

   a. What did you learn about the implications of the larger practice context in the assessment process in social work practice from the articles?

2. Use the phrase "interprofessional collaboration in the assessment process in social work practice" to search the internet, and carefully read and analyze at least two scholarly articles about this topic.

   a. What did you learn about the interprofessional collaboration in the assessment process in social work practice from the articles?

Reflective Writing Practice

In a few sentences, outline a plan integrate your knowledge of the implications of the larger practice context in the assessment process and use interprofessional collaboration in the assessment process during practicum.

_____

_____

_____

_____

Application Follow-Up

Date you were able to integrate your knowledge of the implications of the larger practice context in the assessment process and use interprofessional collaboration in the assessment process during practicum: _____

In a few sentences, describe what you learned from the process of integrating your knowledge of the implications of the larger practice context in the assessment process and engaging in interprofessional collaboration in the assessment process during practicum.

Self-Evaluation

Successful	I can effectively demonstrate these competency requirements during practicum, and I can explain how these competency requirements contribute to effective social work practice.
Developing	I can identify the information I need and am able to apply it in some practicum situations, but I am also aware of some knowledge and skill gaps that I need to address.
Unsuccessful	Currently, I am not able to successfully demonstrate these competency requirements in practicum.

Competency 7

Assess Individuals, Families, Groups, Organizations, and Communities

Social workers are self-reflective and understand how bias, power, privilege, and their personal values and experiences may affect their assessment and decision making.

Identify Key Concepts, Search for the Meaning of Those Concepts, and Critically Examine the Requirements of the Competency

1. Use the phrase "self-reflection and the assessment process in social work practice" to search the internet, and carefully read and analyze at least two scholarly articles about this topic.

    a. What did you learn about self-reflection and the assessment process in social work practice from the articles?

2. Use the phrase "bias, power, privilege, and the assessment process in social work practice" to search the internet, and carefully read and analyze at least two scholarly articles about this topic.

    a. What did you learn about bias, power, privilege, and the assessment process in social work practice from the articles?

3. Use the phrase "social workers' personal values and experiences and the assessment process in social work practice" to search the internet, and carefully read and analyze at least two scholarly articles about this topic.

   a. What did you learn about social workers' personal values and experiences and the assessment process in social work practice from the articles?

4. Use the phrase "assessment and decision-making in social work practice" to search the internet, and carefully read and analyze at least two scholarly articles about this topic.

   a. What did you learn about assessment and decision-making in social work practice from the articles?

Reflective Writing Practice

In a few sentences, outline a plan use self-reflection to manage your bias, power, privilege, and personal values and experiences to ensure that assessment decisions are based on valid assessment results.

_____

_____

_____

_____

Application Follow-Up

Date you were able to use self-reflection to manage your bias, power, privilege, and personal values and experiences to ensure that assessment decisions were based on valid assessment results: _____

In a few sentences, describe what you learned from the process of using self-reflection to manage your bias, power, privilege, and personal values and experiences to ensure that assessment decisions were based on valid assessment results.

_____

_____

_____

_____

Self-Evaluation

Successful	I can effectively demonstrate these competency requirements during practicum, and I can explain how these competency requirements contribute to effective social work practice.
Developing	I can identify the information I need and am able to apply it in some practicum situations, but I am also aware of some knowledge and skill gaps that I need to address.
Unsuccessful	Currently, I am not able to successfully demonstrate these competency requirements in practicum.

Demonstrating the Ability to Assess Individuals, Families, Groups, Organizations, and Communities

The knowledge, values, and skills necessary to effectively assess clients are an essential component of social work practice. Without these abilities, social work interventions are unlikely to effectively address clients' needs.

Apply theories of human behavior and person-in-environment, as well as other culturally responsive and interprofessional conceptual frameworks, when assessing clients and constituencies.

Demonstrating Competency 7 With the Smith and Johnson Family	Demonstrating Competency 7 During your Practicum
1. If you are assessing the needs and strengths of the Smith and Johnson family, what theoretical perspective are you using? 2. How would the assessment process differ if you were using a behaviorist, cognitive, constructivist, or humanist theoretical perspective in the client assessment process? 3. If the Smith and Johnson family belongs to a minority population, how would you ensure that the assessment process is culturally appropriate? 4. If your clients are Alyssa and Daniel, how would having a good understanding of human development theories help you identify the appropriate assessment process? 5. If your practicum is at a health clinic and your client is Mrs. Smith, how would you use health behavior theory as you assess her needs and strengths?	1. How are the needs and strengths of clients assessed in your social work practicum setting? 2. What theoretical perspective is used at your practicum setting in the client assessment process? 3. What would you need to know and be able to do to ensure that the assessment process at your practicum setting is culturally appropriate? 4. What steps are you taking to increase your understanding of human development theories and their role in the client assessment process? 5. Describe how you have used theories of human behavior and person in environment, as well as other culturally responsive and interprofessional conceptual frameworks, when assessing clients during your social work practicum experience.

Demonstrate respect for client self-determination during the assessment process by collaborating with clients and constituencies in developing a mutually agreed-upon plan.

Demonstrating Competency 7 With the Smith and Johnson Family	Demonstrating Competency 7 During Your Practicum
1. If the Smith and Johnson family is your client, how would you include the client's self-determination during the assessment process?	1. Think about the clients served at your practicum. How would you include the client's self-determination during the assessment process?
2. When the social worker asked to complete a genogram to explore potential resources on the father's side of the family, Mrs. Smith reported that Mr. Johnson wanted the children to remain in the care of Mr. and Mrs. Smith because his sister lives too far away and it would diminish his ability to see his children. As long as Mr. and Mrs. Smith are able to care for Alyssa and Daniel, there is no need to explore the father's side of the family. However, can you think of an advantage in knowing that the children have an aunt that could be of support to them? What else would be important to know about the children's aunt?	2. Describe an occasion when an assessment instrument might not be used because it assesses a treatment option the client is not interested in.
3. Based on the biopsychosocial assessment, this family might benefit from community support. However, community services should be offered and not imposed, since the client needs to be willing to participate in the intervention process to benefit from services.	3. Identify an intervention proven to work with most clients but that some clients might not be willing to participate in. What steps can you take to develop a mutually agreed-on plan with those clients?
4. How would you demonstrate your ability to collaborate with clients during the assessment process in this case?	4. How would you demonstrate your ability to collaborate with clients during the assessment process in your practicum?

Competency Development Topics for the Social Work Practicum Seminar

▶ Competency 7 Field Seminar Topics

- The dynamic and interactive assessment process
- Theories of human behavior and person in environment that can be used in a culturally responsive assessment process
- The collaborative client assessment process
- The interprofessional collaboration assessment process
- Self-reflection strategies and the influence of personal values and bias, power, and privilege on the client assessment process

▼ Prior Planning

- Use your notes in this chapter and identify the parts of competency 7 that you have not been able to successfully demonstrate.
- Review your work with clients at your practicum setting and consider the client assessment process. Have you completed a client assessment? If not, have you observed the assessment process? If not, are you able to review clients' records and read about the client assessment

process? If not, you might need to consult with your field practicum faculty to explore options for developing client assessment skills during your practicum.

- Prepare specific questions that will help you explore your client assessment skills during seminar.

◀ **During Seminar**

- Listen attentively to your peers, because they will probably be using a different client assessment process and different tools during their practicum.
- Be ready to contribute by sharing your struggles as well as your successes in implementing client assessments during your practicum.
- Reflect on your professional growth. What have you learned about assessing clients since you started your practicum experience?

Competency Development Topics for the Educational Supervision Meeting

▶ **Competency 7 Social Work Practicum Instructional Supervision Meeting Topics**

- The assessment process and tools used in the practicum setting
- The theories of human behavior and person in environment that are used in the practicum setting to facilitate the assessment process
- The collaborative client assessment process used in the practicum setting
- The interprofessional collaboration assessment process used in the practicum setting
- Self-reflection strategies and the influence of personal values and bias, power, and privilege on the client assessment process

▼ **Prior Planning**

- Review the assessment process and tools used in the practicum setting. Are you able to complete an assessment? If you are using a questionnaire, do you understand the purpose and utility of every question? If you are not allowed to complete a client assessment, can you review the assessment process so that you understand what is being evaluated and how the evaluation process works?
- Use your notes in this chapter and identify the parts of competency 7 that you have not been able to successfully demonstrate.
- Prepare specific questions that will help you explore your assessment skills with your social work instructor during supervision.

◀ **During the Instructional Supervision Meeting**

- Be prepared to ask questions that will help you develop and practice competency 7.
- Share your struggles as well as your successes as you attempt to evaluate clients during your practicum. If you are not allowed to complete a client evaluation, explore the possibility of observing a client evaluation.

- In some social work settings, there are no formal client evaluation instruments. If that is the case in your practicum placement, make sure to explore the informal client assessment process with your social work instructor during supervision.

Summary

Competency 7 is about having the ability to assess clients. As you can see in Figure 7.4, although you will need to learn how to use different assessment instruments and engage different assessment processes depending on the different levels of social work practice, the purpose of assessing clients remains the same. You need to identify the client's goals, strengths and resources, cultural perspectives, and priorities as well as screen for challenges, safety, and risk. The goal of social work practice is to help people address their needs and achieve success, and identifying their strengths is an essential step in helping them recognize their own assets and capacity.

As with every aspect of social work practice, who you are and how you respond to difficult circumstances matters. Your ability to use self-reflection and self-regulation during the entire assessment process, including the ability to collaborate with clients and across professional disciplines, as well as your ability to use analytical skills to assess evaluation procedures and instruments, will affect the process and outcome of the evaluation. Continuous learning is an essential requirement if your goal is to become a proficient social worker.

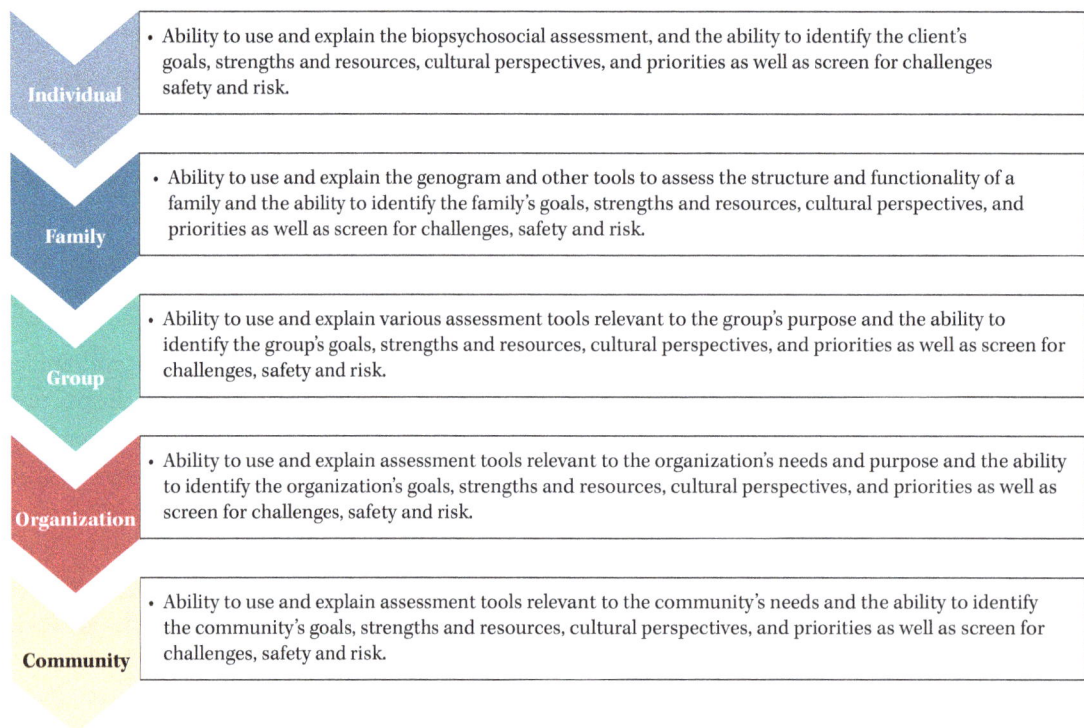

Individual
- Ability to use and explain the biopsychosocial assessment, and the ability to identify the client's goals, strengths and resources, cultural perspectives, and priorities as well as screen for challenges safety and risk.

Family
- Ability to use and explain the genogram and other tools to assess the structure and functionality of a family and the ability to identify the family's goals, strengths and resources, cultural perspectives, and priorities as well as screen for challenges, safety and risk.

Group
- Ability to use and explain various assessment tools relevant to the group's purpose and the ability to identify the group's goals, strengths and resources, cultural perspectives, and priorities as well as screen for challenges, safety and risk.

Organization
- Ability to use and explain assessment tools relevant to the organization's needs and purpose and the ability to identify the organization's goals, strengths and resources, cultural perspectives, and priorities as well as screen for challenges, safety and risk.

Community
- Ability to use and explain assessment tools relevant to the community's needs and the ability to identify the community's goals, strengths and resources, cultural perspectives, and priorities as well as screen for challenges, safety and risk.

FIGURE 7.4   Social work assessment skills at different levels of practice.

Recommended Reading Materials

Books	Description
Corcoran, J., & Walsh, J. (2019). *Mental Health in Social Work: A Casebook on Diagnosis and Strengths Based Assessment*. Pearson Education.	The author uses a case-based approach to discuss evidence-based clinical assessment and intervention skills. She emphasizes gaining competency in the and uses the Diagnostic and Statistical Manual of Mental Disorders (DSM-5) to discuss diagnoses of mental disorders that are commonly seen in clinical and social service settings.
Jordan C., & Franklin C., (2020) *Clinical Assessment for Social Workers: Quantitative and Qualitative Methods*. Oxford University Press.	The authors discuss the use of evidence-based methods to formulate assessments and intervention plans and they emphasize the biopsychosocial-spiritual framework and the importance of the strengths perspective in assessment process. They cover approaches to assessment and how to assess various client populations, including clients who experience adverse childhood experiences, trauma, and clients from underrepresented minority backgrounds.
McGoldrick, M., & Gerson, R. (2020). *Genograms: Assessment and Treatment*. Norton.	The authors provide a standard method for constructing a genogram, doing a genogram interview, and interpreting the results.
Lukas, S. (2012). *Where to Start and What to Ask: An Assessment Handbook* (Enhanced ed.). Norton.	The author provides a framework for thinking about the information you need and how to formulate a thorough assessment.
Pipher, M. (2016). *Letters to a Young Therapist*. Basic Books.	The author uses storytelling and observation to describe what she has learned in 30 years as a therapist.
Bodenheimer, D. R. (2017). *On Clinical Social Work: Meditations and Truths From the Field*. New Social Worker Press.	The author encourages you to think critically about everything from assessment, diagnosis, intervention, and clinical supervision to the social worker's self-care.
Richmond, M. E. (1917). *Social Diagnosis*. Russell Sage Foundation.	This book provides a historical account of social work and the need to use evidence to develop diagnostic skills and provide accurate treatment in case work.
Foo, S. (2022). *What My Bones Know: A Memoir of Healing From Complex Trauma*. Random House.	The author offers a personal account of PTSD and connects the science behind complex PTSD to explain that you don't move on from trauma, but you can learn to move with it.
Winfrey, O., & Perry, B. D. (2021). *What Happened to You? Conversations on Trauma, Resilience, and Healing*. Flatiron Books.	The authors offer a shift from asking "What's wrong with you?" to "What happened to you?" Understanding trauma and adversity is a key component of social work practice, and this book offers a view of resilience and healing.

References

Council on Social Work Education. (2022, May 23). *2022 EPAS*. https://www.cswe.org/accreditation/info/2022-epas/

National Association of Social Workers. (2022, May 23). *NASW Code of Ethics*. https://www.socialworkers.org/About/Ethics/Code-of-Ethics/Code-of-Ethics-English

CREDIT
Fig. 7.1: Adapted from Educational Policy and Accreditation Standards. Copyright © 2022 by Council on Social Work Education.

CHAPTER 8

Competency 8

Intervene with Individuals, Families, Groups, Organizations, and Communities

In this chapter you will examine the eighth of the nine social work competencies provided by the CSWE. Competency 8 outlines the essential intervention skills required to become an effective social worker. It will be helpful for you to review your social work skills course and human behavior and social environment coursework. Those courses provide the theoretical knowledge you need to engage clients in the intervention process. A review of your practice skills textbooks should also refresh your understanding of the different intervention modalities you can use with individuals, families, groups, organizations, and communities.

Social work intervention requires collaboration between the client and the social worker. Interventions cannot be imposed on clients, and we must examine potential interventions for compatibility with clients' goals and readiness to participate in the intervention process. A client who does not want the intervention is unlikely to follow it. We must also identify the resources and skills needed to appropriately implement the intervention. If you are using a good intervention but do not have the knowledge and skills to appropriately implement it, you are not likely to get the results you seek.

Competency 8 Description as Provided by CSWE: Intervene with Individuals, Families, Groups, Organizations, and Communities

Competency 8

Intervene with Individuals, Families, Groups, Organizations, and Communities

Social workers understand that intervention is an ongoing component of the dynamic and interactive process of social work practice. Social workers understand theories of human behavior, person-in-environment, and other multidisciplinary theoretical frameworks, and they critically evaluate and apply this knowledge in selecting culturally responsive interventions with clients and constituencies, including individuals, families, groups, organizations, and communities. Social workers understand methods of identifying, analyzing, and implementing evidence-informed interventions and participate in interprofessional collaboration to achieve client and constituency goals. Social workers facilitate effective transitions and endings.

Social workers:

a. engage with clients and constituencies to critically choose and implement culturally responsive, evidence-informed interventions to achieve client and constituency goals and

b. incorporate culturally responsive methods to negotiate, mediate, and advocate, with and on behalf of clients and constituencies.

Figure 8.1 shows the relationship of the intervention process to the other eight competencies. We cannot identify or implement a successful intervention without effectively engaging with the client and conducting an appropriate assessment. Social policy also guides the intervention process, and thus we need to research clients' cultural needs and utilize ethical and inclusive social work practices.

Competency 1:

Intervene with Individuals, Families, Groups, Organizations, and Communities in ways that demonstrate ethical and professional behavior

Competency 9:

Intervene with clients in ways that incorporate the evaluation of social work practices

Competency 2:

Intervene with clients in ways that advance the human rights and social, racial, economic, and environmental justice

Competency 8:

What are the knowledge, values and skills necessary to effectively intervene with individuals, families, groups, organizations, and communities?

Competency 8 Intervene with Individuals, Families, Groups, Organizations, and Communities

Competency 3:

Intervene with clients in ways that demonstrate anti-racism, diversity, equity and inclusion in social work practice

Competency 4:

Intervene with clients in a way that demonstrates the use of practice-informed research and research-informed practice

Competency 7:

Intervene with clients in ways that demonstrate the ability to effectively assess clients

Competency 6:

Intervene with clients in ways that demonstrate the ability to effectively engage with clients

Competency 5:

Intervene with clients in ways that demonstrate the ability to engage in policy practice

FIGURE 8.1 The relationship of competency 8 to the rest of the competencies.

Applying Competency 8

Competency 8 requires the ability to intervene with clients. As you consider how you might help the Smith and Johnson family, think about the clients you serve at your social work practicum. What kind of interventions are you implementing? How do you know whether they are culturally appropriate? What steps are you taking to gain the knowledge and skills necessary to accurately implement social work interventions?

Reflective Questions on Competency Application

Competency 8 is about the client intervention process. Therefore, we will explore interventions that might benefit the Smith and Johnson family in this section.

The Smith and Johnson family presents several issues that might need intervention. A school social worker could refer the family to community services and may also contribute to a school-wide bullying prevention program. A social worker at a prison might assist Mr. Johnson to stay in touch with his children and lead psychoeducational groups to help inmates prepare for reentry into society once their sentence is over. A social worker in a community agency might work with the family to identify community support or provide direct assistance.

Case work

Based on the biopsychosocial assessment completed in the last chapter, you know that both Mr. and Mrs. Smith need community supports to help them manage their diabetes, and they might also benefit from accessing after-school programs for Alyssa and Daniel since their physical stamina has diminished.

A local clinic offers home visits for people with diabetes, and Mr. and Mrs. Smith qualify for services, but Mrs. Smith is hesitant about having strangers come into her home.

A community agency offers psychoeducational group interventions to help grandparents cope with the stress of raising grandchildren and activities for the children while the grandparents are in the group.

An after-school program near the school will help Alyssa and Daniel with homework and provide snacks, but transportation would need to be arranged.

Bullying prevention

Based on the biopsychosocial assessment completed in the last chapter, you know that Daniel has been a victim of bullying and the school staff was unaware of the problem. There is a zero-tolerance bullying policy in the school but not much in place to enforce it. It seems that bullying often occurs on the school bus.

Since Daniel's safety needs must be addressed immediately, the children involved will receive a written warning, and their parents will be notified of the zero-tolerance bullying policy. Another incident of bullying will result in their children not being allowed to use the school bus for transportation.

This might resolve the issue, or it can also exacerbate it since the bullies might want to retaliate. Therefore, an assessment is needed to identify the safety risks to address school wide:

- The social worker and the school counselor can collaborate to conduct focus groups with bus drivers to identify what they need to keep the children safe.
- The Parent Teacher Organization can lead a meeting with parents and teachers to discuss the issue and possible solutions.

- A bullying prevention team would need to include professional staff, support staff, students, and parents, but it is difficult to get everyone together. The social worker and the school counselor will ask for nominations from each group to hold a focus group, develop a plan, and report back to the wider community.
- The social worker and the school counselor need to work with the school principal to review state laws and school board policies to make sure a bullying prevention program is legal.
- The social worker and the school counselor need to review the research literature to identify the most successful bullying prevention programs and share that information with the bullying prevention team.
- The social worker and the school counselor need to identify the resources necessary to implement the bullying prevention program. If the school district does not have the funds to support the program, are there other sources of funding?

As you consider the interventions for addressing the needs of the Smith and Johnson family, think about the interventions used at your practicum and the knowledge and skills you need to develop.

What theories of human behavior and person in environment could you use to inform the intervention process with this family?

How would your awareness and understanding of your personal bias and privilege affect the intervention process?

What steps can you take to ensure that the interventions you use are appropriate with racial and cultural minority clients?

How do you feel about bullying? If you are completing your social work practicum at a school, you will probably have to work with children who are victimizing other students. How would you establish a positive rapport with hostile clients?

What steps can you take to demonstrate self-reflection, integrity, reliability, and empathy as you engage in culturally responsive social work practice with clients?

Investigating Each Sentence in the Competency Description

In this section, you will closely read each sentence of the competency description to identify key concepts, explore the meaning of those concepts, and critically examine the requirements of competency 8. In Figure 8.2, the intervention process necessary in generalist social work practice is illustrated to highlight the fact that intervention skills need to be tailored to the social work practice level. Although the focus of client intervention in this book is at the individual and family levels, keep in mind that social work with groups, organizations, and communities will require the development of additional intervention skills and abilities.

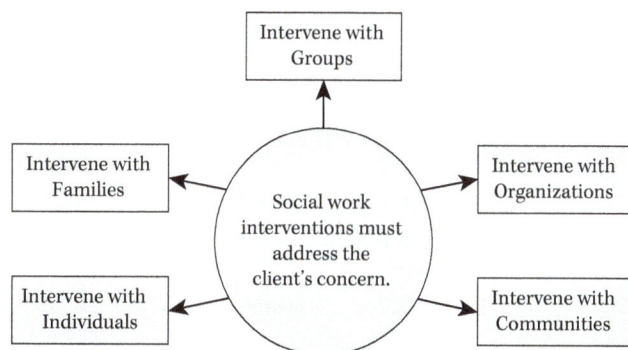

FIGURE 8.2   The client intervention process at different levels of social work practice.

Competency 8

Intervene with Individuals, Families, Groups, Organizations, and Communities

Social workers understand that intervention is an ongoing component of the dynamic and interactive process of social work practice.

Identify Key Concepts, Search for the Meaning of Those Concepts, and Critically Examine the Requirements of the Competency

1. Use the phrase "social work intervention process" to search the internet, and carefully read and analyze at least two scholarly articles about this topic.

   a. What did you learn about the social work intervention process from the articles?

2. Use the phrase "dynamic and interactive social work intervention process" to search the internet, and carefully read and analyze at least two scholarly articles about this topic. Or explore your social work practice textbooks for a description of the dynamic and interactive social work intervention process.

   a. What did you learn about the dynamic and interactive social work intervention process from the articles?

Reflective Writing Practice

In a few sentences, describe your plan to develop your capacity to implement interventions during your practice using the dynamic and interactive process of social work practice.

_____

_____

_____

_____

Application Follow-Up

Date you identified an opportunity to implement an intervention in your practice using the dynamic and interactive social work process: _____

In a few sentences describe what you learned from implementing an intervention in your practicum using a dynamic and interactive social work process.

_____

_____

Self-Evaluation

Successful	I can effectively demonstrate these competency requirements during practicum, and I can explain how these competency requirements contribute to effective social work practice.
Developing	I can identify the information I need and am able to apply it in some practicum situations, but I am also aware of some knowledge and skill gaps that I need to address.
Unsuccessful	Currently, I am not able to successfully demonstrate these competency requirements in practicum.

Competency 8

Intervene with Individuals, Families, Groups, Organizations, and Communities

Social workers understand theories of human behavior, person-in-environment, and other multidisciplinary theoretical frameworks, and they critically evaluate and apply this knowledge in selecting culturally responsive interventions with clients and constituencies, including individuals, families, groups, organizations, and communities.

Identify Key Concepts, Search for the Meaning of Those Concepts, and Critically Examine the Requirements of the Competency

1. Use the phrase "theories of human behavior and person in environment and intervention" to search the internet, and carefully read and analyze at least two scholarly articles about this topic.

    a. What did you learn about the use of theories of human behavior and person in environment and the intervention process from the articles?

2. Use the phrase "critically evaluate interventions" to search the internet, and carefully read and analyze at least two scholarly articles about this topic.

    a. What did you learn about the process to critically evaluate interventions from the articles?

3. Use the phrase "social work interventions with clients and constituencies" to search the internet, and carefully read and analyze at least two scholarly articles about this topic.

    a. What did you learn about social work interventions with clients and constituencies from the articles?

Reflective Writing Practice

In a few sentences, outline a plan to critically evaluate the human behavior theories you can use to facilitate the intervention process with clients during your practicum.

_____

_____

_____

_____

Application Follow-Up

Date you had an opportunity to use theories of human behavior to facilitate the client intervention process during your practicum: _____

In a few sentences, describe what you learned from using human behavior theories to facilitate the client intervention process during your practicum.

_____

_____

_____

_____

Self-Evaluation

Successful	I can effectively demonstrate these competency requirements during practicum, and I can explain how these competency requirements contribute to effective social work practice.
Developing	I can identify the information I need and am able to apply it in some practicum situations, but I am also aware of some knowledge and skill gaps that I need to address.
Unsuccessful	Currently, I am not able to successfully demonstrate these competency requirements in practicum.

Competency 8

Intervene with Individuals, Families, Groups, Organizations, and Communities

Social workers understand methods of identifying, analyzing, and implementing evidence-informed interventions and participate in interprofessional collaboration to achieve client and constituency goals.

Identify Key Concepts, Search for the Meaning of Those Concepts, and Critically Examine the Requirements of the Competency

1. Use the phrase "evidence-informed interventions in social work" to search the internet, and carefully read and analyze at least two scholarly articles about this topic.

   a. What did you learn about evidence-informed interventions in social work from the articles?

2. Use the phrase "identifying evidence-informed interventions in social work" to search the internet, and carefully read and analyze at least two scholarly articles about this topic.

   a. What did you learn about identifying evidence-informed interventions in social work from the articles?

3. Use the phrase "analyzing evidence-informed interventions in social work" to search the internet, and carefully read and analyze at least two scholarly articles about this topic.

   a. What did you learn about analyzing evidence-informed interventions in social work from the articles?

4. Use the phrases "implementing evidence-informed interventions" to search the internet, select at least two articles that are relevant to your social work practicum, and carefully read and analyze those articles.

   a. What did you learn about implementing evidence-informed interventions from the articles?

Reflective Writing Practice

In a few sentences, outline a plan to implement evidence-informed interventions during your social work practicum.

_____

_____

_____

_____

Application Follow-Up

Date you were able to implement evidence-informed interventions during your social work practicum: _____

In a few sentences, describe what you learned from implementing evidence-informed interventions during your social work practicum.

_____

_____

_____

_____

Self-Evaluation

Successful	I can effectively demonstrate these competency requirements during practicum, and I can explain how these competency requirements contribute to effective social work practice.
Developing	I can identify the information I need and am able to apply it in some practicum situations, but I am also aware of some knowledge and skill gaps that I need to address.
Unsuccessful	Currently, I am not able to successfully demonstrate these competency requirements in practicum.

Competency 8

Intervene with Individuals, Families, Groups, Organizations, and Communities

Social workers facilitate effective transitions and endings.

Identify Key Concepts, Search for the Meaning of Those Concepts, and Critically Examine the Requirements of the Competency

1. Use the phrase "effective client transitions in social work practice" to search the internet, and carefully read and analyze at least two scholarly articles about this topic.

   a. What did you learn about effective client transitions in social work practice from the articles?

2. Use the phrase "treatment termination in social work practice" to search the internet, and carefully read and analyze at least two scholarly articles about this topic.

   a. What did you learn about treatment termination in social work practice from the articles?

Reflective Writing Practice

In a few sentences, describe how you will use your understanding of effective transitions and endings in your social work practicum.

_____

_____

_____

_____

Application Follow-Up

Date you were able to assist a client transition or end the social work intervention during your social work practicum: _____

In a few sentences, describe what you learned from the process of assisting a client transition or end the social work intervention during your social work practicum.

_____

_____

_____

_____

Self-Evaluation

Successful	I can effectively demonstrate these competency requirements during practicum, and I can explain how these competency requirements contribute to effective social work practice.
Developing	I can identify the information I need and am able to apply it in some practicum situations, but I am also aware of some knowledge and skill gaps that I need to address.
Unsuccessful	Currently, I am not able to successfully demonstrate these competency requirements in practicum.

Demonstrating the Ability to Intervene with Individuals, Families, Groups, Organizations, and Communities

Having the knowledge, values, and skills necessary to effectively intervene with clients is an essential component of social work practice. Without an ability to identify and implement effective interventions, social work practice is at best ineffective and at worst damaging.

> Engage with clients and constituencies to critically choose and implement culturally responsive, evidence-informed interventions to achieve client and constituency goals.

Demonstrating Competency 8 With the Smith and Johnson Family	Demonstrating Competency 8 During Your Practicum
1. Imagine that you are completing your practicum at a school. Your work with the Smith and Johnson family includes helping the family identify community services and addressing the concern with Daniel being bullied. 2. The first step is to identify the Smith and Johnson family's cultural identity and explore the role of culture in the intervention process. Has their cultural background made them vulnerable to oppression? If so, how would you identify culturally responsive interventions? 3. We know that Daniel has been a victim of bullying and that he was targeted in part due to his skin color. How would you use that knowledge as you share intervention options with this family? 4. What steps can you take to identify culturally responsive bullying prevention programs? 5. You identified a local clinic that offers home visits for people with diabetes, and Mr. and Mrs. Smith qualify for services, but Mrs. Smith is hesitant about having strangers come into her home. How would you explore culturally responsive, evidence-informed interventions to help Mr. and Mrs. Smith?	1. Identify a specific social work practicum case you are familiar with and the intervention or interventions that this client is being offered. 2. Identify the cultural identity of the client. Do you know if the intervention or interventions being offered to the client are culturally responsive? 3. Has the cultural background of the client made them vulnerable to victimization in society? 4. What steps can you take to identify culturally responsive interventions that are relevant to your practicum case? 5. If a client is hesitant to participate in an intervention, what steps can you take to explore culturally responsive, evidence-informed interventions with them?

Incorporate culturally responsive methods to negotiate, mediate, and advocate, with and on behalf of clients and constituencies.

Demonstrating Competency 8 With the Smith and Johnson Family	Demonstrating Competency 8 During Your Practicum
1. Imagine that the Smith and Johnson family is a Native American family. There is a long history of oppression and discrimination against Native Americans in the United States. 2. How would you incorporate culturally responsive methods to negotiate the intervention process? 3. If you need to mediate between the family and the school system, how would you incorporate culturally responsive methods to mediate? 4. Advocating for Native Americans requires an understanding of forced assimilation, the loss and reclaiming process of native languages and traditions, historical trauma, social justice and jurisdictional issues within native lands, the diversity of religious practices among Native American tribes, including sacred sites, and their own vision of self-determination. What steps can you take to increase your awareness of the social issues that affect Native American families? 5. When you consider the needs of the Smith and Johnson family as well as their Native American affiliation, how would you incorporate culturally responsive methods to negotiate, mediate, or advocate, on behalf of this family?	1. Identify the ethnic background of the clients served at your social work practicum. 2. Does your practicum agency serve a client population that has been historically oppressed? If not, why not? 3. If yes, how would you incorporate culturally responsive methods to negotiate the intervention process? 4. Advocating on behalf of minority clients requires an understanding of the issues that have affected them within the social environment. What steps can you take to increase your awareness of the social issues that affect the client populations you serve? 5. When you consider the needs of the clients at your practicum as well as their ethnic identity, what steps are you taking to incorporate culturally responsive methods to negotiate, mediate, or advocate on behalf of your clients?

Competency Development Topics for the Social Work Practicum Seminar

▶ **Competency 8 Field Seminar Topics**

- The dynamic and interactive process of social work intervention
- Selecting culturally responsive theories of human behavior, person in environment, and other multidisciplinary theoretical frameworks relevant to the intervention process
- Methods of identifying, analyzing, and implementing evidence-informed interventions
- The process to facilitate effective transitions and endings

▼ **Prior Planning**

- Review your notes in this chapter and identify the key concepts related to each of the seminar discussion topics.
- Identify the parts of competency 8 that you have not been able to successfully demonstrate.
- Review your work with clients at your practicum setting and consider the client intervention process. Have you contributed to a client intervention? If not, have you observed the intervention process? If not, are you able to review client's records and read about the client intervention process? If not, you might need to consult with your field practicum faculty to explore options for you to develop client intervention skills during practicum.
- Consider the interventions used with clients at your practicum setting and identify any concerns you might want to discuss in seminar.

◀ **Seminar**

- Listen attentively to your peers because they will probably be implementing different interventions at their practicum.
- Be ready to contribute by sharing your struggles as well as your successes in implementing social work interventions during your practicum.
- Reflect on your professional growth. Think about the difference between your skills and abilities before practicum and now; you are likely to identify some areas of development. If you cannot identify any competency development gains, you need to discuss the issue with your social work field faculty as soon as possible.

Competency Development Topics for the Educational Supervision Meeting

▶ **Competency 8 Social Work Practicum Instructional Supervision Meeting Topics**

- The intervention process used in the practicum setting
- Culturally responsive theories of human behavior, person in environment, and other multidisciplinary theoretical frameworks relevant to the practicum setting

- Evidence-informed interventions used in the practicum setting
- The process to facilitate effective transitions and endings in the practicum setting

▼ **Prior Planning**

- Review your notes in this chapter and identify the parts of competency 8 that you have not been able to successfully demonstrate.
- If you are struggling to develop or implement intervention skills, explore the reasons for the struggle. Have you had the opportunity to participate in the client intervention process? Have you been able to observe the client intervention process? Have you been able to review a client's file to study the client intervention process?
- Formulate specific questions that will help you discuss your ability to practice intervention skills with your social work instructor during supervision.

◀ **During the Instructional Supervision Meeting**

- Be prepared to ask questions that will help you develop and practice competency 8.
- Sometimes the intervention role that social work students are allowed to take is limited, but you should be able to develop the intervention skills needed to demonstrate competency. Having a professional relationship with your social work field instructor and asking questions about competency development tasks you can complete during practicum is an essential part of becoming a social work professional.

Summary

Competency 8 is about developing the ability to intervene with clients. As you can see in Figure 8.3, although you will have to learn to select and implement different interventions depending on the level of social work practice, the goal of the intervention process remains the same at different levels of social work practice. You need to identify the client's concerns and be able to explain the client's role in the intervention process and be aware of the skills and knowledge you need to have to implement the intervention appropriately. The goal of social work intervention is to provide clients with a process to address their concerns and achieve success.

Social work intervention is a dynamic and interactive process because clients can reject an intervention option or adopt and reject parts of the intervention. As you engage with clients and assess their ability to participate in the intervention process, as well as whether the intervention is working as intended, adjustments might need to be made. The important thing to remember is that you should not impose an intervention on a client. The client needs to be committed to engage in the intervention process, and that is more likely to occur if the client understands how the intervention will address their needs and help them achieve their goals. As you develop your client intervention skills, you will gain the ability to explain to clients how particular interventions work, the intervention implementation process, and the client's role in the implementation of the intervention.

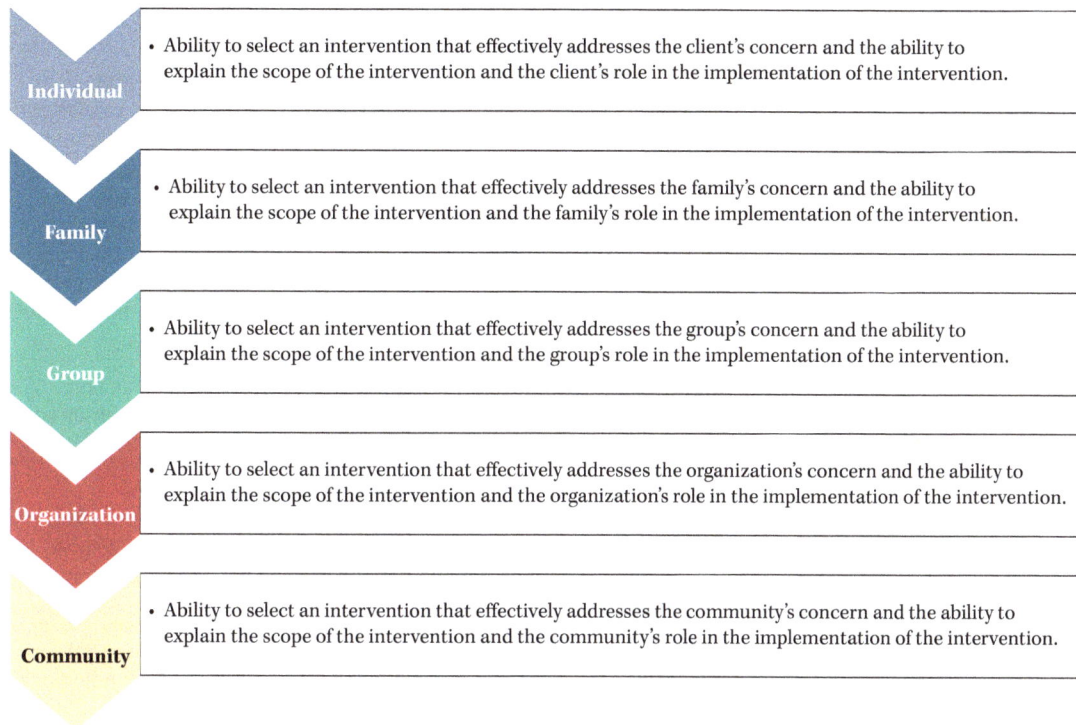

- **Individual** • Ability to select an intervention that effectively addresses the client's concern and the ability to explain the scope of the intervention and the client's role in the implementation of the intervention.

- **Family** • Ability to select an intervention that effectively addresses the family's concern and the ability to explain the scope of the intervention and the family's role in the implementation of the intervention.

- **Group** • Ability to select an intervention that effectively addresses the group's concern and the ability to explain the scope of the intervention and the group's role in the implementation of the intervention.

- **Organization** • Ability to select an intervention that effectively addresses the organization's concern and the ability to explain the scope of the intervention and the organization's role in the implementation of the intervention.

- **Community** • Ability to select an intervention that effectively addresses the community's concern and the ability to explain the scope of the intervention and the community's role in the implementation of the intervention.

FIGURE 8.3 Social work intervention at different levels of practice.

Recommended Reading Materials

Books	Description
Vang, P. D., Hepworth, D. H., Blakey, J. M., Evans, C., & Schwalbe, C. (2022). *Empowerment Series: Direct Social Work Practice.* Cengage Learning.	The authors provide case examples of effective ethical and anti-oppressive direct social work practice and explain the role of theory to real-world applications.
Garces Carranza, C. M. (2019). *Hospital Social Work Interventions.* Goldtouch Press.	The author describes the different interventions used by social workers who work with families in hospital settings.
Garces Carranza, C. M. (2019). *School Social Work: Practice, Policy, and Research.* Oxford University Press.	The authors propose that school social work practice impacts academic, behavioral, and social outcomes for both youths and the broader school community. They focus on evidence-informed school social work practices and include content related to antiracist practice and trauma-informed care.
McInnis-Dittrich, K. (2019). *Social Work With Older Adults: A Biopsychosocial Approach to Assessment and Intervention.* Pearson Education.	The authors describe the major areas of social work with older adults and explain the basics of biopsychosocial functioning, the assessment of older adults' strengths, and the design of both traditional and alternative interventions to treat a wide variety of challenges facing older adults.

(Continued)

Books	Description
Reisch, M. (2018). *Macro Social Work Practice: Working for Change in a Multicultural Society.* Cognella.	The author provides case examples to illustrate the role of macro social work practice in social service and human organizations, health care settings, communities, social networks, and social movements. He proposes that principles of social justice, empowerment, and cultural awareness can be applied in different cultural contexts and discusses how recent political events, cultural developments, and social changes have altered both the context and the content of macro social work practice in the United States.
Corcoran, J. (2014). *Collaborative Cognitive-Behavioral Intervention in Social Work Practice: A Workbook.* Oxford University Press.	The author provides examples of the diverse range of applications cognitive behavioral interventions in social work and how CBT can be a collaborative process.
Sokol, L. (2019). *The Comprehensive Clinician's Guide to Cognitive Behavioral Therapy.* PESI.	The author provides step-by-step plans and activities to teach clients effective coping skills and proposes that those tools will help clients become their own therapist and sustain recovery across a variety of mental health issues.
Curran, L. A. (2013). *101 Trauma-Informed Interventions: Activities, Exercises and Assignments to Move the Client and Therapy Forward.* PESI.	The author provides over 100 approaches to deal with trauma that can be used in both group and individual settings.

References

Council on Social Work Education. (2022, May 23). *2022 EPAS*. https://www.cswe.org/accreditation/info/2022-epas/

National Association of Social Workers. (2022, May 23). *NASW Code of Ethics.* https://www.socialworkers.org/About/Ethics/Code-of-Ethics/Code-of-Ethics-English

CREDIT

CHAPTER 9

Competency 9

Evaluate Practice with Individuals, Families, Groups, Organizations, and Communities

In this chapter you will examine the ninth of the nine social work competencies provided by the CSWE. Competency 9 summarizes the process to critically analyze social work practice outcomes. An evaluation of social work practices is a necessary step if our goal is to ensure that the services we offer clients are appropriate and beneficial. Even proven interventions can be ineffective for some populations or in some circumstances. For example, we know that 12-step programs such as Alcoholics Anonymous can be very effective for some people, but not everyone benefits from support groups. Therefore, 12-step programs should be an option for clients, but not be the only one if the aim is to help clients successfully address an issue like alcoholism.

Because social work's mission is to help people from diverse cultural backgrounds, we also need to be aware that clients will have different views about what is appropriate and what is not. Therefore, interventions that are effective with one group might not be with another.

The aim of competency 9 is to develop an awareness that we must explore the effectiveness of social work processes and practices and adjust those that are ineffective or even harmful to clients if we want to maintain the credibility and effectiveness of the social work profession.

Competency 9 Description as Provided by CSWE: Evaluate Practice with Individuals, Families, Groups, Organizations, and Communities

Competency 9

Evaluate Practice with Individuals, Families, Groups, Organizations, and Communities

Social workers understand that evaluation is an ongoing component of the dynamic and interactive process of social work practice with and on behalf of diverse individuals, families, groups, organizations, and communities. Social workers evaluate processes and outcomes to increase practice, policy, and service delivery effectiveness. Social workers apply anti-racist and anti-oppressive perspectives in evaluating outcomes. Social workers understand theories of human behavior and person-in-environment, as well as interprofessional conceptual frameworks, and critically evaluate and apply this knowledge in evaluating outcomes. Social workers use qualitative and quantitative methods for evaluating outcomes and practice effectiveness.

(Continued)

Social workers:

a. select and use culturally responsive methods for evaluation of outcomes; and
b. critically analyze outcomes and apply evaluation findings to improve practice effectiveness with individuals, families, groups, organizations, and communities.

Figure 9.1 shows the relationship of the social work practice evaluation process to the other eight competencies. Social work practice evaluation is the process of identifying effective social work practices, as well as practices that need to be reexamined or eliminated to ensure that clients are not harmed. Each one of the competencies contributes to the competent delivery of social work services, and competency 9 provides a process to examine if we are in fact integrating the competencies in a way that increases the effectiveness of social work practice.

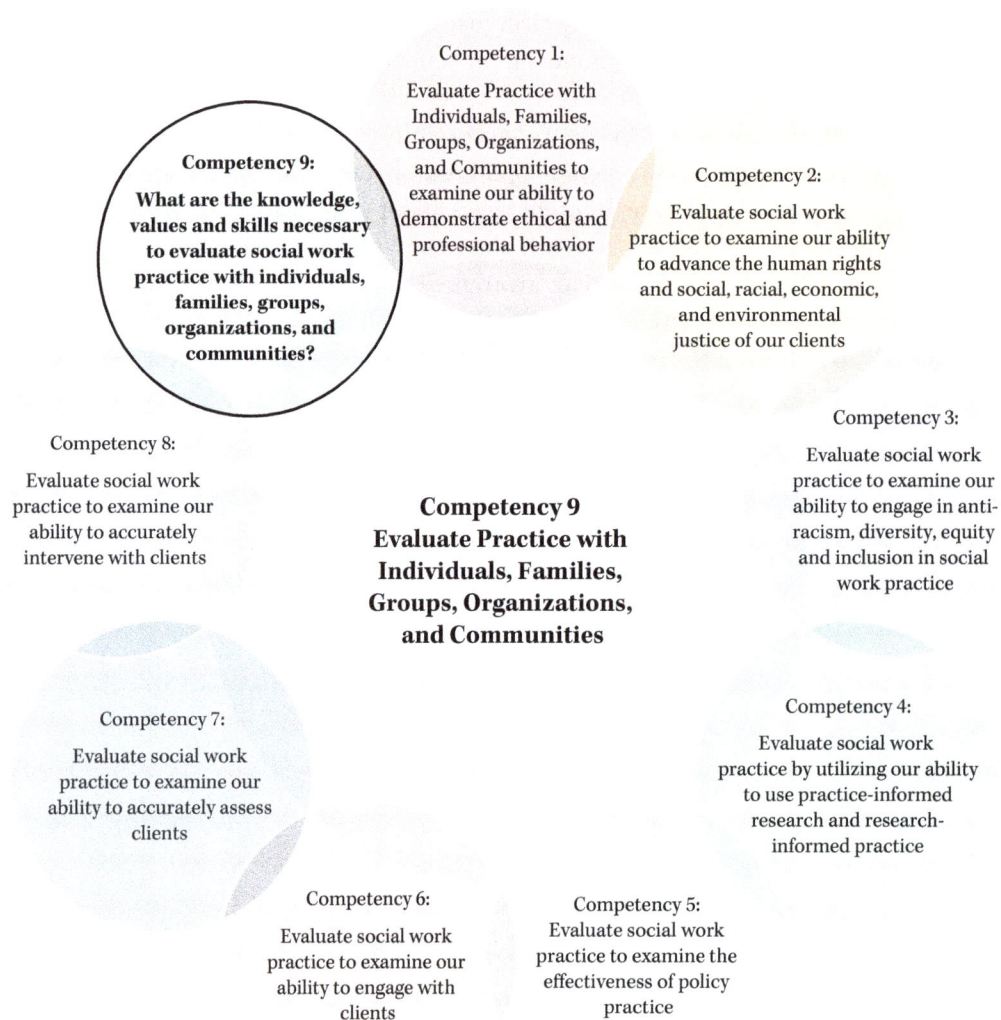

FIGURE 9.1. The relationship of competency 9 to the rest of the competencies.

Applying Competency 9

The Smith and Johnson family's case is fictitious, but as in real cases in social work practice, all nine competencies need to be integrated if the goal is to provide good social work services. Without an evaluation of social work practice, it would be difficult to know if the services provided are beneficial, effective, and efficient.

Reflective Questions on Competency Application

Since competency 9 is about evaluating social work practice, let's explore the social work practices that were relevant to the Smith and Johnson family.

If the Smith and Johnson family were your client and you interacted with this family mainly in a school setting, you would need to evaluate the outcome of case work and the school's bullying prevention program.

Case work evaluation: Did the Smith and Johnson family benefit?

- Did the assessments conducted with the family identify the specific needs to be addressed? If not, how would you know the interventions provided will address the client's concerns?
- Are you familiar with community resources, the professionals who offer services, and the policies and procedures that guide those services? If not, how would you know the referrals you are providing to the Smith and Johnson family are appropriate?
- Do you have a process to follow up on the outcome of your referrals? If not, how would you know whether the clients you refer are accessing those services and benefitting from them?

Bullying prevention program evaluation: Did the program reduce bullying incidents?

- Was an assessment conducted to identify the specific safety risks that needed to be addressed, the specific groups at risk, and where and how bullying occurs? If not, how would you know that the bullying prevention program will address the problem?
- Was a bullying prevention team created and inclusive of all professional staff, support staff, students, and parents? If not, why not? Would those who were excluded feel disrespected and unwilling to cooperate?
- Did the bullying prevention program incorporate widely shared, fair, clearly stated, and consistently applied school policies in compliance with state laws and school board policies, and did it hold everyone accountable? If not, how would you ensure compliance?
- Were evidenced-based interventions identified, coordinated, and implemented school wide? If not, why not, and how would you know whether the intervention was appropriate and implemented correctly?
- Were there sufficient resources (including trained staff) to implement the intervention? If the resources are insufficient and/or staff do not have the knowledge and skills to appropriately implement the intervention, are you really implementing the intervention?

General questions about the evaluation of social work practice in your practicum:

Are you familiar with the agency policies regarding the collection of data for the purpose of outcome evaluation?

Are there clear agency guidelines regarding the difference between evaluating individual client progress and using general outcomes data to evaluate program effectiveness?

How is client confidentiality protected when using technology to keep track of client participation and progress?

(Continued)

If clients belong to a marginalized minority group, how are antiracist and anti-oppressive perspectives incorporated into the evaluation of outcomes?

Is there a process to evaluate the role of theories to inform the intervention process?

Do you know how qualitative and quantitative research methods are used to evaluate social work intervention outcomes?

As you consider these questions, think about the interventions and programs offered at your practicum agency. How would you evaluate the outcomes of those programs or interventions?

Investigating Each Sentence in the Competency Description

In this section, you will closely read each sentence of the competency description to identify key concepts, explore the meaning of those concepts, and critically examine the requirements of competency 9. Social work aims to serve a wide range of clients, and a large portion of social work clients are low income. Thus, social services are often funded through grants whose funders usually ask for evidence of effectiveness and efficiency to continue underwriting the programs they support. Consequently, social work practice evaluation has three purposes.

First, we have an ethical responsibility to provide appropriate services to clients, and without evaluating outcomes we would not know whether we were fulfilling that responsibility. Second, we need to demonstrate effectiveness and efficiency to secure further funding for social programs. Third, we want to maintain our professional standing, and we cannot do that without identifying social work practices that need to be improved and taking the necessary steps to improve them.

Figure 9.2 highlights that the evaluation of social work practice must be tailored to the social work practice level. Although the focus of client intervention in this book is at the individual and family levels, keep in mind that social work with groups, organizations, and communities will require the development of additional evaluation of social work practice skills and abilities.

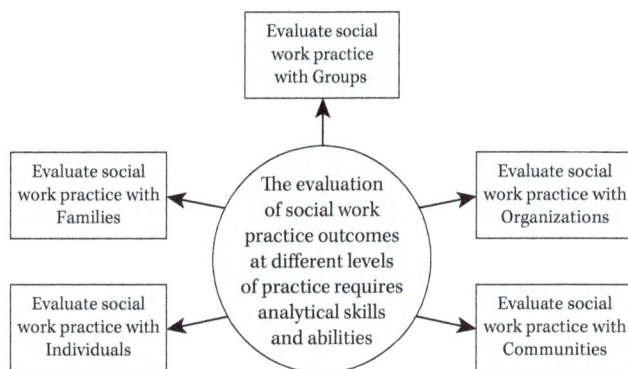

FIGURE 9.2 The evaluation of social work practice process at different levels of practice.

Competency 9

Evaluate Practice with Individuals, Families, Groups, Organizations, and Communities

Social workers understand that evaluation is an ongoing component of the dynamic and interactive process of social work practice with and on behalf of diverse individuals, families, groups, organizations, and communities.

Identify Key Concepts, Search for the Meaning of Those Concepts, and Critically Examine the Requirements of the Competency

1. Use the phrase "evaluation of social work practices" to search the internet, and carefully read and analyze at least two scholarly articles about this topic.

    a. What did you learn about the process of evaluating social work practices from the articles?

2. Use the phrase "dynamic and interactive evaluation" to search the internet, and carefully read and analyze at least two scholarly articles about this topic.

    a. What did you learn about dynamic and interactive evaluation processes from the articles?

Reflective Writing Practice

In a few sentences, outline a plan to engage in the evaluation of social work practices.

_____

_____

_____

_____

Application Follow-Up

Date you were able to engage in the process of evaluating social work practices: _____

In a few sentences, describe what you learned from the process of engaging in the evaluation of social work practices.

_____

_____

_____

_____

Self-Evaluation

Successful	I can effectively demonstrate these competency requirements during practicum, and I can explain how these competency requirements contribute to effective social work practice.
Developing	I can identify the information I need and am able to apply it in some practicum situations, but I am also aware of some knowledge and skill gaps that I need to address.
Unsuccessful	Currently, I am not able to successfully demonstrate these competency requirements in practicum.

> **Competency 9**
>
> ### Evaluate Practice with Individuals, Families, Groups, Organizations, and Communities
>
> Social workers evaluate processes and outcomes to increase practice, policy, and service delivery effectiveness.

Identify Key Concepts, Search for the Meaning of Those Concepts, and Critically Examine the Requirements of the Competency

1. Use the phrase "social work process evaluation" to search the internet, and carefully read and analyze at least two scholarly articles about this topic.

   a. What did you learn about social work process evaluation from the articles?

2. Use the phrase "social work outcomes evaluation" to search the internet, and carefully read and analyze at least two scholarly articles about this topic.

   a. What did you learn about social work outcomes evaluation from the articles?

3. Use the phrase "evaluation of social work service delivery effectiveness" to search the internet, and carefully read and analyze at least two scholarly articles about this topic.

   a. What did you learn about evaluation of social work service delivery effectiveness from the articles?

Reflective Writing Practice

In a few sentences, outline a plan to engage in the process of evaluating social work service delivery effectiveness.

_____

_____

_____

_____

Application Follow-Up

Date you were able to engage in the process of evaluating social work service delivery effectiveness: _____

In a few sentences, describe what you learned from the process of evaluating social work service delivery effectiveness.

_____

_____

_____

_____

Self-Evaluation

Successful	I can effectively demonstrate these competency requirements during practicum, and I can explain how these competency requirements contribute to effective social work practice.
Developing	I can identify the information I need and am able to apply it in some practicum situations, but I am also aware of some knowledge and skill gaps that I need to address.
Unsuccessful	Currently, I am not able to successfully demonstrate these competency requirements in practicum.

Competency 9

Evaluate Practice with Individuals, Families, Groups, Organizations, and Communities

Social workers apply anti-racist and anti-oppressive perspectives in evaluating outcomes.

Identify Key Concepts, Search for the Meaning of Those Concepts, and Critically Examine the Requirements of the Competency

1. Use the phrase "using an antiracist lens to evaluate social work practice outcomes" to search the internet, and carefully read and analyze at least two scholarly articles about this topic.

   a. What did you learn about using an antiracist lens to evaluate social work practice outcomes from the articles?

2. Use the phrase "using an anti-oppressive lens to evaluate social work practice outcomes" to search the internet, and carefully read and analyze at least two scholarly articles about this topic.

   a. What did you learn about using an anti-oppressive lens to evaluate social work practice outcomes from the articles?

Reflective Writing Practice

In a few sentences, outline a plan to use antiracist and anti-oppressive perspectives to evaluate social work outcomes.

_____

_____

_____

_____

Application Follow-Up

Date you were able to use an antiracist and anti-oppressive perspectives to evaluate social work outcomes: _____

In a few sentences, describe what you learned from the process of using an antiracist and anti-oppressive perspective to evaluate social work outcomes.

_____

_____

_____

_____

Self-Evaluation

Successful	I can effectively demonstrate these competency requirements during practicum, and I can explain how these competency requirements contribute to effective social work practice.
Developing	I can identify the information I need and am able to apply it in some practicum situations, but I am also aware of some knowledge and skill gaps that I need to address.
Unsuccessful	Currently, I am not able to successfully demonstrate these competency requirements in practicum.

Competency 9

Evaluate Practice with Individuals, Families, Groups, Organizations, and Communities

Social workers understand theories of human behavior and person-in-environment, as well as inter-professional conceptual frameworks, and critically evaluate and apply this knowledge in evaluating outcomes.

Identify Key Concepts, Search for the Meaning of Those Concepts, and Critically Examine the Requirements of the Competency

1. Use the phrase "theories of human behavior and person in environment and the evaluation of social work outcomes" to search the internet, and carefully read and analyze at least two scholarly articles about this topic.

   a. What did you learn about theories of human behavior and the person in environment and the evaluation of social work outcomes the articles?

2. Use the phrase "critically evaluate social work" to search the internet, and carefully read and analyze at least two scholarly articles about this topic.

   a. What did you learn from the articles about the process of critically evaluating social work?

3. Use the phrase "interprofessional conceptual frameworks and the evaluation of social work outcomes" to search the internet, and carefully read and analyze at least two scholarly articles about this topic.

   a. What did you learn about interprofessional conceptual frameworks and the evaluation of social work outcomes from the articles?

Reflective Writing Practice

In a few sentences, outline a plan to evaluate social work outcomes using an interprofessional conceptual framework.

_____

_____

_____

_____

Application Follow-Up

Date you were able to evaluate social work outcomes using an interprofessional conceptual framework: _____

In a few sentences, describe what you learned from the process of evaluating social work outcomes using an interprofessional conceptual framework.

_____

_____

_____

_____

Self-Evaluation

Successful	I can effectively demonstrate these competency requirements during practicum, and I can explain how these competency requirements contribute to effective social work practice.
Developing	I can identify the information I need and am able to apply it in some practicum situations, but I am also aware of some knowledge and skill gaps that I need to address.
Unsuccessful	Currently, I am not able to successfully demonstrate these competency requirements in practicum.

Competency 9

Evaluate Practice with Individuals, Families, Groups, Organizations, and Communities

Social workers use qualitative and quantitative methods for evaluating outcomes and practice effectiveness.

Identify Key Concepts, Search for the Meaning of Those Concepts, and Critically Examine the Requirements of the Competency

1. Use the phrase "qualitative methods to evaluate social work outcomes" to search the internet, and carefully read and analyze at least two scholarly articles about this topic.

   a. What did you learn about qualitative methods to evaluate social work outcomes from the articles?

2. Use the phrase "quantitative methods to evaluate social work outcomes" to search the internet, and carefully read and analyze at least two scholarly articles about this topic.

   a. What did you learn about quantitative methods to evaluate social work outcomes from the articles?

Reflective Writing Practice

In a few sentences, outline a plan to use qualitative and quantitative research methods to evaluate social work practice outcomes.

_____

_____

_____

_____

Application Follow-Up

Date you were able to use qualitative and quantitative research methods to evaluate social work practice outcomes: _____

In a few sentences, describe what you learned from the process of using qualitative and quantitative research methods to evaluate social work practice outcomes.

_____

_____

_____

_____

Self-Evaluation

Successful	I can effectively demonstrate these competency requirements during practicum, and I can explain how these competency requirements contribute to effective social work practice.
Developing	I can identify the information I need and am able to apply it in some practicum situations, but I am also aware of some knowledge and skill gaps that I need to address.
Unsuccessful	Currently, I am not able to successfully demonstrate these competency requirements in practicum.

Demonstrating the Ability to Evaluate Social Work Practice with Individuals, Families, Groups, Organizations, and Communities

Having the knowledge, values, and skills necessary to effectively evaluate social work practice will give you the opportunity to become an ethical and proficient social work professional. Without these abilities, the possibility of engaging in ineffective or even harmful social work practices is huge. Most social workers would not intentionally engage in harmful practices, but we are all capable of making errors, and if we do not have a process to identify and address those errors, the likelihood of replicating them is obvious.

Select and use culturally responsive methods for evaluation of outcomes.

Demonstrating Competency 9 With the Smith and Johnson Family	Demonstrating Competency 9 During Your Practicum
1. In the last chapter we imagined that the Smith and Johnson family is a Native American family. We considered issues such as forced assimilation, the loss and reclaiming process of native languages and traditions, historical trauma, social justice and jurisdictional issues within native lands, the diversity of religious practices among Native American tribes including sacred sites, and their own vision of self-determination. Taking all this into consideration, how would you select a culturally responsive method to evaluate outcomes in this case? 2. An evaluation of social work practice outcomes would need to include the extent to which these issues were addressed during the engagement, assessment, and intervention process. What steps can you take to evaluate the engagement, assessment, and intervention process considering the family's cultural background? 3. What steps can you take to increase your knowledge and skills to effectively engage, assess, and intervene with Native American clients?	1. Consider the cultural background of the clients served at your practicum. What steps have you taken to develop an awareness of the issues that have affected their life? Considering your clients cultural background, how would you select culturally responsive methods to evaluate social work outcomes? 2. Identify an intervention implemented in your social work practicum setting. What steps can you take to evaluate the intervention you selected using the cultural perspective of a minority client population served at your practicum setting. 3. What steps can you take to increase your knowledge and skills to effectively engage, assess, and intervene with diverse client populations during your social work practicum?

Critically analyze outcomes and apply evaluation findings to improve practice effectiveness with individuals, families, groups, organizations, and communities.

Demonstrating Competency 9 With the Smith and Johnson Family	Demonstrating Competency 9 During your Practicum
1. The Smith and Johnson family was offered the opportunity to access community support services. How familiar are you with community resources? Do you know how to evaluate the utility and effectiveness of community programs? 2. To critically analyze the outcomes and apply evaluation findings to the improvement of practice effectiveness, you would need to follow up with Mrs. Smith to see whether she was able to access and benefit from community support services. What questions would you ask to evaluate the effectiveness of community support services? 3. You would also need to consider the effectiveness of the services offered to Mrs. Smith at two different levels. First, was she able to achieve a positive outcome? And if not, what factors interfered with her ability to benefit from those services, and what alternative interventions might benefit her instead? 4. At another level, you need to evaluate the effectiveness of the intervention overall. If research has been conducted on the effectiveness of the community support services she received, you can review it to identify the factors that make the intervention effective and those that make it ineffective. Knowing the intervention's strengths and limitations would help make informed decisions about its implementation.	1. Identify the intervention practices used at your practicum. Do you know how to evaluate the utility and effectiveness of those interventions? 2. Identify one intervention you want to evaluate and conduct an internet search to see whether any research studies have already been conducted to evaluate the outcomes of the intervention you selected. 3. Review at least a couple of cases to explore the outcomes of the intervention. Make sure not to focus only on positive outcomes. Poor outcomes can be very useful in providing you with an insight regarding the intervention's limitations. 4. Explore alternative interventions that address the same issue and examine their strengths and limitations. Describe how you would use the knowledge you gained by evaluating the intervention you selected. How would you apply evaluation findings to improve practice effectiveness?

Competency Development Topics for the Social Work Practicum Seminar

▶ **Competency 9 Field Seminar Topics**

- The social work practice evaluation process
- The dynamic and interactive process of social work practice evaluation
- The evaluation of practice, policy, and service delivery effectiveness
- Antiracist and anti-oppressive perspectives in evaluating social work practice outcomes
- Theories of human behavior and person in environment that can be used to critically evaluate social work practice outcomes
- The use of qualitative and quantitative research methods to evaluate social work practice effectiveness

▼ **Prior Planning**

- Review your notes in this chapter and identify the key concepts related to each of the seminar discussion topics.
- Identify the parts of competency 9 that you have not been able to successfully demonstrate and formulate specific discussion questions that will help you explore your ability to evaluate social work practice outcomes.
- Consider the social work programs your practicum agency offers and how their effectiveness is evaluated.

◀ **During Seminar**

- Listen attentively to your peers because they will probably be evaluating different social work interventions and programs during their practicum.
- Be ready to contribute by sharing your struggles as well as your successes as you engage in the process of evaluating social work practice outcomes.
- Reflect on your professional growth. Have you found a good social work practice evaluation process? How has your view of social work practice changed since you started to think about evaluating social work practice outcomes?

Competency Development Topics for the Educational Supervision Meeting

▶ **Competency 9 Social Work Practicum Instructional Supervision Meeting Topics**

- The process used to evaluate social work practice outcomes in the practicum setting
- The process used to evaluate social work practice, policy, and service delivery effectiveness in the practicum setting

- Antiracist and anti-oppressive perspectives used in evaluating social work practice outcomes in the practicum setting
- Theories of human behavior and person in environment that can be used to critically evaluate social work practice outcomes in the practicum setting
- The use of qualitative and quantitative research methods to evaluate social work practice effectiveness in the practicum setting

▼ **Prior Planning**

- Review the social work practices, policy, and service delivery process at your social work practicum. Is there anything you think could be improved? Can you identify a social work practice evaluation process you can use to examine the social work practices, policy, and service delivery outcomes?
- Review your notes in this chapter and identify the parts of competency 9 that you have not been able to successfully demonstrate.
- Formulate specific questions that will help you explore the social work practice outcomes evaluation process with your social work instructor during supervision.

◄ **During the Instructional Supervision Meeting**

- Be prepared to ask questions that will help you develop and practice competency 9.
- If your agency has a quality-control unit, ask your instructor if you can participate in the evaluation process.

Summary

Competency 9 is about having the ability to critically evaluate social work practice. As you can see in Figure 9.3, although the evaluation instruments to evaluate social work practice at different levels of practice are very different, as are the knowledge and skills required, there are common factors. At all levels of practice, analyzing the structure and scope of the intervention is a necessary step, because if we do not know the structure and scope of the intervention, we might expect it to cover a bigger range of the problems than it is designed to address, and because its structure might render it inadequate for some settings. For example, self-help groups are usually effective when they are formed to address one issue by inviting participants to provide mutual support, but they are seldom effective when participation is mandated.

The knowledge and skills necessary to appropriately implement the intervention constitute another factor we should evaluate, because whether the social worker has them or not will alter the outcome. We should also evaluate the implementation process itself, because if the process is inadequate the results will likely be as well. We also cannot say if the intervention is adequate if the resources were not sufficient.

Another factor is that although client assessments provide a process to identify the client's needs, both assessments and interventions have the potential to be biased. Finally, we need to be aware that interventions have the potential to produce negative as well as positive outcomes, because if we focus only on positive outcomes, we might ignore potentially dangerous ones.

- **Individual**: Ability to evaluate the outcomes of social work practice by analyzing the structure and scope of the intervention, the implementation processes including client and worker skills and abilities, available and missing resources, benefits and disadvantages of the assessment and intervention as well as positive and negative outcomes.

- **Family**: Ability to evaluate the outcomes of family intervention by analyzing the structure and scope of the intervention, the implementation processes including family and worker skills and abilities, available and missing resources, benefits and disadvantages of the assessment and intervention as well as positive and negative outcomes.

- **Group**: Ability to evaluate the outcomes of group interventions by analyzing the structure and scope of the intervention, the implementation processes including the group and worker skills and abilities, available and missing resources, benefits and disadvantages of the assessment and intervention as well as positive and negative outcomes.

- **Organization**: Ability to evaluate the outcomes of interventions with organization by analyzing the structure and scope of the intervention, the implementation processes including the skills and abilities of the organization and the worker, available and missing resources, benefits, and disadvantages of the assessment and intervention as well as positive and negative outcomes.

- **Community**: Ability to evaluate the outcomes of community intervention by analyzing the structure and scope of the intervention, the implementation processes including the skills and abilities of the worker and the community, available and missing resources, benefits, and disadvantages of the assessment and intervention as well as positive and negative outcomes.

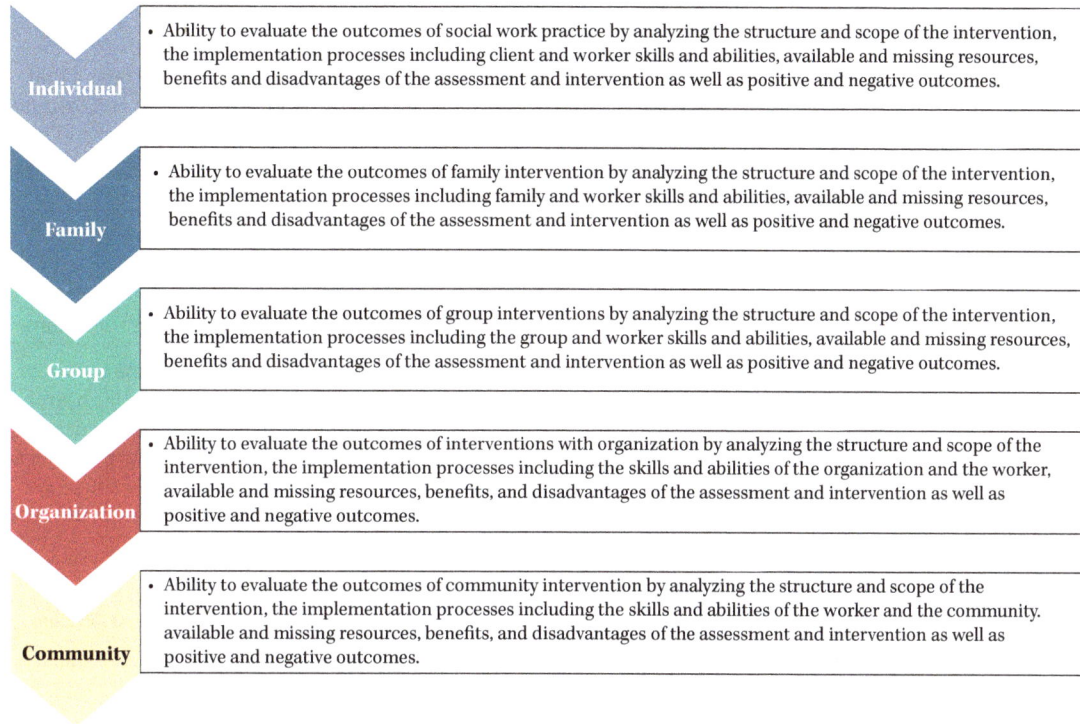

FIGURE 9.3 The evaluation of social work practice outcomes at different levels of practice.

Recommended Reading Materials

Books	Description
Royse, D., Padgett, D., & Thyer, B. A. (2015). *Program Evaluation: An Introduction to an Evidence-Based Approach*. Cengage Learning.	The authors provide a process of learning evaluation techniques and skills to critically analyze evaluation studies conducted by others and simplify the process to gather evidence and demonstrate that their interventions and programs are effective in improving clients' lives.
Specht, H., & Courtney, M. E. (1995). *Unfaithful Angels: How Social Work Has Abandoned Its Mission*. The Free Press.	The authors offer critique of the social work profession and its mission, including the waste of public funds as social workers educated with public money abandon community service.
Dawson, M. P. (2021). *Systems Thinking: A Practical Guide to Improving Your Reasoning*. Blue Hexawolf Limited.	The authors propose that systems thinking provides a framework for defining and solving problems and provide mental models to examine the world from different perspectives to help you become a critical thinker. Understanding systems and being able to analyze them is an essential skill in program evaluation.
Hancock, A. (2004). *The Politics of Disgust: The Public Identity of the Welfare Queen*. NYU Press.	The author proposes that stereotypes and politically motivated misperceptions about race, class, and gender were effectively used to instigate the politics of disgust that paved the way to the reform of the welfare system.

(Continued)

Books	Description
Shaw, D. J. (2016). *The Memory Illusion: Remembering, Forgetting, and the Science of False Memory*. Random House.	The author proposes that memory is fallible and that false memories can be deliberately implanted, leading people to believe things that never happened and how we can improve our memory through awareness of its fallibility.
Rutherford, A. (2020). *The Systems Thinker - Mental Models: Take Control Over Your Thought Patterns. Learn Advanced Decision-Making and Problem-Solving Skills.* United States: Independently Published.	The author proposes that evaluating information correctly is priceless and that systems thinkers have the ability to collect and assess data, which leads to a better understanding of problems and their solutions.
Pelzer, R. B. (2005). *A Brother's Journey: Surviving a Childhood of Abuse.* Grand Central Publishing.	The author is the brother of Dave Pelzer, the author of *A Child Called "It,"* and he reveals that once his brother Dave was out of the house, he became the target of his mother's abusive behavior. The child welfare system is supposed to protect all children from child abuse, yet in this case it rescued one child and left the another behind.
Rhodes-Courter, A. (2009). *Three Little Words: A Memoir.* Atheneum Books for Young Readers.	The author provides a first-person account of the painful memories of her experience in the foster care system.

References

Council on Social Work Education. (2022, May 23). *2022 EPAS.* https://www.cswe.org/accreditation/info/2022-epas/

National Association of Social Workers. (2022, May 23). *NASW Code of Ethics.* https://www.socialworkers.org/About/Ethics/Code-of-Ethics/Code-of-Ethics-English

CREDIT

Fig. 9.1: Adapted from Educational Policy and Accreditation Standards. Copyright © 2022 by Council on Social Work Education.

Conclusion and Next Steps

This guide provided you with a process to examine the requirements of each of the nine CSWE competencies and ways to implement the competency requirements with a fictitious family, as well as in your social work practicum. As you examined the requirements and their relevance to social work practice with the Smith and Johnson family, you experienced a competency development process that you can continue to use as you enter the social work profession. As you can see in Figure C.1, the exercises in every chapter in this book required you to investigate the key concepts in the competency, imagine the utility and implementation of those concepts, identify a date when you implemented them in practice, and evaluate your performance.

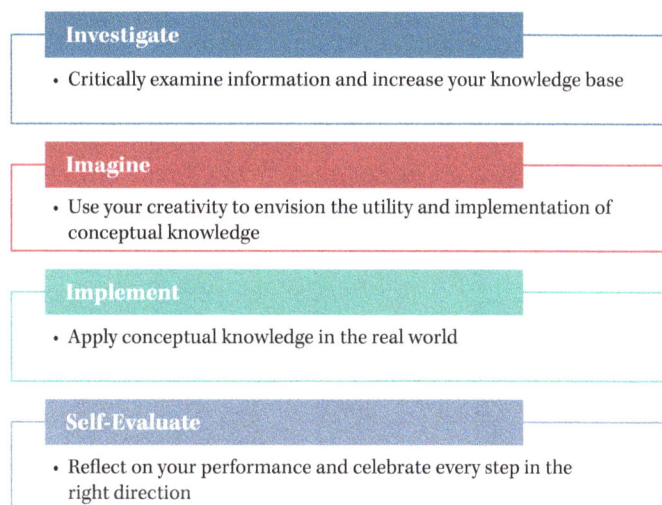

Investigate
- Critically examine information and increase your knowledge base

Imagine
- Use your creativity to envision the utility and implementation of conceptual knowledge

Implement
- Apply conceptual knowledge in the real world

Self-Evaluate
- Reflect on your performance and celebrate every step in the right direction

FIGURE C.1   A competency development process.

In Figure C.2 you can see that the competencies complement each other, but a few of them have more similarities and a specific role to play in the professional development process.

The first three competencies represent the values of the social work profession. The next two provide specific tools you can use to become an effective social work practitioner but are also core professional responsibilities. Without a commitment to lifelong learning, it is impossible to achieve competence.

The next three competencies are all related to client-centered social work practice. They are dynamic and ongoing because you cannot engage, assess, and intervene with a client once and get it over with; you engage, assess, and intervene with clients every time you interact with them. CSWE calls the last competency evaluation, but *review* is a complementary term that implies going back to what you have done to take another look and examine the process and the results of your work with clients.

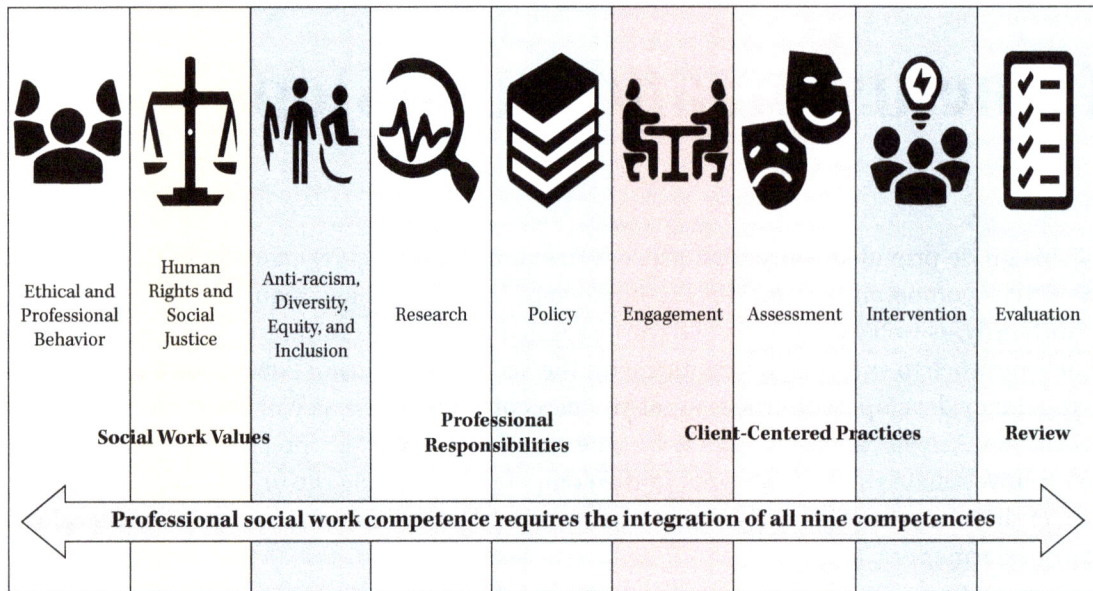

FIGURE C.2 Competent social work practice requires all nine competencies.

In Figure C.3 you will recognize the six values found in the NASW Code of Ethics, because they are all embedded in competency 1. You cannot engage in ethical and professional social work practice while neglecting these six values. Competency 2, "Advance Human Rights and Social,

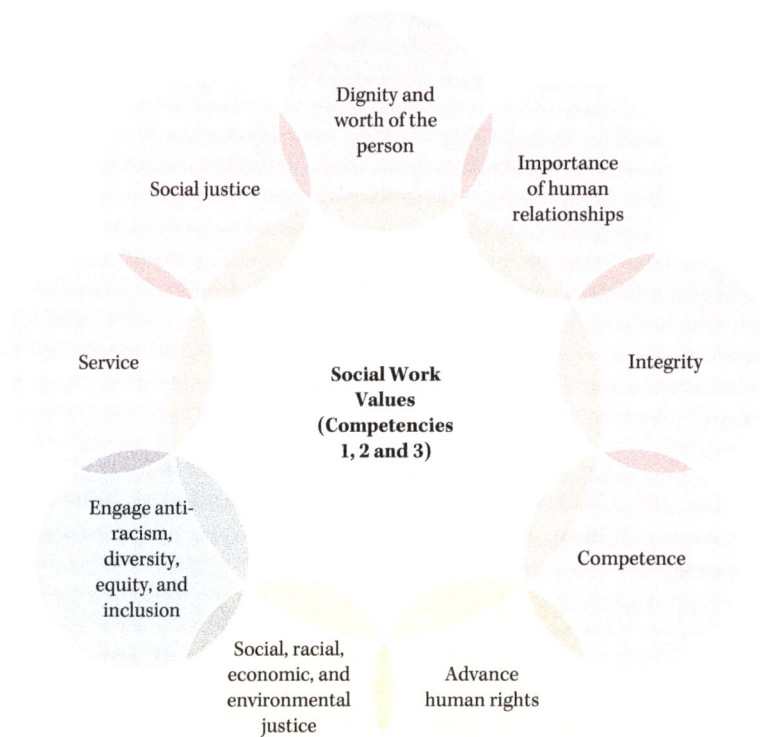

FIGURE C.3. The values of the social work profession.

Racial, Economic, and Environmental Justice," and competency 3, "Engage Antiracism, Diversity, Equity, and Inclusion (ADEI) in Practice," are in fact extensions of most of the original six values. Can you imagine achieving social justice without advancing human rights? Or demonstrating the importance of human relationships without inclusion, equity, and antiracism? Could you be of service and demonstrate integrity without acknowledging the racial disparities that disadvantage minority and marginalized populations in the face of social problems such as the COVID-19 pandemic? The social work profession has embraced the mission to provide services to those who are most in need, and its values are meant to serve as a guiding light.

Personal

- To live a fulfilling life
- To spend rewarding time with family and friends
- To take adequate care of personal business
- To follow a health-promoting routine, including time to rest and recharge

Professional

- To find opportunities to be of service
- To have prospects for growth and development
- To carry a reasonable workload
- To earn appropriate compensation

FIGURE C.4. Life-work balance example.

Competency 1 also requires that "social workers take measures to care for themselves professionally and personally, understanding that self-care is paramount for competent and ethical social work practice." Figure C.4 provides you with a sample of life-work balance that you can tailor to your personal preferences. Try making your own list. What are your personal life goals? How do your professional goals differ from those in the example? The introductory chapter of this book provided a self-care inventory. Did you use it? Have you identified the impact of self-care on your personal and professional life goals? If you have not, you need to do it as soon as possible. Remember the oxygen mask warning on airplanes: "If you are traveling with someone who needs assistance, make sure to put your own mask on first." It makes sense because if you faint you will be useless to those who need you, and the same principle applies on the ground: You cannot effectively help others while neglecting your own needs.

Competencies 1, 2, and 3 represent the values of the social work profession and require that you examine your personal values. Who you are and how you will show up as a social worker are not separate issues. Although part of becoming an effective social worker is setting appropriate boundaries between your work life and your personal life, no matter how successfully you do so, it will be very difficult to engage in antiracist social work practices if your personal beliefs are prejudiced, for instance. Part of the process of achieving the personal-professional balance all of us seek is gaining an understanding of how each side of the equation contributes to our overall life goals. Take an honest look at what you want to achieve in your professional life and the effect of your personal choices on your ability to achieve those goals. It's said that "if you party with the owls, you cannot rise with the eagles," and while you could (occasionally) party all night and show up to school or work the next day, you might not be aware of how you might look or perform after doing so. To consistently demonstrate integrity and competence in the professional world, you need to make sure your personal needs are fulfilled so that you have the stamina to be fully present, engaged, and capable of handling unexpected workplace challenges.

Competencies 4 and 5, shown in Figure C.5, specify necessary professional requirements. If you consider the behaviors related to these competencies, you can see the values of the social work profession clearly embedded. Yet each of these competencies has a specific purpose; the utility of research to improve social work practice, policy, and programs; and the role of policies to ensure access to social services.

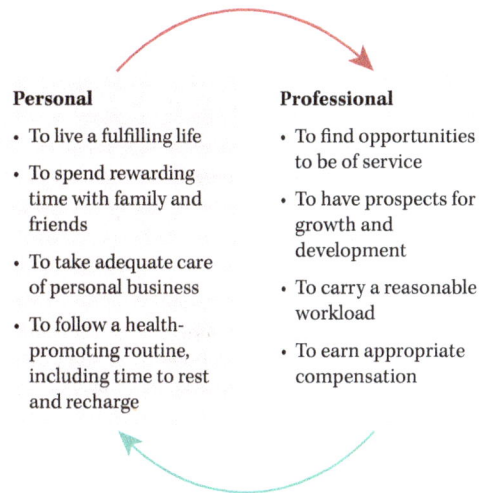

Research   **Policy**

Apply research findings to
inform and improve
practice, policy, and
programs

Use social justice, anti-
racist, and anti-oppressive
lenses to assess how social
welfare policies affect the
delivery of and access to
social services

Identify ethical, culturally
informed, anti-racist, and
anti-oppressive strategies
that address inherent biases
for use in quantitative and
qualitative research
methods to advance the
purposes of social work.

Apply critical thinking to
analyze, formulate, and
advocate for policies that
advance human rights and
social, racial, economic, and
environmental justice.

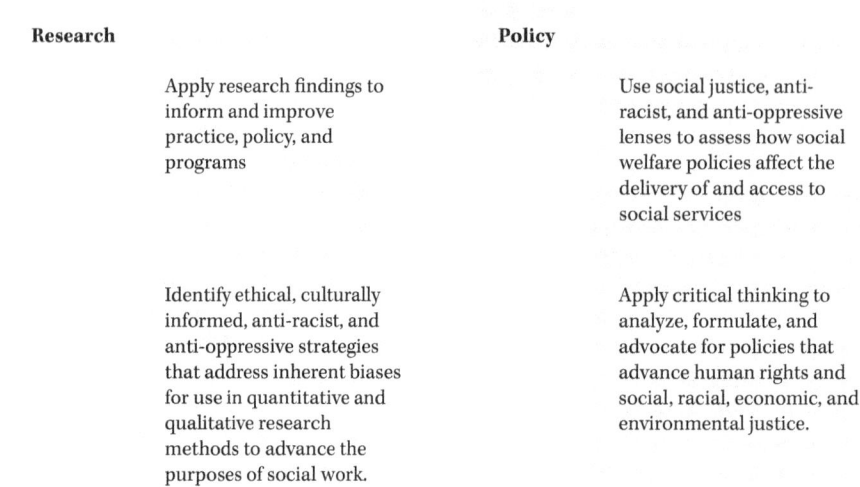

FIGURE C.5. Competency 4: Engage in practice-informed research and
research-informed practice; and competency 5: engage in policy practice.

Research has a huge impact on the development of professional competence. If you completed
the exercises in this field practicum guide, you had to use research skills to explore the meaning
of concepts related to each of the competencies. It is very likely that as you did you discovered
different perspectives and interpretations, and if you have a curious mind, you may have spent
a while exploring them. It is easy to lose track of time when you are learning something that
interests you, and that interest is a sign that you are in the right profession, as you will get many
more opportunities to investigate human behavior and the social environment issues as you
become a competent social worker.

Policy is embedded in all aspects of social life, and social work as a profession has made a
commitment to advocate for social policies that are in line with the values of the profession. As
a beginning social worker, you may find assessing the policies that guide social work practice an
intimidating task, especially the mandate to "use social justice, anti-racist, and anti-oppressive
lenses to assess how social welfare policies affect delivery of and access to social services." When
you considered the role of social policy in the services provided to the Smith and Johnson family,
ideally you gained a better understanding of the importance of this competency. As you develop
your abilities to identify the impact of policies on your work with clients, it will become easier
for you to prioritize learning about any new and changed policies that could create or eliminate
client access to social services.

Competencies 6, 7, and 8 represent the essence of generalist social work practice. Although
each requires specific knowledge and skills, all intertwine during the intervention process. As
you can see in Figure C.6, the engagement process is reciprocal: You can engage with clients only
if they are willing and able to engage with you. As a social worker, you will develop the skills to
engage with clients who might be hesitant to trust you or who might be dealing with other issues
that make engaging difficult. The need to establish an effective working relationship with your
client is an essential first step in initiating the helping process.

In the assessment sphere in Figure C.6, you can see two brains connected to hearts, indicating that
the assessment process is not limited to the social worker. The client's contribution is indispensable

to effectively identifying the client's strengths and challenges. Your analytical skills need to be engaged during the assessment process, but so does your ability to empathize with the client. Your client might be experiencing distress, and no one knows better than the client what is going on in their life. The intervention process is also a team effort. You might be able to identify interventions, but the client must implement those interventions, so it is important to explain the pros and cons of each intervention alternative and give the client an opportunity to choose the one that best fits their goals.

Competency 9 is about evaluating social work practice. This competency has a powerful role because it requires being aware of our professional accountability. If we say that social work is about social justice and that we value evidence-based

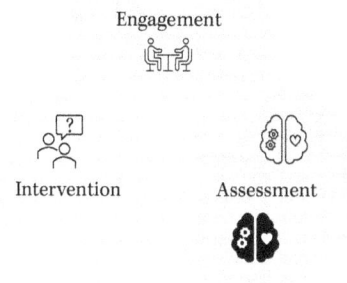

FIGURE C.6. Competencies 6, 7, and 8.

social work practices, competency 9 requires that we examine what we are doing and the results of our work with clients to see if we are in fact delivering appropriate and effective social work services to all clients and that social justice issues were considered and addressed.

In Figure C.7, the evaluation of social work practice requires us to select culturally appropriate methods to evaluate outcomes, use qualitative and quantitative research methods to evaluate practices and outcomes, and apply the analytical skills necessary to critically examine outcomes. We must also use evaluation results to increase practice effectiveness, service delivery effectiveness, and policy effectiveness.

The nine CSWE competencies are always necessary, not just during the educational phase of your career. Consider your growth and development during the social work practicum and multiply it by a case load of clients once you enter the social work profession as a novice social worker. It would be wise to create a learning portfolio for the first 2 years of your career and include all the critical thinking and ethical decision-making tools you accumulated as you completed the exercises in this guide, as well as any tools you received from your social work field instructors. Ideally, when you review Figure C.8, you have a deeper understanding and appreciation of

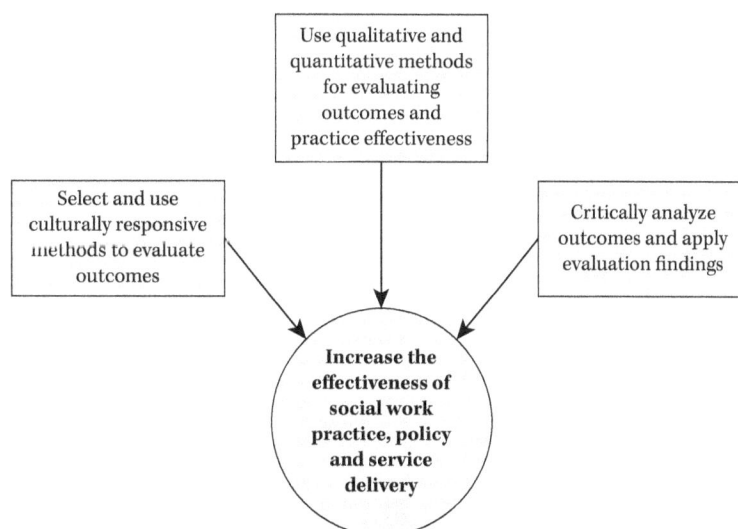

FIGURE C.7. The nine social work competencies.

Competency 1:

Demonstrate Ethical and Professional Behavior

Competency 9:

Evaluate Practice with Individuals, Families, Groups, Organizations, and Communities

Competency 2:

Advance Human Rights and Social, Racial, Economic, and Environmental Justice

Competency 8:

Intervene with Individuals, Families, Groups, Organizations, and Communities

Social Work Competencies from the Counsel on Social Work Education (CSWE) 2022

Competency 3:

Engage Anti-racism, Diversity, Equity, and Inclusion (ADEI) in Practice

Competency 7:

Assess Individuals, Families, Groups, Organizations, and Communities

Competency 4:

Engage in Practice-informed Research and Research-informed Practice

Competency 6:

Engage with Individuals, Families, Groups, Organizations, and Communities

Competency 5:

Engage in Policy Practice

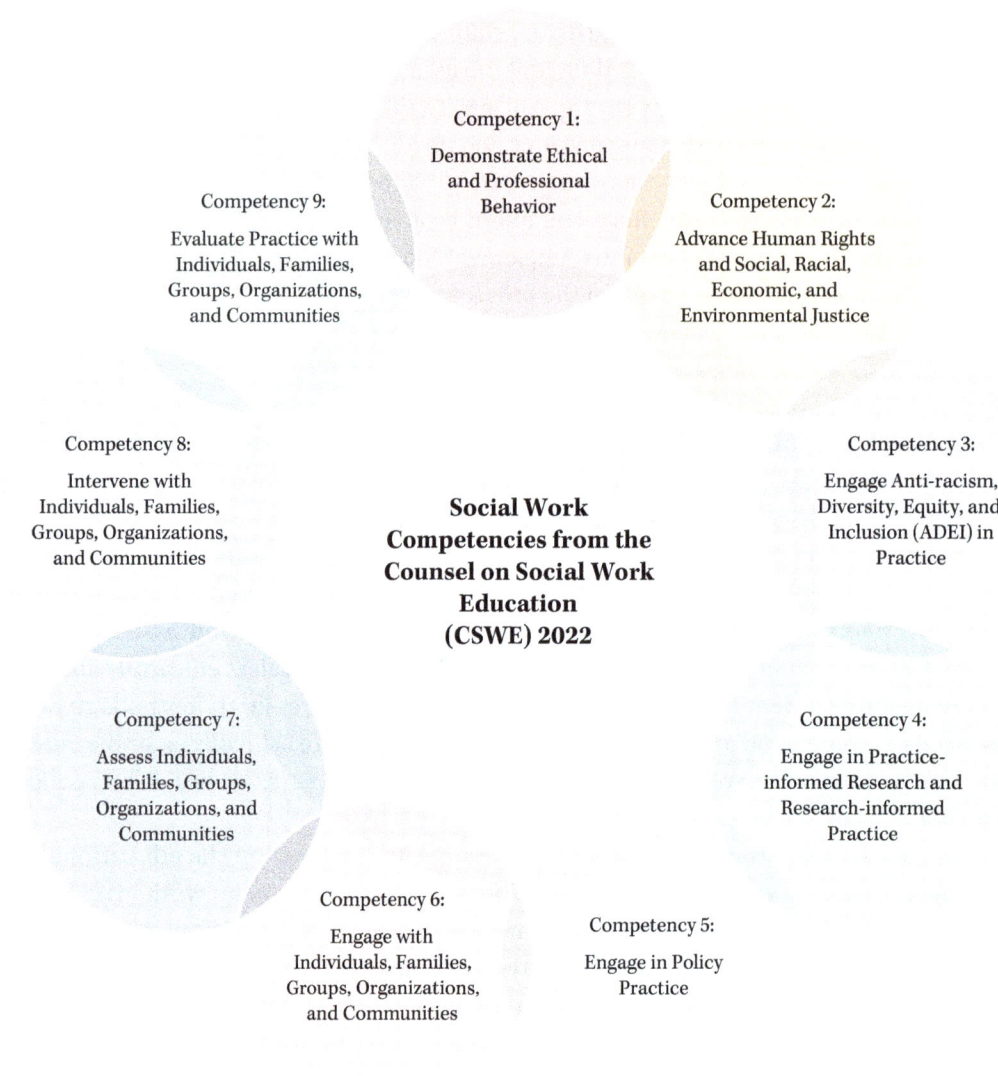

FIGURE C.8. The nine social work competencies.

competency development now than you did the first time you looked at that image. If you completed the majority of the exercises in this guide, I can almost hear you say, "Yes, I can do this."

Recommended Reading Materials

Books/Resources	Description
Rankin, L. (2020). *Mind Over Medicine: Scientific Proof That You Can Heal Yourself (Revised ed.).* Hay House.	The author uses scientific research and spiritual insight to discuss how psychological and physical illness cannot be separated from environmental factors and how unresolved trauma can stand in the way of healing from chronic and life-threatening illnesses and provides tools to heal

Rankin, L. (2022). *Sacred Medicine: A Doctor's Quest to Unravel the Mysteries of Healing*. Sounds True.	The author traveled around the world to meet healers, to investigate the science of healing, and to learn how to stay safe when seeking a healer. From Indigenous cultures for whom healing begins with our sacred connection to Mother Earth to cutting-edge trauma, research the author describes practices and protocols she has found effective.
Tosone, C. (2020) *Shared Trauma, Shared Resilience During a Pandemic: Social Work in the Time of COVID-19*. Springer International.	The contributors are seasoned social work academics, practitioners, administrators, and researchers. Working on the frontlines with patients and families, these social workers have garnered experiences and insights and have developed innovative ways to mitigate the impact of the coronavirus on the psychosocial well-being of their clients and themselves.
Brown, B. (2013). *Daring Greatly: How the Courage to be Vulnerable Transforms the Way We Live, Love, Parent, and Lead*. Brown, B. (2013). Penguin.	The author argues that vulnerability is strength and that when we shut ourselves off from vulnerability—from revealing our true selves—we distance ourselves from the experiences that bring purpose and meaning to our lives.

CREDITS

Index

environment and engagement skills,
112
equity and inclusion in social work, 50
ethical and professional behavior,
1–2, 8
application of, 3–4
demonstrating, 21–24
ethical decision-making, 9
requirements of, 26
ethical decision-making, 10
*Ethical Decisions for Social Work
Practice*, 8
evaluation of social work practices,
155–159
ability to engage in, 165–166
antiracist and anti-oppressive
perspectives, 161–162
critical, 163
interprofessional conceptual
frameworks, 163
outcomes, 160
process, 160
qualitative and quantitative
methods, 164–165
service delivery, 160–161
theories of human behavior, 163
evidence-informed interventions in
social work, 147–148

F
family engagement, 110
federal programs and services, 93–94
figure skaters, 1

G
global injustices, 33
global social welfare, 92

H
Health & Social Work, 63
human behavior theories facilitating
engagement process, 112–113
human rights principles, 8–9, 33

I
inequities in social work practice,
reduction of, 36
injustices against Native Americans, 34
interprofessional collaboration
in research, 79–80
in social work, 115–116
interprofessional work practices, 18
intersectionality and social work,
50–52, 55–56
intervention process, 140–143
ability to engage in, 149–150
dynamic and interactive, 144–145
effective client transitions, 148–149
evidence-informed, 147–148
theories of human behavior in,
145–146
treatment termination, 148

J
Journal of Family Social Work, 63
Journal of Gerontological Social Work, 63
Journal of Law and Social Policy, 63

L
learning-by-doing process, xv–xxv,
xxviii, xxx
lobbyist organizations in the United
States, 97

M
marginalization and alienation, 51
Master of Social Work (MSW) program,
xxx
mutually agreed-on plan, in social work
practice, 131

N
NASW Code of Ethics, xxi, xxx, 5–7, 21,
172

O
oppression and discrimination, in
United States, 33–34, 53

P
policy in social work practice, 86–87,
90–92
ability to engage in policy practice,
98–99
agency policy, 96–97
anti-oppressive social welfare
policy, 94–95, 97
antiracist social welfare policy,
94–95, 97
federal programs and services, 91,
93–94
rights-based social welfare policy,
94–95
Social Security Act of 1935, 91
poverty, 51
practice-informed research, 62
ability to engage in, 80–81
privilege and power, 51, 54–55
professional engagement in social work
practice, 105–106, 120
ability to engage in, 117–118
at different levels of practice, 109
communication skills, 108
community engagement, 110
dynamic and interactive, 109
environment and engagement skills,
112
family engagement, 110
human behavior theories, 112–113
importance of human relationships,
111–112
principles of interprofessional
collaboration, 115–116
self-reflective social worker, 114–115

professional judgment in social work
practice, 12–13

Q
qualitative and quantitative methods of
evaluation, 164
qualitative and quantitative research
methods, 76

R
racial justice and social work, 28–29, 35
racism and oppression in social work
practice, 47–48
racism, in United States, 33–34
reading materials for social work
practicum, xxxi, 26–27, 42, 60, 84–85,
120–121, 139, 153–154, 169–170,
176–177
reflective questions on competency
application
advance human rights and
social, racial, economic, and
environmental justice, 30–31
anti-racism, diversity, equity, and
inclusion (ADEI), 45–46
client assessment process, 125–126
ethical and professional behavior,
4–5
ethical use of digital technology, 20
evaluation of social work practices,
157–158
intervention process, 142–143
policy in social work practice, 88–90
professional engagement in social
work practice, 107–108
research process, 64–65
reflective writing practice, xix–xxii
advocacy process, 37
agency policy, 96
anti-oppressive social work
practices, 17
antiracist social work practice, 49
awareness of intersectional factors,
52
bias, power, and privilege in
assessment, 134
collaborative assessment, 131
connection between global injustice
and needs of clients, 34
critiquing research study, 74
cultural humility, culture privilege,
and power, 55
culturally responsive assessment
with clients, 129
distribution of power and privilege
in society, 36
dynamic and interactive
intervention process, 144
effective client transitions, 148–149
ethical and professional behavior, 7
ethical approaches to conducting
scientific research, 68
ethical decision-making, 10

www.ingramcontent.com/pod-product-compliance
Lightning Source LLC
Chambersburg PA
CBHW081434270326
41932CB00019B/3199